COMEBACK

PRAISE FOR *COMEBACK*

"In this powerful and provocative book, democracy scholar Steven Fish argues convincingly that what liberals need now is strong leadership, with buoyant, vigorous, self-confident messaging, to combat bullying authoritarianism, 'recapture the flag' *for* democracy, and excite people with a positive moral vision of change . . . This is a rallying cry for Democrats to reestablish 'their reputations for superior strength and patriotism.'"

> —**Larry Diamond**, Mosbacher Senior Fellow of Global Democracy at the Freeman Spogli Institute, Stanford University, and author of *The Spirit of Democracy*

"As authoritarianism threatens to take hold in the United States, many Americans have bought into narratives of inevitable decline and found themselves overtaken by despair. Steve Fish is having none of it. *Comeback* is the work of a veteran scholar and happy warrior: Fish not only corrects the record but lays out a battle plan for saving democracy."

> —**Tom Nichols**, Staff writer at *The Atlantic* and author of *The Death of Expertise*

"For all those who want to truly understand the Trump phenomenon, Steven Fish's *Comeback* is revelatory. For those who long to defeat Trump and Trumpism once and for all, *Comeback* is vital reading."

> —**Mark Danner**, author of *Spiral: Trapped in the Forever War*

"From an eminent scholar of democracy and dictatorship comes this crucial, cogent, and impassioned plea for rescuing American democracy. *Comeback* gave me hope that democracy in the United States could survive—if enough people read it and take Fish's critically important findings to heart."

—**Valerie Sperling**, Professor of Political Science, Clark University, and coauthor of *Courting Gender Justice*

"Fish lays waste to a string of narratives that lead to electoral dead ends and provides a script for a campaign to beat back—and dominate—Trump and his miserable vision. If you're a democratic patriot, or a patriotic Democrat, you'll be nodding along as you read. This book could help the right side win."

—**John Carey**, Professor of Government, Dartmouth College, founder of *Bright Line Watch*, and coauthor of *Campus Diversity: The Hidden Consensus*

"A stirring, convincing, and crystal-clear call to action that is both urgently needed and utterly feasible . . . The Democratic Party and its allies need to read this book closely and follow his advice if they are to win in November and preserve our democracy over the long haul."

—**Lucan A. Way**, Distinguished Professor of Democracy, University of Toronto, and coauthor of *Competitive Authoritarianism*

"*Comeback* is a remarkable achievement. Fish mobilizes decades of experience as a leading specialist on democracy and authoritarianism to construct a paradigm-busting explanation for Trump's rise. He offers novel, promising, and feasible prescriptions for defeating Trumpism . . . This is a must-read for politicians, scholars, journalists, and everyone who supports equality and democracy."

—**Marc M. Howard**, Professor of Government and Law, Georgetown University, and author of *Unusually Cruel: Prisons, Punishment, and The Real American Exceptionalism*

"Fish provides the guidebook we need at the moment we need it . . . He offers a fresh and powerful approach to reaching American voters with a message of strength through inclusion and freedom. Those seeking to defend a truly free and liberal America need to take heart and read this book."

—**Jack A. Goldstone**, Professor of Public Policy, Mason University, and author of *Revolution and Rebellion in the Early Modern World*

"Steve Fish presents an original strategy for defeating America's slide toward authoritarian populism, backed by an avalanche of data and incisive analyses of speeches and statements that illustrate how liberal luminaries have defended democracy throughout American history. His causal analysis and policy prescriptions are utterly convincing. *Comeback* is an important, brilliant, and thrilling read."

—**George W. Breslauer**, former Executive Vice Chancellor and Provost, University of California, Berkeley, and author of *The Rise and Demise of World Communism*

"Drawing insights from political psychology, communications, and American political history, Fish issues a rousing call for new strategies of political dominance to defeat democracy's foes. This book is essential reading for all those concerned about the fate of democracy, and what must be done to secure its future."

—**Kenneth M. Roberts**, Professor of Government, Cornell University, and coeditor of *Democratic Resilience*

"Fish has penned a passionate, compelling, and incredibly important work explaining the roots and dynamics of the political malaise that has gripped American democracy. Yet he also offers hope, pointing the way to restoring an America that is fearless, free, united, and unshakably democratic. Every American who cares about democracy should read this book!"

—**Kathleen Collins**, Professor of Political Science, University of Minnesota, and author of *Politicizing Islam in Central Asia*

"Steve Fish takes aim at some of our most cherished explanations for what ails American democracy and offers an impassioned plea for how we can defend it from its foes . . . the Democrats have forgotten how to dominate the arena, to fight rhetorically with the 'gloves off.' It's an aptitude they desperately need to re-acquire. We all do."

—**Jeffrey Kopstein**, Dean's Professor of Political Science, University of California, Irvine, and coauthor of *The Assault on the State*

"Steve Fish issues an urgent call for a new approach on how the Democratic Party messages. Building on studies from psychology and political science, he calls for messaging that embeds the Democrats' appeals in a particular kind of rhetoric that is potentially far more effective than what the Democrats now offer...*Comeback* is a timely intervention at a moment in history when democracy itself is at stake."

—**Ruth Collier**, Heller Professor of the Graduate School, University of California, Berkeley, and author of *Paths toward Democracy*

"In this punchy, provocative book, M. Steven Fish shows that Democrats haven't been losing because of their policies, but because they don't have the confidence to talk about them in clear, powerful language. *Comeback* will be essential reading for political scientists, activists, and anyone who wants to reclaim the rhetorical tradition and fighting spirit that has helped Democrats sell Americans on political change and progress."

—**Rob Boatright**, Professor of Political Science, Clark University, and author of *Getting Primaried: The Changing Politics of Congressional Primary Challenges*

COMEBACK

Routing Trumpism,
Reclaiming the Nation, and
Restoring Democracy's Edge

M. Steven Fish

with Laila M. Aghaie

Rivertowns
B O O K S
IRVINGTON, NEW YORK

Printed in the United States of America · May 2024 · I

Paperback edition ISBN-13: 978-1-953943-52-1
Hardcover edition ISBN-13: 978-1-953943-53-8
Ebook edition ISBN-13: 978-1-953943-54-5

LCCN Imprint Name: Rivertowns Books
Library of Congress Control Number: 2024936365

Rivertowns Books are available from all bookshops, other stores that carry books, and online retailers. Visit our website at www.rivertownsbooks.com. Orders and other correspondence may be addressed to:

Rivertowns Books
240 Locust Lane
Irvington NY 10533
Email: info@rivertownsbooks.com

To the memory of my father, mentor, and hero, Michael P. Fish

Contents

Acknowledgments

I have incurred more debts in writing this book than I can possibly acknowledge here. I owe a special debt of gratitude to Neil Abrams, Sener Akturk, George Breslauer, Ruth Collier, Jack Goldstone, and Valerie Sperling, each of whom provided detailed critiques of earlier drafts. I also received an abundance of helpful feedback from Larry Diamond, Sarah Kadous, Jeff Kopstein, and Lucan Way. Exchanges with John Carey, Jack Citrin, Kathleen Collins, Mark Danner, Marc Howard, Greg Olson, and Omar Wasow helped sharpen my thinking as well.

I profited immensely from membership in a small working group on democracy's crisis that included Dan Abbasi, Rebecca Carpenter, Ken Roberts, and Colin Woodard. Dan and Ken are also lifelong comrades whose friendship has sustained me since our days in "the dungeon," the windowless basement room in which first-year Ph.D. students made our "offices" at Stanford in the mid-1980s.

I also owe Rebecca a shout-out for putting me in touch with the publisher of Rivertowns Books, Karl Weber. Karl's virtuoso editing helped turn an ungainly manuscript into a readable one, and his masterful work as a publisher enabled this book to see the light of day in record time.

For invaluable research assistance, I am indebted to David Cheng, Cassidy Clark, Kaitlyn Lenkeit, Giorgio Riccardi, and Mark Yoo.

I am deeply grateful to my students, and particularly those who have taken my advanced seminar, Democracy's Global Crisis, and my introductory lecture course, Introduction to Comparative Politics. Anyone who sees a trade-off between teaching and research hasn't taught my students. They have been an abiding source of insight and inspiration for this book.

Democracy Hawks, a student group that grew out of the seminar, have been a special source of encouragement and support. The Hawks devote themselves to research, writing, and activism on behalf of democracy in the United States and worldwide. In addition to David Cheng, Cassidy Clark, Kaitlyn Lenkeit, and Mark Yoo, group leaders who I have already acknowledged, I would like to recognize T. J. Ahmed, Emily Bass, Jasmine Lozano Castillo, Eric Castro, Alex Dang, Eric Heilmann, Sameer Kazim, Edward Lee, Kaila Love, Tristan Shaughnessy, Emiliano Silva, and Diego Vital.

A scholar's life isn't just an intellectual venture; it's a spiritual one as well. On this score, my debts to Mitch Houston, Andrew Huberman, Mark Labberton, and Joe Sizer are especially profound and irredeemable.

I wrote this book for my amazing sons, Nate and Max Fish, in hopes that they will spend their lives, as I have, governing themselves and enjoying liberty's blessings. I am also grateful to their mother, Olga, for partnering with me to raise such remarkable exemplars of what human beings can become.

My wonderful mother, Cherrie Robinson, and brilliant sister, Diana Fish, have provided unfailing support for my entire life. The memory of my father, Michael Fish, guides me every day. His widow, Renate Fish, made Dad's life complete, and she continues to sustain Diana and me in all our endeavors.

At about 5 a.m. on November 9, 2016, after hours of ranting and stomping around my apartment in Albany, California following the news of Donald Trump's victory, I collapsed onto the couch, spent and dejected. (If you're reading this book, I'm guessing you might have spent that night much the same way.) I don't remember how much time passed before my partner broke the silence: "You've been studying people fighting for their freedom in other countries your whole career. Did you ever think you would have the responsibility, the privilege, of fighting for democracy in your own country?"

My life's work has been the study of democracy, and in particular how people can get it if they don't have it and keep it if they do. Over the decades, I've seen dictators come and go, democracies born and wane. I've sung in packed churches in Poland, where the faithful alternated hymns to God with anthems to Solidarity, the trade-union-led movement that would later ignite a lightning strike of events that buried communist regimes from Prague to Vladivostok. I've spent long nights swilling vodka with democratic dreamers in overheated, smoke-filled apartments in Volgograd and Tula and glorious days freezing in massive marches of Muscovites as Russians brought the curtain down on Soviet rule.

I've hunkered down at sooty strike headquarters with coal miners in Donetsk who had put down their tools to demand free elections in Ukraine. I've conducted interviews in whispers with a dictator's hidden critics in Uzbekistan and lived among academic, religious, and political leaders in Indonesia, endeavoring to assess how they had buried the rotten notion that Muslims weren't capable of governing themselves. I've interviewed leaders and activists in Mongolia, which has shown the world that neither poverty nor being sandwiched between powerful dictatorships can overcome a people's longing for freedom. And I chronicled Russia's chaotic experience of freedom after the fall of the Soviet Union—and its journey back to unfreedom under Vladimir Putin.

Yet the struggle was always somewhere else, in countries that were relatively new to democracy or never quite got it. Now autocracy is pounding on America's door.

We marvel at the courage of the people in our past who gave their all to secure democracy, but we too often fail to recognize that we must follow their example if democracy is to survive today. The political challenge of our era is nothing less than preserving our right to live in freedom, dignity, and peace. It's a task that requires a new batch of heroes—and any one of us, from any walk of life, can take on that role if only we are willing.

My greatest hero in that quest is my wife, Laila Aghaie, the woman who issued the challenge to me on the night of Trump's election in November 2016. This book is the answer to her call, and she has been my full partner in every step of its creation. Every argument is the product of our late-night kitchen-table conversations and debates; to the extent that any of the arguments herein are convincing, she is to credit. Every line has been crafted with her help and is the product of her masterful editing. Laila's children, Darius, Ayden, and Lena, have furnished a lifetime of inspiration for her, and since I met their mother, they have also inspired me. Where oceans meet, love of my life and partner in everything.

Steve Fish
Berkeley, California
March 2024

Introduction: Democracy on the Line

A t the dawn of the 21st century, the question of who should govern seemed ridiculous. The answer was obvious and the same everywhere: the people, of course! Even the hardest-core autocrats paid lip service to democracy or at least professed their intentions to yield to it eventually.

But by the middle of the 2010s, democracy was in trouble all over the world. In a stunning reversal, autocrats now looked like trendsetters, and democrats like holdouts. The trend reached a crescendo on November 8, 2016, when Donald Trump, who said he would only respect the results of the election "if I win," won the presidency of the United States. During the campaign, he publicly called on Vladimir Putin to hack Hillary Clinton's emails—Putin's operatives obliged. Kathleen Hall Jamieson, the leading scholar of political communication in the United States and a rigorous nonpartisan, concluded that the Russian intervention probably tipped the election to Trump.[1]

Trump then spent his time in office remaking the Republican Party in his own image. He flaunted his contempt for democracy at every turn. He defied congressional subpoenas and laws against leveraging his office for personal gain. He treated foreign policy and national secrets as personal assets to trade for favors, profits, and bragging rights. He cozied up to America's adversaries and lashed out at democratic allies—all under the smug, watchful eye of his Russian idol-sponsor.

In the run-up to his November 2020 reelection bid, Trump had his postmaster general yank mailboxes off streets and remove mail-sorting machines from post offices during early voting. By his own exuberant admission, his goal was to prevent mail-in ballots, which he thought would favor the Democrats, from reaching their destinations in time. At the state and local levels, the Republicans pressed for measures that made it harder to vote.[2]

Joe Biden still managed to beat Trump, winning the Electoral College by a decisive 306 to 232 and the popular vote by over seven million. But accepting defeat was no longer in the Republicans' repertoire. Trump claimed fraud and launched a bizarre venture to overturn the results. He pressured Republican-controlled state legislatures to throw the election to the House of Representatives. To provide some coercive muscle, he incited an insurrection at the Capitol on January 6, 2021. In the aftermath of the violent assault, congressional Republicans emerged from their hiding places in barricaded committee rooms—and joined Trump's plot. In the gravest threat to democracy in modern times, over two thirds of House Republicans voted to delay certification of Biden's election, trying to give Trump more time to carry out his traitorous scheme.

The plot failed, but since then the Republican Party's most sacred truth has become the Big Lie that Trump won. In 2022, all Republican members of Congress who challenged the Big Lie publicly were ousted from leadership positions. In a survey of 552 Republican candidates in the midterm elections, fewer than a third accepted Biden's victory. In a poll of 20 Republican nominees for governor and the Senate two months before the midterm vote, six said they would not commit to accepting the results if they lost and six others refused to answer the question. Rejecting the outcome of any election they do not win has become the Republican way.[3]

In the meantime, Trump has taken to channeling Hitler, attacking opponents as "vermin" whom he intends to "root out." He calls for the execution of generals who criticize his assaults on democracy. He threatens to round up immigrants who are "poisoning the blood of our country" and throw them into detention camps. Abroad, Russia will be given free rein to savage Ukraine, the United States will withdraw from NATO, and dictators will be our new best friends. [4]

The Heritage Foundation's Project 2025 maps Trump's plan to dismantle the "deep state"—meaning the agencies of justice, administration, and law enforcement. These are the bodies that ensure the rule of law—that is, a system in which the rulers, as well as everyone else, must obey the rules. Gutting them will enable the Republicans to steal at will, suppress opposition, weaponize law enforcement, and rig political competition. Trump has already said the Constitution and term limits should be suspended in his case. This is the Republican plan for a second Trump term. [5]

It isn't that the Republicans have become more conservative. Ronald Reagan was a far more consistent God-and-country conservative than Trump. He shrank government spending on social programs, slashed taxes more deeply than current Republicans could dream of doing, and pursued a truly "traditional values" agenda. John McCain, the Republicans' 2008 nominee for president, sponsored legislation that would force the government to balance the budget every year and relentlessly pushed to maximize spending on the military.

But when these leaders lost elections, there was no question of their trying to discredit the outcome or cling to office. Reagan lost his first two attempts at the Republican nomination, and his response was to go home and gear up for the next contest. After losing to Barack Obama, both McCain and Mitt Romney, the Republicans' 2012 presidential nominee, offered gracious concession speeches that were the stuff that democracy is made of. These leaders knew that in the country that invented rule by the people, there's nothing "conservative" about snuffing out democracy.

But since Trump and his Make America Great Again (MAGA) movement took over the party, the Republicans' democratic inclination has flamed out. No matter what Trump does, Republican leaders stand by their man. As political sociologist Jack Goldstone warns,

"Should the Republicans manage to gain control of the House, Senate, and presidency in 2024, building an electoral autocracy to impose their views without challenge will be their top priority."[6] One might add: Even if they don't achieve a lock on government in 2024, the danger of their doing so in subsequent elections—and then pushing for authoritarianism—will remain.

That is why genuine conservatives like Anne Applebaum, David Brooks, Tom Nichols, Jennifer Rubin, Max Boot, George Will, Peter Wehner, and Joe Scarborough have left the Republican Party. As Brooks put it in 2018: "Republican or conservative, you have to choose."[7]

The survival of democracy in America now depends, pure and simple, on the ability of the Democrats to thrash the Republicans in every national election for the foreseeable future. Everything else is details.

How did a reality-show con man who kowtows to a mafia-state don in the Kremlin end up in the Oval Office? And how can it be possible that he and his cult-party now threaten to stamp out free government in the world's oldest and most powerful democracy?

Let's start by revisiting an episode from the 2016 election that holds clues to why the Democrats have faltered. You might recall that in the home stretch of the campaign, Hillary Clinton quipped that half of Trump supporters sit in a "basket of deplorables," which she defined as people who are "racist, sexist, homophobic, xenophobic, Islamophobic—you name it." Clinton called the deplorables "irredeemable" and "not America."

But what about the other half of Trump supporters? That *non-deplorable* basket, Clinton said, is filled with people who

feel the government has let them down, the economy has let them down, nobody cares about them, nobody worries about what happens to their lives and futures; and they're desperate for change. It doesn't really even matter where it comes from. They don't buy everything [Trump] says, but—he seems to hold out hope their lives will be different. They won't wake up and see their jobs disappear, lose a kid to heroin, feel like they're in a dead-end. Those are people we have to understand and empathize with as well. [8]

Why was this moment so significant?

The media fell into a frenzy over Clinton's condemnation of the "deplorables." But what about her doleful depiction of the *non-deplorable* portion of Trump's voters?

Clinton's well-heeled supporters nodded along with her description of the unfortunate but redeemable stiffs who were "desperate for change" and "feel like they're in a dead end." But what would *you* think of someone who characterizes you like that?

Clinton's patronizing depiction of the "people we have to understand and empathize with" might have been at least as important to Trump's edge with working-class voters as their supposed feelings that "nobody cares about them" or fears their kids might drop dead from a heroin overdose. And she is not alone in this; current-day Democrats generally portray working-class voters the same way.

To make matters worse, within hours Clinton walked back her criticism of the deplorables. Instead of bearing down on her fighting words, she and her campaign managers panicked over ruffling the feathers of bigots. But it never occurred to them that her treatment of the non-deplorables was the real problem.

So rather than staying on offense, Clinton shifted to damage control and offered the supposedly desperate, dead-ender redeemables another pat on the head:

> I also meant what I said last night about empathy, and the very real challenges we face as a country where so many people have been left out and left behind. As I said, many of Trump's supporters are hard-working Americans who just don't feel like the economy or our political system are working for them. I'm

determined to bring our country together and make our economy work for everyone, not just those at the top.[9]

So there you have it: It *is* possible to cower, cloy, and condescend—all at the same time.

Ever on offense, Trump reveled in the spectacle, tweeting: "While Hillary said horrible things about my supporters, and while many of her supporters will never vote for me, I still respect them all!" Clinton didn't roll over in her counter-tweet, but she didn't stick it to Trump on behalf of all Americans, either. Instead, she reminded her audience how mean Trump was to the list of particular groups she rattled off practically every time she gave a speech. In answer to Trump's (ridiculous) boast that he respected everyone, she tweeted: "Except for African Americans, Muslims, Latinos, immigrants, women, veterans—and any so-called 'losers' or 'dummies'."[10]

So while Trump projected gleeful self-assurance and claimed to embrace all Americans, Clinton hunkered down and portrayed the Democratic Party as a patchwork of victimized groups.

For their part, analysts agonized over Clinton's deplorables remark for years afterward. Dismay at her insensitivity to bigots ruled liberal commentary. Said journalist Jonathan Allen, "It's very hard to say you have a message of civility and then turn around and talk about how essentially a quarter of the country is, in your view, a basket of deplorables. That is a screeching conflict of her overall message, which is we have a civilized country and we need to be stronger together—that this should be a kinder, gentler, unified country."[11]

Liberals weren't the only ones who focused on the purported gaffe of Clinton's attack on the "deplorables," thereby missing the episode's real significance. A half-decade after the fact, Republican strategist Frank Luntz mulled over just how terribly hurtful the word "deplorable" must have been in the tender ears of the accused. He opined that the term was "as insulting as any word in the English language. To be deplorable means you have no excuse as a human being." He asserted that Clinton's riff "hardened opposition to her instantly as someone who has no heart."

Beyond his remarkable belief that Trump voters see lack of "heart" as a deal-breaker or that Clinton ever had a shot with the deplorables anyway, Luntz never considered that her condescension to the non-deplorables and the lack of temerity she showed by backing down might have been the problem. He ignored the fact that Trump did little *but* insult, attack, criticize, and condemn Clinton's liberal supporters—and ended up electrifying his base, taking over his party, and beating one of the best-qualified candidates for president in modern American history.

The lessons that pundits of all political stripes took from the deplorables debacle were wildly wide of the mark.

Clinton's denunciation of Trump's worst supporters was no gaffe; instead, it was as smart as it was intrepid. Sticking to fierce truth-telling about their intolerance and immorality could have stoked her base and earned respect from the rest of the electorate—even the deplorables themselves. Clinton showed forceful moral discernment—which isn't to be confused with huffy, defensive umbrage. Toughness and a sense of pride in the *real* America shone through her statement and represented a rare moment of authenticity in an otherwise painstakingly scripted campaign.

But she followed it with a string of unforced errors. None were distinctively hers. In fact, each represents a facet of the way post-Bill-Clinton Democrats relate to working-class voters.

First, no sooner had she impressively coldcocked the deplorables than she depicted the rest of Trump's voters as dupes in dire need of a break. How many proud working people in a society famed for its belief in self-reliance want to be portrayed like that—still more by people who are richer and better educated than they are?

Clinton's second blunder was backing down from her attack on the deplorables. She could have reiterated the provocative truths she told to stick it to Trump and his nasties—and to delight her progressive base. Instead, she reinforced her image as a principle-and-passion-free politician. Her defensive, risk-averse, donor-dinner-driven campaign contrasted with Trump's brash, fill-the-stadiums-and-to-hell-with-the-critics approach.

Her third mistake was continuing her patronizing treatment of working-class voters in her follow-up statement. Clinton could have doubled down on her rightful separation of the moral bottom half of Trump voters from the other 75-80 percent of America—and the country's better nature. She also could have cast these potentially persuadable voters as vital members of a glorious country rather than misled dead-enders, a step toward *reclaiming the nation*—something the Democrats continue to neglect.

Finally, in her follow-up response to Trump's sarcastic crowing, she was wrong to carve out categories of people she thought he disrespected. Her identity-group particularism, ever on display during her campaign, singled out groups without embedding their causes in the whole nation's fate. Speaking for certain people and not others based on their ethnicity, religion, gender, or other non-moral, non-political criteria needlessly alienated entire demographics.

The deplorables episode encapsulates the Democrats' struggles to connect with voters in recent decades. Now, even as the Republicans grow more extreme by the day and Trump vows dictatorship, the Democrats continue to flounder.

In this book, we'll show how and why the Democrats' approach has become so ineffective—and exactly what can be done to correct course.

We'll begin by examining the basic assumptions liberals make about American voters—assumptions that have coalesced into a standard story about how Trumpism took over the Republican Party and gained the support of a shockingly large segment of the electorate. That narrative claims the success of authoritarian politics is being driven by a combination of working-class economic distress, the failure of liberal politicians to defend working-class interests,

backlash against cultural change, and a Constitution that is struc-
turally stacked against the Democrats.

As we'll see, these explanations are fundamentally faulty. And
getting the causal story straight is of great importance, because de-
fective explanations for the crisis produce deficient prescriptions for
how to escape it. If we don't grasp what motivates Trump's voters,
as well as how we can impress swing voters and mobilize our own
liberal base, we'll never defeat Trumpism. Like the proverbial drunk
searching for his keys under the lamppost at night because that's
where the light is, we've been looking in all the wrong places. The
keys are somewhere back in the park, and it's time to pull out our
flashlights and find them.

Politics is a dominance game and a contest to capture the flag.
Politicians who seem to be the *strongest* leaders and most *ardent patriots* hold the advantage—and the Republicans never forget it.

Nor did the mighty liberals who democratized America. But current-day Democrats leave dominance and nationalism to democracy's foes. As a result, they fail to assert stable electoral superiority
over a party whose program boils down to groveling before a cheap-
jack dictator wannabe and making America safe for polluters, Proud
Boys, and plutocrats.

First, on *dominance*: Politics is a game of dominance, no less
than business, sports, and war. The Republicans have become specialists in the art of dominance. They take risks, double down on
even unpopular policies, use entertaining, provocative language,
embrace us-versus-them framing, and exude gusto in pursuit of
their goals. They bulldoze the Democrats, often convincing people—
and even many Democratic voters and leaders—that MAGA policies
are more popular than they really are. And while liberals have a hard
time facing the fact, Trump has established a reputation for strong
leadership, even as he deepens divisions, incites chaos, tears down
rights, and threatens free elections.

Trump *owns the libs* who his supporters think look down on
them, and "the libs" respond in a manner that reinforces his

dominance and leaves Trump in charge of the political arena. Ever since Trump entered national politics, liberals have implored him to declare whether he plans to be a dictator. They're still doing so now—as if he'll finally reveal, after all these years, if there are limits to his badness. Trump offers wink-and-nod responses like saying he won't be a dictator "other than day one" of his second term in office.[12] When reporters press him on his Hitleresque language, he responds "I never read 'Mein Kampf'," adding that Hitler said it "in a much different way."[13] While his sickening snark generates applause lines from MAGA enthusiasts, Democratic leaders alternate between yowling see, Trump *admits* he would be a dictator!—and offering still more fervent promises to control prescription drug prices.

Trump says it; scandalized Democrats play it back—*did you hear what he said?!* Trump savors the moment—then says it again, but worse. Frothed-up Democrats take the bait—*can you believe he's saying it again?!* The mainstream media runs Trump's statements and the Democrats' reactions wall-to-wall. Playing their part to a T, FOX and kindred MAGA media roll out reports on the spectacle of liberals in high dudgeon.

Meanwhile, the Democrats have yet to counterpunch—all they've done is *react*. They assume the more they amplify Trump being Trump, the more abhorrent he'll seem—and they would much rather let him discredit himself than take him on directly.

But by now, the whole country has Trump's lines and lies down—after all, they're pretty much all you hear.

Trump on top; libs owned; MAGA mission accomplished.

As John LaClair said of his favorite politician after driving down from Barrington to Durham to attend a Trump rally at the University of New Hampshire, "He's like a guy with a laser pointer, and the left is the cat."[14]

We live in an age of click-bait communication, infotainment, and public addiction to spectacle. If freedom's enemies project more chutzpah than its defenders, democracy will remain in jeopardy—if it survives at all.

The Republicans leverage their dominance advantage to normalize coercion, corruption, and cruelty. But rather than overmatch their dominance to defend dignity, decency, and democracy, the Democrats have become specialists in low-dominance messaging. They have grown pathologically risk-averse and poll-driven, allergic to engaging on hot-button issues except abortion—and more than a little boring. They have forgotten how to claim credit for their accomplishments and too often blame themselves—or, worse, the country as a whole—for problems that are the Republicans' doing. Rather than embracing the fight and giving as good as they get or better, liberals cry foul; they retreat into fact-checking instead of creating new facts on the ground. Timorous over what they wrongly regard as the Republicans' advantage on race, sex, and immigration, the Democrats leave the cultural arena to the Republicans, hoping against hope that another infrastructure bill or healthcare promise will carry them over the finish line.

The second way democracy's opponents have gained the upper hand is by *embracing nationalism*. Politics isn't just a dominance competition; it's also a matter of capturing the flag. For centuries, strong liberal leaders relentlessly tethered the defense of democracy and pursuit of justice to the whole nation's customs, welfare, and fate. The Democrats didn't win seven of nine presidential elections—and control of 16 of 18 Congresses—during the middle third of the 20th century just by convincing voters they were compassionate progressives. Franklin Roosevelt, Mary McLeod Bethune, Harry Truman, John Kennedy, Lyndon Johnson, and Martin Luther King were also unapologetic nationalists. They relied on a vigorous rhetoric of national honor and greatness to justify and build support for Social Security, Medicare, Medicaid, food stamps, federal aid to public education, voting rights, civil rights, liberal immigration policy, environmental protection, consumer protection, and progressive taxation.

Their messaging celebrated the nation's triumphs under liberal leadership and offered a bold vision of a still-greater age to come.

They appealed to the heart, not just the head. This was no less true of 19th-century progressives like Frederick Douglass and Cassius Clay, breakers of slavery and healers of the nation after its near-death experience in the Civil War. These leaders made liberal democracy patriotic—and patriotism liberal and democratic.

Little of this can be said of most liberal leaders today. Their squeamishness about nationalism and failure to embed identity groups' causes in an inspiring national narrative has left Trump's narrow, nativist fable as the main one Americans hear. In the absence of a compelling, inclusive *national-democratic* narrative, *ethnonationalists* like Trump, who identify the nation with a particular ethnic or religious group while treating members of other groups as second-class citizens, convince many Americans that they are the real patriots.

If policy appeals—the sole prop of Democrats' current electoral strategy—aren't embedded in gripping narratives that evoke strong emotions, voters will experience them as bloodless, boring bromides. And if the politicians who promise the policies don't tap into primal preferences for powerful protectors who fervently believe in the nation, voters will doubt their will and ability to enact the measures anyway. That's exactly what's happened to the Democrats today.

This phenomenon isn't uniquely American. Free government has been taking a tumble around the globe since about 2010, when Viktor Orbán, a right-wing demagogue who aligns with Putin while alienating EU partners, was elected prime minister of Hungary. In 2014, the imperious, anti-Muslim Narendra Modi and his Hindu nationalist BJP party won control of government in India. In 2015, the Law and Justice Party took power in Poland and spent the next eight years degrading democracy. In 2016, the democracy-busting Rodrigo Duterte won the presidency of the Philippines. In 2018, Jair Bolsonaro, the self-proclaimed "Trump of the Tropics," was elected president of Brazil and spent his time in office imitating his American mentor to a T.

In few of the countries where democracy has come under fire can the trend be attributed to economic crises or poor policy performance by prodemocratic parties. In the quarter-century prior to Modi's takeover in India, GDP per capita tripled under the able leadership of the liberal Indian National Congress party. In the quarter-century leading up to the takeover of Poland by antidemocratic demagogues, the economy grew by an astonishing 160 percent under liberal leaders, posting the strongest performance in Europe. The Philippines' economy fared well under the leadership of a liberal president prior to Duterte's victory. Surveys also reveal liberalization in cultural attitudes, with more people registering acceptance of LGBTQ people and embracing women in political leadership positions. Democracy's adversaries have been winning even where economies and minds are expanding.

What seems to unite the experiences of these countries is leadership. Everywhere they have gained ascendence, authoritarians like Orbán, Modi, and Trump have hammered at their purported superiority as protectors and lovers of the nation. Putin did the same as he won Russians' hearts and reestablished dictatorship at the beginning of the century. Liberal leaders, by contrast, no matter their successes as policymakers, no longer seem *strong*; they no longer appear *buoyant*—and they sometimes don't sound like ardent patriots, either. Ordinary people often don't recognize themselves in the stories liberal politicians tell about them, while the authoritarians speak a language of dominance and national greatness that connects.

With Biden in trouble despite a robust economy and a slew of policy accomplishments, and liberals struggling to capitalize on Trump's limitless liabilities, the Democrats as they currently operate may be out of bullets. And while Biden beat Trump in 2020, it's unclear what the outcome would have been if COVID hadn't intervened and the economy hadn't posted its worst performance since 1946. It's possible that the Republicans' abortion bans and attachment to a narcissistic grifter who faces 91 felony charges will prevent them from capturing power in 2024. But what will become of democracy if they then quit pressing widely loathed policies and re-place Trump with a more talented demagogue—perhaps someone in the mold of Orbán, Duterte, or Modi?

Whether or not Trump recaptures the White House in 2024, Trumpism will still be a force to contend with. As David Brooks says of the Republicans, "Trumpism now pervades the deepest recesses of their minds and governs their unconscious assumptions...the party of Eisenhower, Reagan, and McCain is stone cold gone."[15] This is a long-term struggle, and the Democrats have got to be better equipped for the fight than we are right now.

Defeating the forces of authoritarianism is the political combat task of our age, and we must take it up with the certitude and bold-ness that our eminent forebears did. Rebuilding the Democrats' ap-peal by reestablishing reputations for superior strength and patriotism is a challenge. But the fact that democracy's plight is due to flaws in liberals' leadership and messaging rather than economic crises, popular prejudices, or a faulty Constitution is good news. It means that the Democrats can turn the tables on Trumpism *now*.

In the following pages, we'll see how to do just that.

Part One of this book evaluates the standard explanation for how we got Trump. It shows that the conventional account is fundamen-tally unsound and yields recommendations for Democrats that hold little promise. Part Two examines the Republicans' embrace of a high-dominance political style and the Democrats' retreat to low-dominance messaging. It probes why liberal politicians have turned away from dominance and reveals the consequences of that trend. It then spells out how liberals can reclaim their dominance edge. Part Three investigates the Democrats' failure to "reclaim the nation" from democracy's enemies. It shows how the Democrats can seize the flag and propagate a powerful national-democratic narrative that beats the Trumpian tale. In Part Four, we'll see how distin-guished partisans of democracy throughout history have defended freedom and promoted justice. They defeated the forces of darkness in their day—and we, inspired by their example, *can do the same now.*

PART ONE

UNDERSTANDING THE CRISIS: WHAT'S WRONG WITH THE STANDARD STORY

1. The Standard Story in Brief

How did we get President Trump, and why is his authoritarian turn attracting support among so many Americans? Explaining this stunning development is an essential first step toward addressing the problem.

Many people believe that escalating economic insecurity and inequality have generated disillusionment with democracy, particularly among working-class voters. Others argue that alarm over rapid cultural change is to blame.

Or perhaps it's a toxic interplay between the two. As *Atlantic* staff writer Derek Thompson wrote on the eve of the 2016 election:

> First . . . Older non-college white men might not be desperately poor, but their economic fortunes are clearly in decline. They are watching their incomes stagnate, their children's income fall behind, and their cultural status wither. Second, Trump is fanning their anger by scapegoating poor minorities, thus making many of his economic messages fundamentally racial. Third, cultural and economic anxiety reinforce each other in ways that are invisible, yet obvious . . . racism's latent virus blooms into fullest view when majority groups fear the scarcity of their winnings.[16]

We social scientists are drawn to these kinds of accounts. Political explanations for political phenomena strike us as superficial. So rather than consider that misguided or unimaginative liberal leadership—a purely political factor—might be the root cause of working-class voters' turn to Trump, we look for structural causes. The idea that deep trends in the economy determine cultural attitudes, which in turn drive political behavior, is the kind of causal story we are comfortable with—perhaps *too* comfortable.

Liberal journalists, activists, and Democratic Party operatives often accept these basic tenets but also focus on political agents. They tend to blame right-wing leaders who resist or roll back reforms, liberal leaders who have supposedly drifted away from their progressive commitments, and benighted ordinary folks who choose leaders who appeal to their prejudices rather than serving their true interests.

These explanations for Trumpism have come together in a narrative that now dominates mainstream thinking. In a nutshell, it runs something like this:

The early postwar decades were a golden era for prosperity, class justice, and democracy. Between 1945 and 1980 or so, the economy grew briskly, and the middle class expanded apace. Job security and satisfaction were high, and income inequalities were low. Taxes were steeply progressive, so most people felt justice was tolerably served.

The Democrats pursued progressive economic policies that differed starkly from the Republicans'. We stuck with the working people, and they stuck with us.

Authoritarian demagogues came and went, but they didn't capture the top offices. Prosperity was widely shared, so most people had little reason to back politicians who sought to overturn the system.

But then the Golden Age began to wane. Gone were the days of Dwight Eisenhower, Richard Nixon, and Gerald Ford, Republican presidents who knew that state intervention to temper markets would benefit almost everyone and bind society together. Ronald Reagan turned away from responsible conservatism, hollowing out social programs to fund tax cuts for the rich. The economy began to experience periods of prolonged stagnation, and even when it grew the top earners captured all the gains. The real value of the minimum wage deteriorated. Inequality exploded—and neoliberal policies just made it worse.

The increasingly knowledge-based economy created abundant prospects for the well-schooled. But those without a higher education felt their anxieties mount as their job security ebbed.

Satisfaction with work flagged. He used to manufacture the finest steel in the world, but now he's making lattes. She didn't have to work outside the home unless she chose to do so. But now she has to take an unsatisfying desk job—and spend most of what she makes on daycare for the kids.

Their self-worth took a hit. They used to feel like they were in the middle of the pack and had plenty of room to rise. But now they felt the American Dream was fading. The hollowing out of the middle class fueled a steep rise in "deaths of despair."

The folks might still have kept thinking democracy worked for them if only one of the parties had stuck by them. But the Democrats, enthralled by globalization and increasingly focused on the upwardly mobile, converged with the Republicans on economic policy. They now prioritized economic growth and technological innovation. Equity brought up the rear.

The Golden Age gave way to the New Gilded Age of the 1980s-2020s. Rightists like Reagan and Newt Gingrich might have founded the new order, but neoliberalism-friendly Democrats like Bill Clinton and Barack Obama extended it.

The Democrats ignored class justice and became preoccupied with lifting up immigrants, women, and ethnic and sexual minorities. To native-born working-class people from the ethnic majority, liberal leaders now seemed to care more about political correctness and the rights of refugees than ordinary folks' livelihoods. The apparent rise in the status of people of color, exemplified by Obama's presidency, left white working-class people feeling further diminished.

Enter Trump, the outsider. He blamed the struggles of working people on minorities, immigrants, foreign exporters, and out-of-touch liberal elites. Whites who lacked a college education found Trump's blame game compelling. He played on their resentments, deepening their prejudices and polarizing the electorate. The result was Trump's shocking 2016 victory and the rise of authoritarianism in the years since.

Steeped in this standard story, liberals often conclude that the way to reverse the drift toward Trumpism is to double down on our traditional economic justice agenda. To the extent that we bear responsibility for democracy's plight, the logic goes, we need to return to the ways of a bygone era when we focused more resolutely on the working man's jam.

If you buy this story, you're in good company. Most liberal scholars and politicos believe some version of it, too. As a liberal social scientist, I believed it as well. I began to question it only after I saw that the measures it calls for—pursuing progressive economic policies and ramping up shows of concern for the working person's plight—were failing to put a dent in the Trumpian threat. Studying cases of democratic crisis outside the United States deepened my doubts.

Some elements of the standard story are true. But on the whole, is the cause-and-effect narrative it offers logically sound and empirically well-supported? Has economic decline fueled working-class despair, cultural resentment, and a turn toward authoritarianism? Let's examine the evidence.

2. The Economy Has Not Declined and Injustice Has Not Surged

I f the standard story is correct, the decades leading up to the election of Trump must have been a period of deepening economic suffering, especially for middle- and working-class people. There should be hard evidence for this distress in the data.

Has the American economy fallen behind? No. Except for a handful of tiny luxury-states like Luxembourg and Qatar, the United States is the richest country in the world.[17] GDP per person is much higher than anywhere else, including the rich European and East Asian countries where democracy hasn't come under serious threat. When Trump was elected in 2016, GDP per person stood at $59k, compared to $42k in Germany, $37k in France, and $35k in Japan.

America's economic performance during the quarter-century leading up to Trump's election was relatively strong, with GDP per person rising by roughly 50 percent. That rate was faster than in Germany, France, and Japan, where it increased by 35, 30, and 20 percent respectively. Since then, the American economy has expanded while the others have not. In 2022, GDP per person stood at $66k in the United States, $43k in Germany, $39k in France, and $36k in Japan.

Is the *typical* American person or family hurting compared to people in other rich countries? No. One argument in the standard story is that while *average* incomes (which track GDP per person) have risen robustly, *median* incomes have not, so pay has flatlined or fallen for the typical person.

It's true that median figures tell a more meaningful story than averages. The *average* is calculated by adding all values and dividing by the number of cases. The *median* is the value for which half of the cases are larger, and half are smaller. To see the difference, consider this example involving a community of five people: Two earn $40k per year, one makes $50k, and two make $1 million. The average salary in this group is $426k. That looks like a pretty rich group if you take the average number. But it's actually two very rich guys and three who are busting their butts to bring home the bacon. The median number is $50k—that's the typical guy.

An even better measure is *median disposable income* per person—the money a person has to spend after she's paid her taxes and received government transfers, adjusted for purchasing power parity (meaning what you can buy for your money).

So how does America look when viewed through this lens? In 2021, the median disposable income per person was roughly 40 percent higher than in Germany, 50 percent higher than in France, and 70 percent higher than in Japan. The typical non-college-educated American can buy more with what she makes than the typical college-educated German, French, or Japanese person.

Have incomes stagnated or fallen for everyone but the rich? No. Figure 2.1 graphs real median personal income in the United States. In 1980, it was $25k per year. In the year Trump was elected, it stood at $37k, rising to $40k in 2022. So between 1980 and 2022, the typical American's income rose by about 60 percent.

One could certainly hope for better. But are these numbers bad enough to explain the rise of politicians seeking to overthrow democracy?

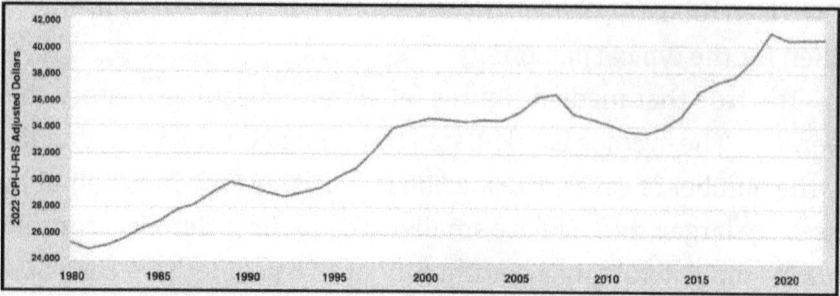

Figure 2.1. Real Median Personal Income, 1980-2022

What about in the years just prior to Trump's election? Incomes did fall during the financial crisis of 2008 and its aftermath, but they rebounded strongly thereafter—and much more robustly than in other rich countries. Between 2012 and 2016, median household income grew by 12 percent; Obama's second term was the best on record. So incomes were rising significantly—under a Democratic president—at the time Trump was elected.

Has joblessness grown more severe? Just the opposite. The financial crisis drove unemployment up to 10 percent in 2010, the highest level since 1983. But it then declined steadily, falling to five percent when Trump was elected in 2016. As of March 2024, with Biden trailing Trump in the polls, it's been under four percent for two years. It hasn't been this low for that long since the late 1960s.

Is income inequality especially severe in the United States, and has it been escalating? It's higher than in other wealthy countries but hasn't changed substantially in three decades. To measure income inequality, analysts use Gini scores, which range from 1-100. In the 1960s and 1970s, America's score ranged in the mid-high 30s. It hit its low in 1980, bottoming out at 35. Under Reagan and George H. W. Bush, it grew to 40. But ever since Bill Clinton terminated Reaganism in the mid-1990s, it's remained steady, fluctuating within a very narrow range. It was 41 the year Trump won and 40 in 2021. That's just two points higher than in 1964, roughly the midpoint of the standard story's Golden Age.

Liberals rightly regard these numbers as too high. The Europeans' Gini scores are generally in the low 30s, and we have plenty of work to do to make the United States a more egalitarian society. But as with the data on income, it's hard to see why this trendline would spark an unprecedented crisis of democracy.

Have American workers been cut out of gains in productivity? They've been getting less than they used to and less than they deserve, but they haven't done worse than workers in some other rich countries. The OECD published a study on this issue that covered 1995-2013. The numbers are presented in Table 2.1.[18]

Country	Labor productivity	Real average wages	Real median wages
Sweden	2.4	2.7	2.6
United States	**1.8**	**1.2**	**0.5**
France	1.1	1.1	1.4
Canada	0.9	0.4	0.2
Germany	0.7	0.6	0.5
Japan	0.7	0.3	0.2

Table 2.1. Growth of Labor Productivity and Wages, 1995-2013, Select OECD Countries (average annual growth rates, percent)

The Swedes did much better than we did, and they should be an example for us. Not only was their productivity growth high, but real median wages also grew along with it. But the American pattern, in which the median earner captured only between one third and one fifth of productivity gains, isn't unique to the United States. It's also visible in Japan and Canada. In both countries, moreover, productivity grew slowly, and the absolute growth of the median wage was just 40 percent of the American rate. Decoupling of productivity and wages was less dramatic in Germany. But as in Japan and Canada, productivity grew at just 40 percent of the American rate. As a result, median income rose half a percentage point per year, the same as in the United States.

So in absolute terms, the median American wage earner did as well as her German counterpart and substantially better than her

Japanese and Canadian counterparts. Yet no one like Trump reached the pinnacle of power in any of these other countries.

Has the real minimum wage been falling? A superficial glance at the numbers can create that impression. While the federal minimum wage is $7.25 today, its inflation-adjusted worth was $10.25 when Reagan won office. Hence the frequent appearance of stories like "After Inflation, People Making U.S. Minimum Wage Are Earning Less Now Than 60 Years Ago," reported by *CNBC* in 2022.[19] No wonder Jack and Diane are turning to Trump.

But those numbers tell us practically nothing about actual incomes, because only *one* percent of American earners make federal minimum wage today, compared to 15 percent in 1980.[20] That's largely because 30 states and the District of Columbia, where 63 percent of Americans live, now set their own higher minimum wages. In West Virginia, it's $8.75; in Ohio, $10.45; in Arkansas, $11; and in Colorado, $14.42. Many localities set it higher than their state's minimum. The California minimum wage is $16, but in San Francisco, it's $18.07.[21]

Weighting the minimum wage for states' populations, even without accounting for the higher rates in many localities, the minimum wage in 2023 was $10.81—56 cents higher in real terms than when Reagan took office. In 2020, economist Ernie Tedeschi estimated that the "effective minimum wage" hit $11.80 in 2019—higher, by his calculations, than it's ever been—and it's risen since then.[22] (By the way, Tedeschi is a liberal who Biden appointed chief economist on the White House Council of Economic Advisers in 2023.) So simply comparing today's federal minimum wage with what it used to be is blatantly misleading.

We could go round and round with numbers all day, and it's certainly not hard to find some bad news as well. While the average American lives in a bigger house, drives a larger and newer vehicle (we love our monster trucks and SUVs), watches wider TV screens, and can afford to eat out more often than the average European or Japanese, we have less time to enjoy these things since our life expectancies lag behind—and our vacation times are shorter. We are also less likely to enjoy what time we have feeling safe: Legacies of racial oppression and ludicrously lax gun laws contribute to murder rates that run about five times the European norm.

But at the very least, the data we've seen suggest the need to reexamine our assumptions. The fact that they are often systematically overlooked in the standard story of how Trumpism has taken hold is significant. If we're to really understand why so many working-class voters seem less concerned about the predations of the one percent than we think they should be, we need to look at a fuller picture.

That leads us to how folks perceive their own circumstances.

3. Working-Class People Have Not Felt That Their Well-Being Is Eroding

E ven if people haven't done nearly as poorly as you might think from listening to the standard story, perhaps working in a globalized, technology-driven economy has made them *feel* less satisfied and secure now than in the past. Has it?

For answers, let's look at data from the General Social Survey (GSS), which has tracked Americans' perceptions since the 1970s.[23] Having data that stretch back that far affords a look at people's subjective feelings and beliefs during the last decade of what the standard story characterizes as the Golden Age of working-class welfare and middle-class expansion.

We'll focus primarily on whites who lack a college degree (we'll call them "non-college"). This is the largest ethnic-educational demographic in the United States, accounting for about one third of voters. It is this group whose feelings of well-being, job security, job satisfaction, and optimism are said to have eroded. And it is this group's turn to Trump that has posed the gravest challenge to democracy. To test whether Republican voters might have felt especially hard-hit, I sort respondents by party affiliation and present those numbers in graphs and accompanying tables.

We can start with people's overall feelings of life satisfaction. The GSS asks: "Taken all together, how would you say things are these days—would you say that you are very happy, pretty happy, or not too happy?"

Americans, including those lacking a college education, register a high degree of contentment, and there has been no meaningful change over time. In 2018, 88 percent of non-college-credentialed whites said they were happy, three points higher than in 1972.

Were Republicans less content? As Figure 3.1 and the accompanying table show, non-college white Republicans' happiness rates averaged three points *higher* than the Democrats, a trend that held even during Obama's time in office.

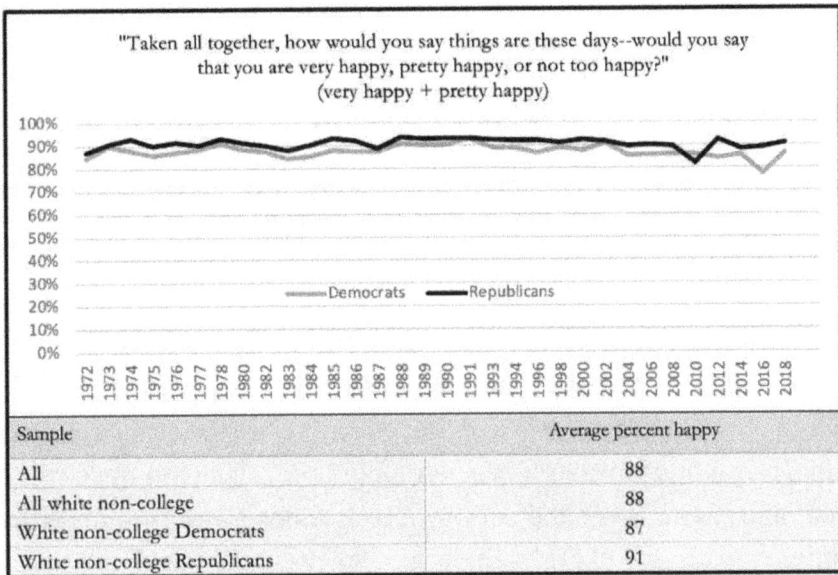

"Taken all together, how would you say things are these days--would you say that you are very happy, pretty happy, or not too happy?"
(very happy + pretty happy)

Sample	Average percent happy
All	88
All white non-college	88
White non-college Democrats	87
White non-college Republicans	91

Figure 3.1. Non-College-Educated Whites'
Assessments of Personal Happiness

What about job security? The number of non-college whites who felt they were *unlikely* to lose their jobs over the next 12 months fluctuated between 83 and 93 percent. There was no downward trend over time, and between 2012 and 2016 the numbers topped 90 percent—as high as any other equivalent stretch of time. Non-college white Republicans, on average, registered slightly higher feelings of job security than non-college white Democrats, including during Obama's presidency, as shown in Figure 3.2.

"Thinking about the next 12 months, how likely do you think it is that you will lose your job or be laid off--very likely, fairly likely, not too likely, or not at all likely?" (not at all likely + not too likely)

Sample	Average percent secure in job
All	90
All white non-college	89
White non-college Democrats	88
White non-college Republicans	91

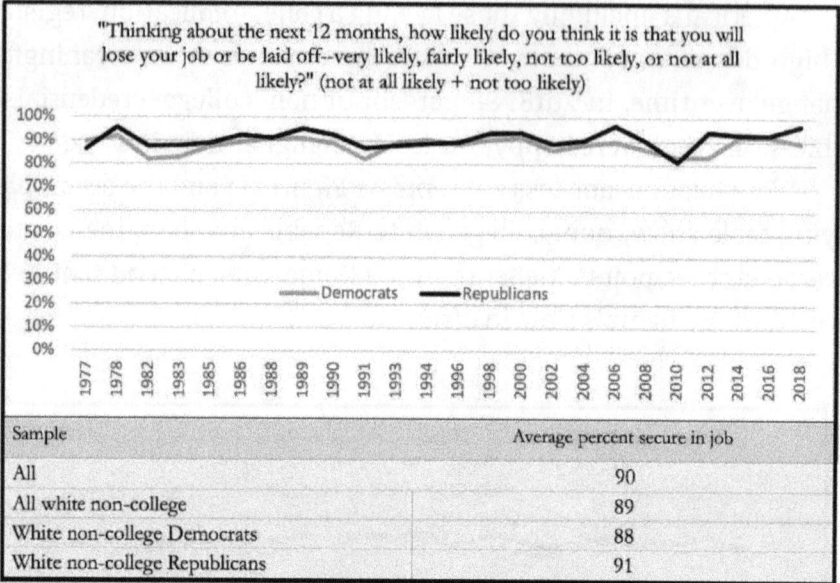

Figure 3.2. Perceptions of Job Security among Non-College-Educated Whites

Still, bread, butter, and benefits aren't everything. Contentment with work also matters, and many observers assume it's been declining for people who lack a higher education. In the story that Donald Trump and Elizabeth Warren alike tell, folks who once mined coal and manufactured steel now stock shelves and ring up orders for Glazed Cheesy BBQ Meatballs and Spicy Garlic Chicken Rollers at the 7-Eleven. That can devastate feelings of efficacy and dignity on the job.

Yet job satisfaction was high and stable over the entire period. Between 78 and 87 percent of non-college whites said they liked what they did. In the year of Trump's election, 83 percent said they were satisfied with their work—four points higher than in 1973, when steel production reached its zenith and over a half-million Americans worked in the industry, compared to 80k in 2016. It was also four points higher than in 1987, when 150k Americans mined coal, a number that had fallen to one third that level at the time of Trump's election. And over the four surveys taken during Obama's presidency, non-college white Republicans exceeded their Democratic counterparts in job satisfaction by an average of four points. Figure 3.3 graphs the numbers.

Many analysts regard jobs in the age of coal and steel as superior to those that have multiplied since the 1980s. For example, economists Anne Case and Angus Deaton attribute what they claim is "the rising tide of despair" among non-college whites partly to "the fall in good jobs, those that offer a sense of belonging, meaning, and purpose and prospects for advancement."[24] But in light of the data showing no overall decline in non-college whites' satisfaction with life, job security, or quality of work, it makes sense to revisit that premise.

Jobs for steel workers and coal miners have indeed declined precipitously. But those for industrial machine mechanics, who earn about 50 percent more than steelworkers and miners, are growing fast. Positions for wind turbine technicians also pay more and are

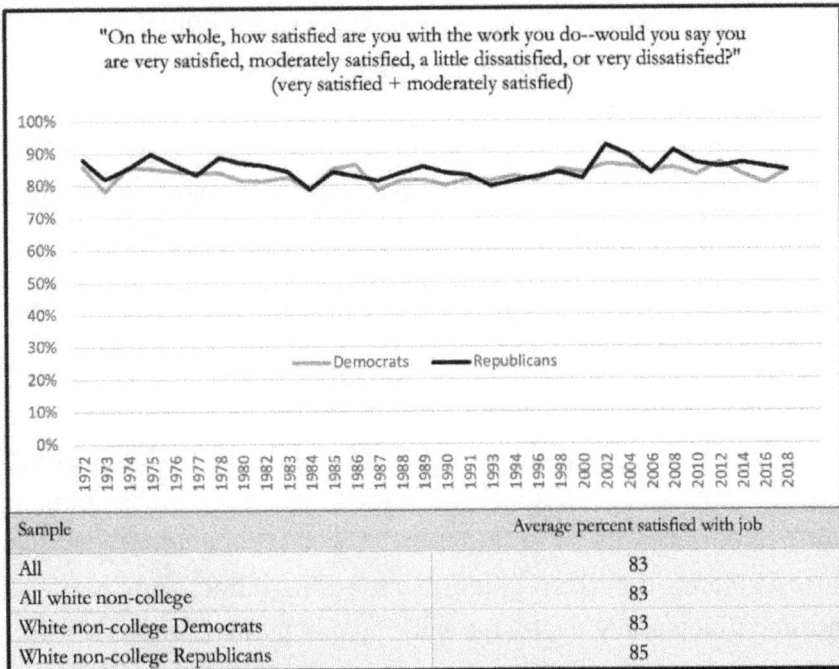

"On the whole, how satisfied are you with the work you do--would you say you are very satisfied, moderately satisfied, a little dissatisfied, or very dissatisfied?" (very satisfied + moderately satisfied)

Sample	Average percent satisfied with job
All	83
All white non-college	83
White non-college Democrats	83
White non-college Republicans	85

Figure 3.3. Job Satisfaction among Non-College-Educated Whites

expected to expand by 70 percent during the 2020s. More workers are now employed as airline mechanics and service technicians (130k) than in coal (40k) and steel (80k) combined, and they pay twice as much as the mills and the mines ever did. None of these jobs requires an hour of college, and they are not geographically concentrated.[25]

Businesses that make pharmaceuticals, medical supplies, computer equipment, furniture, and ice cream are currently adding a multitude of jobs amidst booming demand. Many don't require a college degree, and employers are scrambling to fill them.[26]

Ten months after Trump's election, Gallup's principal economist, Jonathan Rothwell, published findings on the effects of manufacturing job losses on life satisfaction.[27] He aimed to answer the following question: "Is there a particular psychological price that is paid when manufacturing jobs disappear—one that could in turn have an effect on how people view the world and vote for political candidates?" He hypothesized that "manufacturing downturns may create lower life evaluation, even for people or communities who apparently did not experience large losses in overall employment rates or average income."

To test that possibility, Rothwell used data from over 173k Americans interviewed by Gallup. He measured manufacturing exposure for every county in America and found that, "Overall, the data simply don't support the hypothesis that a decline in manufacturing jobs in an area has an unusually negative effect on how individuals who live in that area evaluate their lives—any more so than a decline in jobs in general."

When Rothwell analyzed the same variables by region, he found that "shifting jobs from manufacturing to other sectors is not damaging to community life evaluation...There is no evidence in these data to indicate that the regional decline of manufacturing per se has resulted in lower life evaluations for people living in those communities." He concluded: "Manufacturing jobs can be good jobs, of course, but there doesn't appear to be anything unique about them in terms of the way people look at their lives when other jobs are developed to replace them."

It's fair to ask whether our elite liberal nostalgia for the mills and the mines—places few of us or our parents ever worked, but which we assume were the beloved occupational rocks of Gibraltar for those who did—is really shared by the people who labored there themselves. Do most of the sons and grandsons of men who worked at U.S. Steel and Westmoreland Coal really wish to return to those jobs?

Billy Joel no doubt captured a gloomy reality when he crooned: "Well we're living here in Allentown/And they're closing all the factories down/But they've taken all the coal from the ground/And the union people crawled away."

But that song came out in 1982. Today Allentown is the fastest-growing metro area in Pennsylvania. It's home to 785k people, twice the population in 1982. Like all places, it has its problems, but it's a humming medium-sized metropolis with a diversified economy, minor-league baseball and hockey teams, and a vibrant housing market. Allentowners have moved on.

Common belief also holds that trends associated with globalization have shortened the time people spend on the same job and thereby reduced opportunities for advancement, job security, and belonging in the workplace. But according to a 2022 report by the Employee Benefits Research Institute: "While some believe current American workers change jobs more frequently than was the case for past generations, the data on employee tenure show that career jobs (individuals holding only one job for their entire career) never actually existed for most workers and continue not to exist for most workers." The report concludes: "Over the past 40 (or nearly 40) years, the median tenure of all wage and salary workers ages 25 or older has stayed at approximately five years."[28]

Let's now consider how people evaluate their ability to get ahead. If morale has diminished, we might expect people to have grown less confident in their ability to shape their own fortunes. The

GSS poses a question that's directly on point: "Some people say that people get ahead by their own hard work; others say that lucky breaks or help from other people are more important. Which do you think is most important?"

Figure 3.4 graphs the proportion of non-college whites who think people get ahead by their own hard work. It shows a moderate *upward* trend over time. In the year of Trump's election, it stood at 77 percent, 12 points higher than in 1973. In 2018, it notched up again, with four out of five respondents holding that hard work had a bigger effect on their lives than luck and breaks. White working-class Americans' average scores were a bit *higher* than those of Americans as a whole. And again, Republicans are slightly more upbeat than Democrats. These aren't the numbers we'd expect if people felt their lot was plummeting.

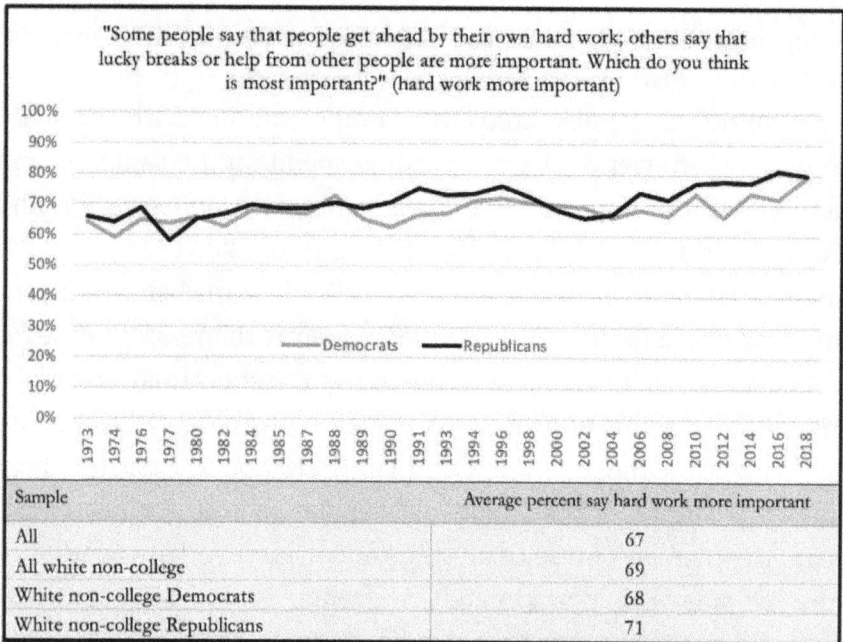

"Some people say that people get ahead by their own hard work; others say that lucky breaks or help from other people are more important. Which do you think is most important?" (hard work more important)

Sample	Average percent say hard work more important
All	67
All white non-college	69
White non-college Democrats	68
White non-college Republicans	71

Figure 3.4. Non-College-Educated Whites' Perceptions That Hard Work Matters More Than Luck and Connections

In short, the data show no sign that white Americans who lack a college degree have felt their personal happiness, job security, quality of employment, or personal efficacy has fallen. In the years just prior to Trump's election, their views of their own situation were actually improving.

Nor is there any indication that non-college Republicans from the ethnic majority have grown more dissatisfied or insecure than their Democratic compatriots. If working-class G.O.P.ers had become particularly unhappy, we might have at least a partial explanation for why they would turn their party into a democracy-battering hate machine. But they offered slightly *higher* evaluations of their circumstances than Democrats, even while Obama was in office.

Needless to say, some people have felt that their lot has deteriorated, and their numbers are no doubt substantial in certain occupations and geographical areas. That fact alone, as well as liberals' principled commitment to aiding those in need, are reason enough to mind the concerns of those who have fallen behind. But nowhere in the data do we find compelling evidence that rising working-class demoralization explains Trumpism.

Now, you don't have to be a statistician to know that these numbers might miss vital trends among certain pockets of disgruntled voters. But if the standard story of Trump riding a wave of working-class resentment over economic decline had merit, we would expect to see *some* evidence of growing discontent in the aggregate data, perhaps especially among Republican voters. But there's no sign of that in the numbers.

We do have more fine-grained data that are of immediate relevance to the 2016 election, and they too provide little evidence that Trump rode to power on a tide of working-class economic frustration. In the 2018 VOTER Survey, Robert Griffin and John Sides used a new measure of economic distress and found that "working-class white people are not distinctively distressed relative to other groups" and that economic anxiety was actually falling in the years leading up to the election. Furthermore, when they checked data sources from before the election, they found that levels of economic distress among Trump supporters were not higher than those of Clinton supporters. As the survey data went back to 2012, the authors showed that "there was no difference in economic distress between Obama-Trump voters and Obama-Clinton voters." They concluded that "this pattern does confirm evidence from earlier surveys showing that economic distress was not a distinctive feature of support for Donald Trump."[29]

For another angle, let's examine subjective perceptions of social status. The matter is relevant not only to the United States but also to other countries where illiberal parties that might threaten democracy have made inroads in elections. There's been a wave of excellent scholarly articles recently that try to grapple with the matter.[30] But a 2022 paper by Daniel Oesch, a leading specialist on occupational change, social stratification, and political behavior, and coauthor Nathalie Vigna, is the first major study to really attack the big question directly: Whatever prevailing economic conditions might be, have working-class people felt their social status is slumping?[31]

The authors use the following question from the International Social Survey Programme: "[I]n our society there are groups which tend to be toward the top and groups which tend to be toward the bottom. Where would you put yourself on a scale from the bottom to the top?" The data run from 1987 to 2017.

Respondents are separated into five categories: upper-middle class, small business owners, unskilled working class, skilled working class, and lower-middle class. As one might expect, the authors find that the subjective status of workers is lower than that of upper-middle-class people and small business owners. But the finding on change over time "contradicts our expectations. The subjective social status of the unskilled and the skilled working class remained basically constant in Britain, Poland, Sweden, and Switzerland. It possibly even increased in Germany (between 2002 and 2015) and the US (between 1987 and 2005)."

Mindful that working-class men might have experienced a greater sense of status deflation than working-class women, Oesch and Vigna repeat the analysis by gender. But they find that "the time trends do not reveal any systematic decline in subjective status among either men or women."

How does educational attainment affect perceived social status? The authors replicate their analysis using three groups: people who lack a high-school education, those who have one but lack a university degree, and people who have a university degree. They report: "[T]he evolution over time in social status is again flat. The social status of both the low- and the mid-educated group seems constant over time. Despite some fluctuations, the dominant trend is stability."

These relationships may obscure shifts in the composition of classes. To take these factors into account, Oesch and Vigna analyze the evolution of social status by education and class, holding gender and age constant. They report: "[T]hese estimates contradict the idea of an absolute decrease in the subjective social status of the unskilled working class in six out of eight countries. . . . In the US, their status even seems to have increased." When they compare the evolution in social status between the upper-middle class and the skilled working class, "there is no relative status decline for the skilled working class in the United States, but a status increase."

The authors further test whether status decline differed between production and service workers. They find essentially no difference between the groups' subjective status relative to members of the upper-middle class, either over time or in absolute terms.

The authors conclude: "[O]ur findings throw doubt on the narrative that sees workers' falling subjective social status as a prominent driver behind the radical right. . . . [W]e may need to find another explanation for the radical right's rise than the status loss of the working class."

It's easy, of course, to find stretches of America where communities have been decimated by industrial decline. The geographical concentration of "left-behind communities" in some swing states is and should be of concern to Democrats. But given the numbers we've seen here, combined with the fact that Trump didn't restore jobs to those communities but remains the white working-class favorite anyway, there are ample grounds to question whether his appeal is based mainly on his ability to feel or express their economic pain, let alone to ease it.

Could it be that those who are unpampered by the refinements of higher learning are more resilient than we assume—and more than their espresso- and Chardonnay-swilling would-be benefactors are ourselves?

4. There Is No Epidemic
of "Deaths of Despair"

In a 2015 paper, Anne Case and Angus Deaton popularized the term "deaths of despair," and in 2020, they published a book, *Deaths of Despair and the Future of Capitalism*.[32] The ominous black-and-white photo on the book's cover shows a middle-aged man in a plain T-shirt—presumably despairing and non-college-educated—leaning over a table, his face buried in his hands. The misery is palpable.

The book won countless awards, made bestseller lists, and achieved instant-classic status. It became a centerpiece—really, a kind of summary—of the standard story about why democracy is imperiled in America.

The phenomenon the authors identify is indeed disturbing. Age-adjusted deaths of despair as they define them—suicides, fatalities from "alcohol-related causes," and fatalities from "drug-related causes"—rose appreciably during the 1960s and then stabilized in the 1980s and 1990s, fluctuating within a narrow range between about 23 and 25 people per 100k per year. But then, in the 21st century, they began climbing steeply, and by the end of the 2010s stood at about 45 people per 100k.[33] The authors focus in particular on the rise in mortality among those who lack a college education, and especially a narrow slice of middle-aged whites.

Case and Deaton attribute the apparent rise to "American capitalism," which they say "is now destroying the lives of blue-collar

America." They hold: "For the White working class, today's America has become a land of broken families and few prospects."[34]

Of course some people are hurting, and it stands to reason that those with a higher education have better life prospects. The question is whether people are hurting economically more than in the past. The evidence for that claim, as we've seen, is lacking.

How, then, can we account for the skyrocketing rates of these deaths that Case and Deaton identify? At this point, we must start placing "deaths of despair" in quotation marks, since closer examination reveals that most of these events are not deaths of despair at all.

When we disaggregate the numbers, several noteworthy facts emerge. One is that the suicide rate has indeed been on the rise during the 21st century, from 10.4 per year per 100k people in 2000 to 13.5 in 2020.[35] But in the longer term, we see that the rate has waxed and waned moderately over the postwar period. In 2020, it was virtually the same as in 1950 (13.2) and 1975 (13.6), before globalization and neoliberalism are said to have laid the working person low.[36] The same pattern holds for alcohol-related deaths, the second of the three types of deaths tracked in Case and Deaton's index.

In reality, the *entire* long-term rise in "deaths of despair" is driven by growth in drug-related causes.[37] Figure 4.1 graphs the numbers.

Suicides are definitely deaths of despair. Alcohol-related deaths have also been seen to stem from unhappiness and probably make for a reasonably sound indicator of despair as well.

But deaths from drug-related causes are another matter entirely. They result from *accidental* overdoses. Drug-induced intentional suicides are classified as suicides and are reflected in the data on that factor; deaths from "drug-related causes" are unintentional. They precisely track the flooding of the American market with legal, doctor-prescribed opioids in the first decade of the century and then with illegal opioids (mainly fentanyl) over the past decade.

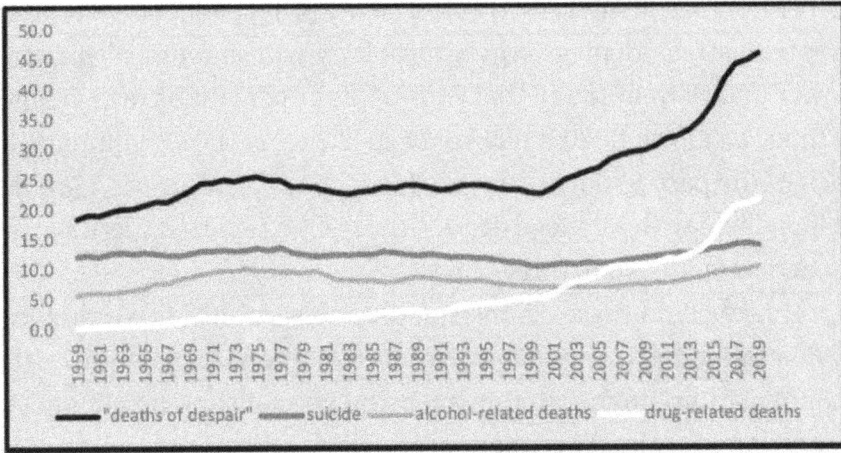

Figure 4.1. "Deaths of Despair" (per 100k)

Classification of accidental poisoning from these drugs as "deaths of despair" is based on the claim that people use these drugs to medicate their "despair." So even if deaths arising from their use are accidental, Case and Deaton argue that they are due to rising despondency. But there's a highly plausible alternative explanation: the drugs became much more dangerous and accessible.

To support their "demand-side" explanation, Case and Deaton cite several factors. One is that deaths from drug overdoses have risen fastest in areas where economic conditions are worse and/or declining, which are also areas that disproportionately support the Republicans.

Second, according to Case and Deaton, we would expect demand for potentially deadly drugs to be increasing more generally given a rise in unhappiness indicated in life satisfaction surveys. The authors hold: "One such measure [of rising dissatisfaction] is the fraction of the population who report that they are 'not too happy' in the GSS. From 1972 to 1990, this fraction showed no clear trend, but it has trended upwards sharply since about 1990, and much more so among those with less education."

Third, Case and Deaton refer to a study that apparently shows a rise in psychic pain. They rely on a survey conducted by David

Blanchflower and Andrew Oswald that asked respondents how often they felt "stress, depression, and problems with emotions." Blanchflower and Oswald found that in 1993, four percent of respondents without a college degree reported experiencing these symptoms in each of the past 30 days, compared to eight percent in 2019. Among respondents with a college degree, those who reported these symptoms rose from two to three percent.[38]

How well do these claims stand up to scrutiny? In a statistical evaluation of the claim that economic conditions explain the crisis, economist Christopher Ruhm, a leading specialist on health policy, found that counties that experienced deteriorating financial circumstances between 1999 and 2015 did post a higher rise in drug deaths. But he also found that "changes in economic conditions accounted for less than one tenth of the rise in drug-related deaths." Once he controlled for other relevant factors, even that modest relationship disappeared.

Ruhm concluded that "supply-side" factors—namely, the increased availability of potentially deadly drugs—and not "demand-side" factors, such as growing despondency, accounted for the rise in drug-related deaths. He reports: "These results suggest that the 'deaths of despair' framing, while provocative, is unlikely to explain the main sources of the fatal drug epidemic and that efforts to improve economic conditions in distressed locations, while desirable for other reasons, are not likely to yield significant reductions in drug mortality."[39]

In a 2017 study, sociologist Ryan Masters and colleagues pointed instead to obesity-related metabolic diseases, combined with the opioid epidemic, as the key drivers of rising mortality rates. As Masters put it in an interview, "The despair death narrative caught fire and has since begun to inform mortality research and media coverage, and shape dialogue among policymakers and politicians. Yet our research shows it is demonstrably incorrect."[40] Other researchers have also found that cardiovascular disease, which is highly correlated with obesity rates, checked gains in life expectancy after 2010.[41]

What about Case and Deaton's claim that GSS data showed a sharp upward trend in unhappiness starting in the 1990s? Examination of the GSS data, however, shows no appreciable upward trend, still less a sharp, lasting one. In 2018, the proportion of unhappy non-college Americans was 14 percent, three percent lower than in 1972.

As for the report on the rise of distress among non-college respondents, of course that may be happening. Yet these reports also might reflect greater comfort with expressing negative feelings and admitting to mental illness. According to a recent study by sociologist Bernice Pescosolido and colleagues, in the past several decades, there has been a substantial rise in Americans who believe that mental health issues are due to brain disruptions and genetic factors rather than flaws in character or upbringing, as well as a significant fall in social rejection of people who suffer from depression.[42]

In fact, the data strongly suggest that "supply-side factors," especially the widespread availability of fentanyl beginning around 2013, explain the rise of drug deaths. Data from the National Institute on Drug Abuse show that the explosion in drug deaths after 2014 was due to the exponential rise in fentanyl overdose fatalities.[43]

Even the much lower absolute levels and the far smaller increases in deaths from other drugs are, for the most part, driven by their being laced with fentanyl. Specialists cannot always say precisely how often users who die from overdoses were unaware that their drugs were cut with fentanyl, but by all accounts, the frequency of such cases is very high and rising.[44]

Evidence of this problem is found by examining deaths from other drugs where fentanyl was also present in the deceased person's system. Given the drug's unrivaled lethality—it's 50-100 times stronger than heroin—specialists consider fentanyl a likely cause of death when it's present. For example, while cocaine-involved deaths multiplied by about six times between 2006 and 2021, virtually the entire rise was due to the presence of fentanyl. Over the same period, prescription opioid-involved fatalities rose by about 30 percent, but fentanyl lacing accounts for the change. Deaths from prescription opioids alone, without the presence of fentanyl, declined by about 40 percent.[45]

The demographic profile of those who are dying from overdoses adds to the evidence that an explosion in the availability of deadly drugs, rather than escalating despondency, drives the epidemic of fatalities. In Case and Deaton's account, the despairing parties are middle-aged, working-class whites. Supposedly, they are especially victimized by capitalism and prone to despair.

But in 2015, after fentanyl began to flood the streets and dealers *en masse* started cutting their cocaine, heroin, and meth with it, Black fatalities began to rise precipitously. In 2020, deaths of Blacks surpassed those of whites as a proportion of their group's population. And while suburban, small-town, and rural areas previously had suffered more deaths per capita from fentanyl than large cities, urban centers became the largest sites of death in 2020.[46]

The victims of fentanyl poisoning are also rapidly becoming younger. The proportion of drug-related deaths among Americans under 45, who use recreational drugs at a higher rate than older cohorts, rose from half to two thirds between 2010 and 2021. In 2021, 84 percent of teen overdose deaths involved fentanyl-laced drugs. The leading cause of death for Americans 18–45 years of age is now fentanyl overdose, and the CDC reported that fentanyl poisoning, along with COVID, was driving down life expectancy in the United States.[47] That leaves the question of whether accidental drug overdoses can be classified as "deaths of despair" at all. It's evident that the answer is no. As we've seen, accidental drug deaths are qualitatively different from suicides and alcohol-related deaths. What's more, the sudden, astronomical rise in one cause of death (accidental drug overdoses) and the absence of such change in the other two (suicide and alcohol) suggests that they are not measuring the same thing. A more valid measure of deaths of despair would include suicides and alcohol-related deaths alone.

That leads us back to the core causal claim of the "deaths of despair" argument. It's that "American capitalism," in Case and Deaton's wording, "is now destroying the lives of blue-collar America." According to this argument, American-style capitalism is much harder on those who lack privilege than the type of capitalism found in countries we think of as social democracies. In Case and Deaton's words, "Both the safety net and the financing of health care are radically different in other rich countries where—with few exceptions—*there are few deaths of despair*" (emphasis added).

Are there?

Table 4.1 reports deaths from suicide and alcohol-related causes in 10 rich countries. The numbers are for 2019, the most recent year reported by the World Health Organization.[48]

The United States does not suffer from unusually high mortality from these causes. European countries with the world's most generous welfare states, as well as Canada and Japan, have rates that are higher than or just a bit lower than the United States.

Country	Suicides	Deaths from alcohol-related causes	Total deaths of despair (suicides plus alcohol-related causes)
Finland	13.0	6.7	19.7
Belgium	15.0	3.0	18.0
Denmark	8.4	8.7	17.1
France	12.5	3.8	16.3
United States	**11.7**	**3.2**	**14.9**
Austria	11.3	3.5	14.8
Japan	14.2	0.3	14.5
Germany	9.5	4.5	14.0
Canada	11.0	2.5	13.5
Sweden	10.7	2.2	12.9

Table 4.1. Deaths of Despair (Suicide and Alcohol-Related Causes, per 100k per year), Select Advanced Industrialized Countries, 2019

The "deaths of despair" narrative, and the broader story of rising working-class despondency, fits the assumptions of most social scientists and other analysts who are trained to think of economic circumstances as the ultimate determinant of political behavior. It also appeals to the liberal's natural compassion for the less fortunate.

But the facts tell another story.

5. Cultural Backlash Does Not Explain Democracy's Reversal

S o far we've seen the tenuousness of the evidence on which the "economic distress" thesis is based. But what about the "culture shock" theory? Do resentment and dismay over a Black president, immigrants pouring over the southern border, and Heather having two mommies (one of whom blurs the binary) explain the rise of MAGA? Can democracy's plight be attributed to growing backlash from cultural conservatives?

One study that touts a cultural explanation for the rise of Trump is Daniel Cox, Rachel Lienesch, and Robert P. Jones's "Beyond Economics: Fears of Cultural Displacement Pushing the White Working Class to Support Trump." The work is based on surveys conducted around the time of Trump's election in November 2016.[49]

The authors did find that working-class whites who supported Trump held more conservative views and that people without a college degree were generally more concerned that America was in danger of losing its cultural identity. There's nothing surprising about these numbers. But a closer examination complicates the picture. Let's begin with a look at attitudes about immigration—a central cultural dispute of our time and Trump's signature issue.

Beyond the headline of the study by Cox, Lienesch, and Jones, their research actually found that working-class whites largely shared in the liberal consensus about immigration. Fifty-nine percent (compared to 63 percent of all respondents) said they favored granting citizenship to immigrants living in the country illegally, provided they met certain requirements. Fewer than half as many (27 percent) advocated deportation. Data like these call into question the thesis that the white working class was being pushed to support Trumpism by fear of cultural displacement.

Other studies show how Americans' attitudes toward new arrivals have undergone dramatic liberalization. In 1994, 63 percent agreed that immigrants "burden the country by taking jobs, housing, and health care" while 31 percent agreed that they "strengthen the country because of their hard work and talents." Over the succeeding quarter-century, those numbers more than reversed: In 2019, 66 percent said immigrants strengthened the country, while just 24 percent said they were a burden.[50]

Most Americans regard immigration as a critical component of national identity. In a 2021 Pew survey, two thirds agreed that "America's openness to people from all over the world is essential to who we are as a nation," while just one third held that "If America is too open to people from all over the world, we risk losing our identity as a nation."[51] While Trump's anti-immigrant stance no doubt delights the deplorables, Diana Mutz, a leading specialist in political psychology and communication, found that Trump's extreme stance on immigration harmed his overall electoral performance in 2016.[52]

Opinions depend on whether immigrants are in the country lawfully. In a 2022 Gallup poll, 41 percent said they worried "a great deal" and 19 percent worried "a fair amount" about illegal immigration, versus 23 percent who said they worried "a little" or "not at all."[53] In fact, some of the same surveys that indicate majority support for a path to citizenship for those who reside in the country illegally also express support for beefing up border controls and even deportations.[54] These surveys reflect a widespread embrace of immigration but distaste for breaking the law and policies that fail to rein in disorder at the border.

Over recent decades, American attitudes on race have also liberalized dramatically. In 1978, a decade after passage of the Fair

Housing Act, just 37 percent of non-Black Americans favored requiring owners to rent and sell to people regardless of their race. In 2016, the year of Trump's election, that number had more than doubled, rising to 76 percent. The opinions of non-college whites track and almost match those of all respondents.[55]

Attitudes on gender have liberalized dramatically as well. One item in the GSS asks respondents whether they agree that "Most men are better suited emotionally for politics than most women." In 1974, 49 percent of respondents disagreed, rising to 83 percent in 2018. There is virtually no difference between non-college-educated whites and Americans as a whole.

The same striking progressive trend holds in attitudes toward sexual minorities. In a 2022 Gallup poll, 71 percent said that "marriages between same-sex couples should be recognized as valid, with the same rights as traditional marriages." That's up from 27 percent in 1996 when Gallup started asking the question.[56]

As for dealing with sex and sexuality in schools, a 2022 Harris-APNORC survey asked: "Are teachers in your local public school discussing issues related to sex and sexuality too much, too little, or about the right amount?" Seventy-one percent answered "too little" or "about the right amount," compared to just 23 percent who said "too much."[57]

Most Americans also support trans rights. In a 2022 Pew survey, 64 percent "strongly favor" or "favor" "policies that protect transgender individuals from discrimination in jobs, housing, and public spaces such as restaurants and stores," while just 11 percent "oppose" or "strongly oppose" such protections. Sensitivity about bias runs high as well: 78 percent say trans people face "a great deal," "a fair amount," or "some" discrimination in society, versus 14 percent who think they face "a little" or "none at all."[58]

Scholars who lead the way in gauging popular attitudes, including Ronald Inglehart, the founder of the World Values Survey, generated much of the data that reveal these liberalizing trends. Yet

Inglehart himself believed that changing cultural attitudes explain the rise of Trumpism. How is that possible?

In *Cultural Backlash: Trump, Brexit, and Authoritarian Populism*, Inglehart and coauthor Pippa Norris spell out the logic.[59] Marshaling a spate of data gathered since the 1970s, they detect a "silent revolution" in values as attitudes have grown more liberal. But they hold that once liberal values became predominant, an "inflection point" or "tipping point" was reached, triggering an "authoritarian reflex." They argue: "The tipping point—as formerly predominant majorities become a steadily shrinking but still sizeable share of the population and the electorate—is predicted to trigger the latent authoritarian reflex. Resentment against the silent revolution has spawned a counter-revolutionary conservative backlash." According to this theory, as cultural attitudes tipped into liberal territory, conservatives became so resentful they started supporting politicians like Trump.

But is there anything new about cultural backlash? Do we have reason to think its political effects are stronger today than 20, 50, or 100 years ago when authoritarian demagogues came nowhere near the White House?

There are several reasons for skepticism. First, for cultural attitudes to explain democracy's reversal, the political effects of the backlash would have to exceed the political effects of the broader liberalization that elicited it. An implication would be that fury at the liberalization in attitudes that made possible the election of a Black president, more women in high office, and the legalization of same-sex marriage is so acute among a shrinking minority that it overwhelms in its political effects the liberalization itself. But that point is difficult to demonstrate, and neither Norris and Inglehart nor anyone else has done so.

The second basis for questioning the cultural backlash hypothesis is the difficulty of locating the "tipping point." When has a society passed it and become vulnerable to a democracy-endangering backlash from irate conservatives? Norris and Inglehart say we can't know where the tipping point is, but they suggest that it is crossed when "[p]eople with socially conservative values have lost their cultural hegemony, activating feelings of resentment toward groups blamed for change."

Fair enough, but we need to ask: When and where have people with what are considered conservative values by the standards of their times *not* been losing their cultural hegemony? When are we *not* in a "tipping point era"? When are culture wars *not* raging in America—and most other countries where people have the right to voice and act on their opinions?

Consider racial attitudes in the United States. In the early and mid-20th century, people who were culturally conservative by the standards of the day supported segregation of schools. In 1956, white Americans were evenly split: 49 percent favored it, and 49 percent opposed it. Over the next decade, attitudes tipped: In 1968, just 26 percent of whites supported segregation, while 71 percent opposed it.[60]

So not only were segregationist whites suddenly forced to send their kids to school with Black kids. Now they also felt their ranks dwindling fast. They had plenty to be pissed about.

And pissed they were. White mob and police violence against African American civil rights activists raged at a level few Americans under 70 can imagine today. In 1968, George Wallace, the Alabama governor and race-baiter *extraordinaire*, made the second of his three bids for the White House. Running on the slogan *Stand Up for America*, he pledged to allow state governments to segregate.

In the summer of 1967, as Wallace plotted his run and about nine months before Martin Luther King was gunned down in Memphis, my 27-year-old father was managing a gas station in downtown Detroit. From our apartment on the city's edge, I remember watching the sky over the burning city turn orange at night. In the 1967 Detroit Rebellion, sparked by police violence against African Americans, the nation suffered its largest-scale riot since 1863.

As the fires raged, my Dad thought it was time to explain to his five-year old son the reason for the unfolding horror. He took me outdoors after dark and, pointing to the eerie glow on the horizon, told me of an alleyway that ran behind his gas station. In that space, he recounted, a certain "game" was played. Police officers would make a sport of dragging young Black men into the alley, telling them to "run for it," and then shooting at them as they fled. He filed a complaint at the local police headquarters, but it didn't go down very well. He even got in trouble with his boss for "stirring things up." The attacks in the alley stopped, but no cops were ever prosecuted, and he heard rumors that they had just moved their "game" to other streets.

Eight years later, I was an eighth grader in a Jefferson County, Kentucky, public school when U.S. District Judge James Gordon ordered the county to desegregate. I watched the riots and demonstrations on the local news. Some classmates' families moved to neighboring counties to escape being bused to integrated inner-city schools. (My family stayed put, and I was bused from my formerly almost all-white school to formerly nearly all-Black Central High School). I recall the proliferation of "TO HELL WITH JUDGE GORDON AND BUSING" bumper stickers. I remember, too, the much smaller number of pro-busing stickers. They had a picture of a school bus and read: "Nobody Wins When You Lose Your Cool."

My mother had one of those. She had to replace several car windows.

But laws were changing and attitudes were tipping. Until the Supreme Court abolished the so-called anti-miscegenation laws in the 1967 *Loving v. Virginia* decision, 16 states still banned interracial sex and marriage. The court's decision was not popular. In 1969, only 17 percent of whites approved of interracial marriage. But over the next quarter-century, that number crept up by an average of about one percent per year and then jumped from 45 percent in 1995 to 61 percent in 1997.[61] At that point, whites who still loathed interracial unions had to live with them—both as a legal fact and as something most other whites endorsed.

These days, interracial relationships and integrated schools and housing are taken for granted. Opinion has long since "tipped."

So where was the tipping point on race? Did the liberalization of opinion on integrated schools in the 1950s-1960s count? Or was it the shift to white support for integrated housing in the 1980s? Or did the tip come in the 1990s, when white opinion moved decisively in favor of interracial marriage? Or were they all tipping point eras? Why didn't George Wallace or some other Trump-like figure make it to the White House in those times? Are culture wars in the age of Colin Kaepernick and George Floyd more heated and disruptive than in the times of Martin Luther King and Medgar Evers?

We could ask related questions about gender and sex. We can't know for sure, but the tip in attitudes that led to women's enfranchisement might have been at least as traumatic for cultural conservatives in the early 20th century as the tip that enabled the near-election of a woman president—and the election of a woman vice president—a century later. And, just in case you're old enough to remember it, you might agree that the transformation in values that enabled gay people to come out of the closet and form visible communities in the 1970s was as momentous in its time as the tip in opinion that made same-sex marriage possible in the 2010s.

Disillusionment over cultural change runs deep in every society and in any era. If values are changing at all (and where aren't they?), conservatives are always giving ground to people who embrace the change. In fact, "socially conservative people" are *perpetually and by definition* "losing their cultural hegemony."

In short, the passage of "tipping points" is a constant, not a variable. Attributing democracy's misfortune to it makes sense only if we can demonstrate that cultural backlash is stronger and more politically consequential these days than in other periods of change when democracy was not threatened. Neither the data nor common sense yield that conclusion.

Evidence that progress overpowers backlash is visible in the data on racial attitudes and voting. In an interview, Justin Grimmer summarized the results of research he and fellow political scientists William Marble and Cole Tanigawa-Lau found on racial attitudes in the 2016 and 2020 elections: "Trump's supporters were less xenophobic than prior Republican candidates, less sexist, had lower animus to minority groups, and lower levels of racial resentment. Far from deplorables, Trump voters were, on average, more tolerant and understanding than voters for prior Republican candidates."[62]

How is that possible? Grimmer and colleagues do find that Trump holds special appeal among bigots. So how can Trump's voters be less racist than those who supported Republican moderates like Mitt Romney?

The answer is that racism overall has markedly declined, so fewer people bear strong racial animus in the electorate as a whole. According to Marble:

> [B]etween 2012 and 2016, the number of people who scored at the high end of the racial resentment scale declined significantly. As a result, there were simply fewer high racial resentment voters for Trump to win in 2016 and 2020 than there were in earlier eras. At the same time, the number of people scoring at moderate levels of racial resentment increased. Trump was not as popular among this voting bloc, compared to those with high racial resentment. But because this group is larger, whites with moderate racial resentment scores ended up contributing more net votes to Trump.

Of the authors' finding that "Trump voters were, on average, more tolerant and understanding than voters for prior Republican candidates," political scientist Ruy Teixeira, a leading analyst of working-class voting, notes: "To say this is not how most Democrats think about the Trump-voting white working class is to considerably understate the case." The evidence, Teixeira suggests, should lead the Democrats to question their common assumption that they are faltering among white working-class voters due to these folks' intolerance. The fact that the Democrats do poorly with this demographic, he holds, "represents a real failing on their part, not a noble stand against the barbarians at the gates."[63]

None of the numbers show that America has overcome its grave, centuries-old racism problem; the deplorables soldier on. Nor do the numbers prove that bigoted demagoguery never pays at the polls. In some scenarios, even messages that flop with majorities can yield returns if precisely targeted to specific constituencies. But the evidence does suggest the wisdom of treating the cultural backlash explanation for democracy's quandary with some skepticism.

6. The Democratic Party Has Not Abandoned the Working Class

S o far, we've found little to support the standard story about the causes of democracy's woes. But the evidence we've examined largely pertains to economic and social conditions. We need to delve into the political side of the equation as well. Whatever people's objective conditions and subjective perceptions, they could conceivably forsake prodemocratic politicians who aren't representing their interests. Thomas Frank, the author of *What's the Matter with Kansas?*, is a prominent proponent of the widely accepted belief that liberals' neglect of working-class economic welfare paved the way for demagogues.[64]

In this account, the left converged with the right on economic policy and quit sticking up for labor unions and other bulwarks of the working class. Bill Clinton and the Democratic presidents who succeeded him are blamed for embracing globalization with more than a little too much zeal, to the detriment of the working person's material interests and her loyalty to the Democratic Party. Writes Robert Reich, Bill Clinton's (obviously estranged) secretary of labor, "Bill Clinton and Barack Obama helped shift power away from the people towards corporations. It was this that created an opening for Donald Trump."[65]

Another exponent of this view is journalist George Packer. He blames Trump's rise to power on—Bill Clinton's optimistic embrace of free trade and technological innovation. Says Packer in his otherwise ingenious "How America Fractured into Four Parts":[66]

> At one point [Bill] Clinton informed the participants [in a 2000 White House conference on the economy] that Congress was about to pass a bill to establish permanent trade relations with China, which would make both countries more prosperous and China more free. "I believe the computer and the internet give us a chance to move more people out of poverty more quickly than at any time in all of human history," he exulted.
>
> You can almost date the election of Donald Trump to that moment.

Indeed, Packer claims that the fracturing of America into four parts—Free America, Real America, Smart America, and Just America—was due to "America's failure to sustain and enlarge the middle-class democracy of the postwar years."

Let's look at the logical and empirical bases of what these critics are saying.

First, the "middle-class democracy" of the early postwar decades that Packer lauds featured a far less inclusive middle class and political system than we have today. During the first two decades of the supposed Golden Age, few Blacks were allowed to vote in the South. Blacks and women (the latter as individual earners, not necessarily members of households) were largely excluded from the middle class as well.

In 1960, two percent of women and Blacks worked in what economists classify as "high-skill" jobs that pay good salaries, such as medicine, law, and engineering. But between 1960 and 2021, the proportion of medical doctors who were white men fell from 94 to 29 percent. Women now make up a majority in this, America's best-paying and most secure profession. In the workforce at large, the female-to-male earnings ratio held at around 60 percent during the Golden Age and rose steadily after 1980, reaching 84 percent in 2021.[67]

Educational opportunities also burgeoned. In 1980, one third of Americans aged 25 or older lacked a high-school education; in 2020, one tenth did. Over the same period, the proportion of Americans overall aged 25 or older with a college education more than doubled; the number for Blacks more than tripled. [68]

Second, it's important to pose the counterfactual: What was the alternative to embracing the technological revolution and integration into the global economy? Should Clinton and his successors have tried to restrict the development of computers and the internet? Should they have walled America off from exports from China and other developing countries?

The second option was perhaps possible. But that would have made it much harder for a billion-and-a-half Chinese, Indians, Southeast Asians, and Latin Americans to lift themselves out of poverty. Do the lives of non-Americans of color matter, too? What do you say, progressives?

The welfare of these people aside, what would the effects of the presumed alternative to Clinton's approach have been on Americans? Opting out of globalization or trying to tiptoe into it without risking anybody's job would have ruled out what Americans have come to take for granted: unbridled access to inexpensive, high-quality imports. It would have curbed the development of American industries that depend on low trade barriers. They include soybean growers, who export $16 billion worth of their crops to China annually, and manufacturers of mechanical appliances, TVs, and sound recorders, whose exports to China total $36 billion per year.[69]

Rejecting globalization also would have checked the explosive development of American high-tech industries, blunting the growth of businesses and jobs that make the United States the world's innovation capital. The global ascendancy of American universities also would have been jeopardized. In a word, embracing protectionism would have risked turning the United States into a declining, second-rate economic and intellectual power.

Fortunately, that didn't happen. America's share of the G-7's GDP rose from 40 percent in 1990 to 58 percent in 2023. The other rich countries have watched their economies shrink as a proportion of global GDP as China and India took off, but the United States now accounts for a quarter of global output, the same as in 1990.[70]

Would tariffs have been the ticket to protecting the working stiff? They amount to taxes on consumers, and they are proven losers for preserving jobs and boosting incomes, especially in advanced industrialized countries.[71]

Jonathan Rothwell notes that 58 percent of workers in manufacturing indeed voted for Trump in 2016. But he found that Trump's support among manufacturing workers was lower than among workers in construction, which does not compete with low-income exporters, and agriculture, where America runs a large trade surplus. Rothwell also found that Trump's advantage over Hillary Clinton among manufacturing workers was due to them being older, white, Christian, straight men with conservative attitudes on race. When he controlled for these factors, the effect of working in manufacturing disappeared.[72]

It's commonly believed that workers worry that technological innovation or companies moving overseas threatens their jobs. But in a poll taken shortly after Trump won in 2016, Gallup found that just 13 percent of American workers thought their jobs would become obsolete due to technology, while 87 percent did not. Nine percent were concerned that their company might move jobs overseas, versus 90 percent who weren't.[73]

In some evenly divided states and districts, there might be enough folks who fear for their jobs to tip elections. But these voters don't necessarily tilt toward the Republicans. Rothwell found that among workers concerned about losing their jobs to innovation, more disapproved of Trump than approved.[74]

Bill Clinton did turn away from some of the hoary leftist dogmas of earlier decades. But did he and his Democratic successors really abandon the working person's material interests?

The Democrats have fought tooth and nail for healthcare going back to the days of Harry Truman in the late 1940s. Clinton tried and failed to secure universal coverage during his first year in office. In 2010, the Democrats finally took a major step toward achieving it, in the form of the Affordable Care Act ("Obamacare")—and they did so without a single Republican vote. Since then, they have defended it doggedly against relentless Republican assaults. They have also fought to protect and extend every program—Social Security, Medicare, Medicaid, home energy assistance, women/children nutrition (WIC), food stamps included—that drove poverty down to its lowest point on record in 2021.

The Democrats have also worked consistently for fairer taxation.[75] One of the first things Clinton did after arriving in office in 1993 was to boost taxes on top earners, corporations, and gasoline. Spending on the Earned Income Tax Credit, which provides tax cuts for low- and middle-income Americans, rose from $9 billion to $26 billion during Clinton's time in office. Medicaid expenditures grew by 37 percent, the steepest rise of any presidency. In part as a result of these policies, inflation-adjusted incomes of households in the bottom 40 percent grew by 17 percent, better than under any other president of the past half-century. African Americans' median household income expanded by 25 percent, double the (still brisk) pace for all American households. Clinton also left office with the government running a $200 billion annual surplus and paying down the federal debt. Deficit spending returned with a vengeance the year after Clinton departed, and balanced or surplus budgets have never been seen again.[76]

After Clinton's departure, practically every congressional Democrat lined up against George W. Bush's regressive, deficit-ballooning 2001 tax cut. After Obama came to office, the Democrats pushed the rates on the rich back up.

In 2017, every congressional Democrat voted against Trump's regressive, deficit-expanding tax cut. Once Biden got to office, the Democrats raised the rates on the rich to finance massive spending programs on infrastructure, student loan forgiveness, and the development of green technologies. Biden also pays for his programs by requiring large corporations to pay a 15 percent minimum tax on profits and imposing an excise tax on stock buybacks and redemptions.[77]

Democrats aren't to blame for injustices in the tax system. The Republicans are. The first thing that Republican administrations do when they get to office is cut taxes on the rich, and the first thing Democratic administrations do is push them back up again.

Biden's programs constitute the most far-reaching effort on behalf of economic justice since Lyndon Johnson's Great Society programs of the 1960s. He has crafted the most interventionist and ambitious industrial policy since the New Deal, and his programs explicitly target non-college-educated voters who have migrated to the Republicans. The economic results are plain to see: Manufacturing is booming, labor power is escalating, strikes are proliferating, and the economy is adding jobs like it's 1969.[78]

The idea that the Democrats have forsaken the working person, like the notion that working people therefore turned to a party that couldn't care less about their economic interests, strains logic.

That said, even if the Democrats' policies have been radically more progressive than the Republicans', did they leave labor unions behind?

It's true that union membership contracted by half between 1983 and 2021. The fall is due in part to the changing character of work that has accompanied technological innovation. Employment in manufacturing declined by 30 percent between 1990 and 2015, while it grew by 63 percent in the leisure and hospitality business.[79] Travel agents and hotel employees are harder to unionize than auto workers.

Still, impersonal market forces alone aren't at fault. A fall in protections for the right to unionize, together with weakened labor standards, forced arbitration and class action waivers, erosion of overtime protection, and weakened enforcement of labor standards are all products of laws and court rulings.[80]

But these regressive trends and practices are the work of Republican administrations, Republican-sponsored legislation, and Republican-appointed judges. Right-to-work laws, which make it unlawful to require employees to join a union or pay union dues, are present in 28 states—and they are the products of Republican-controlled legislatures and state houses. The governments of the states that do not have right-to-work laws are typically controlled by Democrats.

It's no mystery why the Republicans push anti-union laws, and it's not just about depressing wages to benefit corporate interests. As economist James Feigenbaum, political scientist Alexander Hertel-Fernandez, and social policy specialist Vanessa Williamson have shown, right-to-work laws can impair Democrats' electoral performance: "In presidential elections, we estimate that these laws cost Democratic candidates two to five percentage points in right-to-work counties . . . We find similar effects at other levels of government."[81]

Those effects give both parties a handsome incentive to act when they're in power. And act they do: When Scott Walker and his fellow Republicans won control of Wisconsin in the mid-2010s, the state adopted a right-to-work law forthwith. When the Democrats, led by Governor Gretchen Whitmer, flipped both houses of the Michigan state legislature in 2022, repeal of right-to-work laws ensued immediately.

Still, many liberal observers persist in taking the Democrats to task for, in the words of *Intelligencer* writer Eric Levitz, "letting unions die."[82] But such arguments usually blame the Democrats for failing to overcome Republican opposition or for placing *another* progressive cause before this or that union-friendly bill. Thus, Harold Meyerson, editor of *The American Prospect*, chided Obama for prioritizing the passage of universal healthcare over the pro-union Employee Free Choice Act (EFCA) in 2009—and then failing to have the votes to pass the labor reform bill after the Republicans won control of Congress in 2010. Similarly, Meyerson faults Bill Clinton for "appointing a commission to recommend changes in labor law to the next Congress—which turned out to be run by Newt Gingrich."[83]

Seriously, folks?

It would be difficult to argue, moreover, that unions lack a booster in Biden. Receiving funds from his massive spending policies requires that producers and service providers be staffed with union labor. In September 2023, Biden joined UAW workers on the picket line, an unprecedented act of solidarity by a sitting president.[84]

What about messaging? Have the Democrats pressed for progressive economic policies but moved toward soft, centrist rhetoric? Based on their analysis of presidential campaign speeches from 1932-2012, political scientists Jesse Rhodes and Kaylee Johnson conclude: "Democratic presidential candidates have made increasingly frequent references to the wealthy; have employed a consistently adversarial tone in statements regarding the affluent; have made increasingly frequent criticisms of Republicans' alleged favoritism toward the rich; and have increasingly linked references to the wealthy to promises to assist less fortunate Americans through programmatic reforms."[85] Data like these give the lie to the notion that Democrats have become corporate shills only a little less objectionable than the Republicans themselves.

Finally, let's take a close look at the claim that working-class people turned against the Democrats due to their free-trade policies. If this part of the standard story were true, we'd see a history in which Democrats won majority support from working-class voters prior to 1992, followed by a cratering of that support once Bill Clinton and his successors embraced globalization. What do the data show?

In 15 of the 19 presidential elections held since World War II, the Republicans won more non-college white voters than the Democrats. So contrary to the standard story, this wasn't *our* proletariat to begin with. Other than Harry Truman (1948) and Lyndon Johnson

(1964), the only Democrat to best his or her Republican opponent in this demographic was Bill Clinton—and he did it twice. In 1992, he ended the reign of Reaganism by beating George H. W. Bush by nine points among white, non-college-educated voters. Four years later, he won that group by a five-point margin over the Republican Senate majority leader, Bob Dole.

Bill Clinton's strength among white working-class Americans was unique in the past half-century. And it didn't come at the expense of support from African Americans. Clinton defeated his Republican opponent by over 7-to-1 both times he ran.

His performance among Hispanics was no less impressive. He beat his Republican adversary among Hispanics by 36 points in 1992 and 51 points in 1996. No Democrat before or since has matched Clinton's 1996 performance with America's fastest-growing ethnic demographic.

Thanks to his broad-based appeal, Clinton won West Virginia, Kentucky, Tennessee, Missouri, Arkansas, and Louisiana—twice. He arrested the partisan realignment that tilted the South toward the Republicans in the 1970s and 1980s. It resumed after he left office. He also beat his Republican rivals in crucial swing states. He won Wisconsin by four points in 1992 and 11 points four years later. With NAFTA in full swing and trade with Mexico and China surging, in 1996 Clinton took supposedly trade-averse Ohio and Michigan by 7 and 13 points, respectively.

Rather than accusing Clinton of alienating the white working class and planting the seeds of Trump's rise, liberals should be looking to him for ideas on how to win a bigger slice of that demographic without losing an iota of support among people of color. Democratic abandonment of the working class never happened—which means it can't be blamed for the rise of authoritarianism in America.

7. A Flawed Constitution Is Not to Blame for Democracy's Crisis

S ome scholars look beyond economic and cultural explanations to argue that the Republicans are a "minority party" that gains power by taking advantage of outworn, unfair political institutions.[86] The Senate, for example, is often said to grossly favor the Republicans. The proposed remedy is to abolish it or "reform" its membership to reflect states' populations.

Now, I admit to glancing up at the map of the United States that hangs over my desk, cursing the fact that Wyoming's 600k people have as much representation in the Senate as my California's 40 million.

But for every little red Wyoming, there's also a little blue Delaware. Half of the 10 least populous states—the ones that benefit most from disproportionate representation—went for Biden in 2020, and half went for Trump. Half of the 10 most populous states— the ones most harmed by disproportionality—went for Biden in 2020, and half chose Trump. Disproportionality in representation might be an injustice, but it's not clear that it strongly disfavors the Democrats.

What about the House of Representatives? Many liberals believe that our single-member-district elections and aggressive Republican gerrymandering are the only way the G.O.P. ever stands a chance of winning a House majority. The assumption is that the Democrats consistently get more votes, but institutional distortions prevent their wins from translating into House majorities. One solution is to replace the system prescribed by the Constitution with proportional representation, where voters elect a party list rather than individual candidates.

But in the 2022 midterms, Republican candidates topped the Democrats by three million votes. Such an outcome was hardly a rare event. In the 12 elections for the House that have been held since 2000, Republicans won the popular vote eight times and the Democrats won four times. The mean vote for Republican candidates across elections was 49 percent, to 48 percent for the Democrats.

The Electoral College is another institution liberals believe systematically favors the Republicans. Now, it is undoubtedly archaic and unjust. It's absurd that the popular-vote winner can lose the election. It's no less bizarre and antidemocratic that presidential elections are decided in 6-10 "battleground states," giving candidates an incentive to ignore about three quarters of the electorate. No wonder two thirds of Americans favor doing away with the Electoral College. It's similarly unsurprising that no other democracy has such a thing.[87]

But whether it creates a decisive bias for the Republicans is another matter. Experts estimate that in the 18 presidential elections held since 1952, the Electoral College has favored each party nine times. In the 21st century, it has advantaged the Republicans three times (in 2000, 2016, and 2020) and the Democrats three times (2004, 2008, and 2012). The danger for the Democrats now is that the Republicans' advantage in the past two elections might persist into 2024 and beyond.[88]

But the *New York Times's* chief elections pollster, Nate Cohn, surmised in September 2023 that "Trump's Electoral College edge seems to be fading." National and statewide polls, as well as numbers from the 2022 midterms, lead him to believe that the Republicans' advantage was set to shrink from 2.9 percent in 2016 and 3.8 percent in 2020 to 0.7 percent in 2024.[89] According to political scientists J. Miles Coleman and Kyle Klondik, it's not hard to imagine scenarios where relatively small shifts would return the Electoral College to a Democratic advantage.[90]

The electoral system isn't stacked against the Democrats. The problem isn't institutional injustice; it's that too many people are voting for the Republicans. And even if reforming some institutions might aid democracy, no such changes are possible until the Democrats secure a lasting lock on government. What's more, abolishing the Senate or adopting proportional representation for House elections is never going to happen, regardless of which party is in power. The imperative of winning elections *now*, under the institutions we've enjoyed (or suffered with) for a quarter of a millennium, remains.

8. Mistaken Premises, Unsound Prescriptions

W e've seen how the reasoning of the standard story on the rise of authoritarianism in America works. While the evidence we've examined isn't dispositive, it is highly suggestive—and it forces us to question every link in the story's chain of reasoning.

Economic conditions are as favorable for democracy as they have ever been. White working-class voters, including the two thirds who now vote for the Republicans, aren't despairing over their lives any more than they used to. Their evaluations of their own life satisfaction, job security, quality of employment, and sense of personal efficacy have not deteriorated. They have not moved to the right on social issues like immigration, race, and gender—in fact, their attitudes have become markedly more tolerant. And far from ignoring the needs of the working folks, the Democrats have consistently pushed for policies that would promote their interests.

Why does bungling the explanation for Trump's rise matter so much?

The biggest problem with the standard narrative is that faulty explanations yield ineffectual prescriptions. If the standard story were right, the key to beating Trumpism would be 1) to continue banking on economic policies and performance in hopes of relieving working-class suffering; and 2) either compromise with the right in the culture wars or sit out those struggles and concede that battle to the Republicans. If the standard story is right, this is pretty much all the Democrats are left with. But this thinking is misconceived and paves a path to defeat.

First, regarding economic policies: What more could the Democrats do—especially within the constraints of Republican intransigence—than they're already doing?

Biden is championing a mountain of progressive policies. He has pumped trillions—primarily aimed at hiking working- and middle-class incomes—into the economy. The Democrats have also done everything in their power to aid the afflicted, expanding a host of welfare programs that the Republicans are hellbent on eviscerating. Take the child tax credit. No policy is closer to Biden's heart. It reduced child poverty just as it was intended to do. But it is constantly under threat from the Republicans and has been in jeopardy since the Republicans' takeover of the House in 2023.

In a 2021 survey, half of respondents favored expanding the tax credit, while 38 percent opposed it. Sixty-one percent reported receiving the credit, and fully 39 percent of those people said it had a "major impact" on their "financial security." That included 40 percent of whites.

But here's the rub: When asked, "Who do you feel is responsible for the expanded child tax credit being made possible?," just 38 percent picked "President Joe Biden."[91]

The problem couldn't be more obvious: Even popular legislation that brings immediate benefit doesn't necessarily earn political points.

Second, in terms of economic performance: How much better could the Democrats do than they are already doing?

Throughout Biden's time in office, America's economy has grown at a rate that is the envy of other rich countries. During Biden's first three years in office, the economy added an astonishing 13k jobs per day. That's over twice the average during Trump's first three years, before COVID hit and unemployment skyrocketed. Biden inherited a COVID-induced inflationary disaster, but as of January 2024, average hourly wages had outpaced inflation for nine months running. While he was in office, Trump never quit crowing about how the stock market was faring, but during 2024 the Dow has set records, soaring far above Trump-era levels. Biden's interventionist policies are arguably having the most powerful favorable effect on the economy of any president's since Franklin Roosevelt.[92]

Yet as of March 18, 2024, half of Americans said the economy was "getting worse," compared to a quarter who said it was "getting better."[93]

In a January 2024 NBC News poll, respondents said they trusted Trump more than Biden on managing the economy. Trump enjoyed a 22-point advantage—the biggest edge of any candidate in the poll's history dating back to 1992.[94]

The situation presents a snapshot of a larger picture that spells constant trouble for the Democrats: Despite an avalanche of contrary evidence, Americans tend to think the Republicans are better at managing the economy. While some analysts have made stabs at explanations, the phenomenon remains a mystery.[95]

As we'll see later, the enigma unravels when we focus on *leadership* and *messaging.* The Republicans are winning this game in a walk, as they have for decades. It's not policies, promises, or even performance that decide elections. It's *public perceptions* that count most.

Third, in terms of policies on cultural issues: What are the Democrats supposed to do, move to the right?

The logic of the cultural backlash explanation—if it were correct—suggests the wisdom of compromise. That means tacking to the right on matters like immigration and protections for women and racial and sexual minorities.

The main problem with such remedies is that they are repulsive to most of those who stand at the forefront of the struggle against the authoritarian threat. Let's face it and face it with enthusiasm: We aren't going to compromise with MAGA on Trump's monstrous immigration policies. We want smart and humane immigration laws, not detention camps and kids in cages. We refuse to tolerate women dying in emergency rooms for lack of treatment because they might be pregnant. Nor are we going to honor MAGA's cherished Confederate statues or indulge their adoration of AR-15s, the weapon of choice for school shooters. We want to melt down their Robert E. Lee monuments and machine guns, not abide them. That's never going to change.

Nor should it. At a time when Republicans are trying to make it harder for African Americans to vote and banning books that touch on gender identity from the schools, the Democrats can't scale back on our values and remain ethical democrats. Relentless advancements in social equality, personal freedom, and openness to immigration are built into America's democratic and demographic promise.

What's more, feminists and ethnic and sexual minorities are core Democratic Party constituencies—failing to defend them would ensure Democratic defeats. Beyond that, the majority is on the Democrats' side in the culture wars. There's political gold for us in those conflicts if we only engage in them skillfully. Again, it's public perceptions, not policies, that matter most.

The Democrats shouldn't give an inch on our progressive policies. They have yielded impressive results as measured by economic and social progress.

But by themselves, such policies may not yield the *political* effects we expect. In 2016, 64 percent of non-college-educated white voters chose Trump over a Democrat who ran on promises to pump government resources into working people's pockets. In 2020, after enacting a tax cut and other policies that disproportionately benefited the rich, Trump won 65 percent of non-college whites. After a two-year spending blitz that aimed to boost working-class incomes under Biden, 66 percent of non-college whites voted Republican in the 2022 midterms.

Nor are the Democrats' policy exertions energizing the progressive base or winning over voters of color. In an October 2023 *New York Times*/Siena poll of voting intentions in six battleground states,

22 percent of Blacks and 42 percent of Hispanics said they planned to vote for Trump in 2024. These numbers, which represent a surge toward Trump compared to 2016 and 2020, help explain why Trump led in five of these six states.[96]

Progressive policies *can* boost the Democrats' electoral performance, but any benefit is likely to be limited and it certainly won't happen by default. In order to leverage their great policies for electoral gain, the Democrats are going to have to incorporate them into a larger, optimistic narrative about their contributions to national purpose and glory. They also must start trumpeting the fruits of their policies from the mountaintops, without apologies or qualifications, which they are decidedly not doing.

Finally, there's one other major problem with the standard story. It paints a dismal picture of the typical white working-class voter: Ignorant of his own interests, despairing to the point of self-destruction, desperate for government help, vulnerable to the appeals of racist demagogues—how can we expect to win people over if they see a pathetic, ugly caricature of themselves in the story we tell (or murmur) about them?

This narrative also reinforces the carnage tales that Trump tells of America. Both offer a story of broken dreams and wretched working masses cheated out of their fair share by liberal elites enchanted by globalization.

Trump glorifies a past when America was supposedly truly great. He never says exactly when that was, but the 1950s would be a good guess. It was clearly before the civil rights movement and feminism transformed the social order. It was an age when the immigrant share of the population was falling and the honor of becoming an American was largely limited to whites. It was a period, unique in our history, when just five percent of Americans were born abroad, compared to 15 percent today. It was a time when Ward Cleaver came home from his solid-but-never-specified middle-middle-class job to greet his mischievous son Beaver and his lovely wife June, vacuuming the carpet clad in pearls.

Liberals rightly castigate Trump for his mislaid nostalgia. Yet when we embrace an absurdly idealized picture of America before globalization "hollowed out" the middle class, and we fail to celebrate the much better America that exists today, we reinforce the Trumpian story.

If the Democrats are to roll up the electoral victories needed to defeat democracy's enemies, the time has come to retire the standard story and adopt a new approach. But that doesn't mean playing nice with our opponents' orange hero and his ilk; in fact, just the opposite is called for. That's up next.

PART TWO

EMBRACING THE POLITICS OF DOMINANCE

9. Defining Dominance

What does Donald Trump have that Hillary Clinton didn't? What did Ronald Reagan have that Jimmy Carter didn't? What did Abraham Lincoln have that John C. Breckinridge—his 1860 presidential-election opponent who fled behind Confederate lines after the Civil War started—didn't?

One answer lies in an area that pollsters aren't measuring, liberal strategists aren't considering, and political scientists aren't studying: the politics of dominance. While liberals pore over this week's issue polls and focus on delivering more attractive policies, authoritarians have grasped what neuroscientist Steven Stanton and colleagues have found: "Political elections are dominance competitions."[1]

Dominance is a *style* or a *way* of leadership. Upping one's dominance game doesn't depend on legislative victories—though it can help produce them. Nor do the Democrats need to alter their policies or principles. In fact, compromising on liberal values would be a step in the wrong direction.

Dominance is not inherently good or bad. How it's deployed is up to the user. Republicans under Trump have used high-dominance politics to pursue corrupt, oppressive, authoritarian ends. Democrats, at their best, have mobilized dominance to fight for justice, freedom, and democracy.

Unfortunately, many liberals have come to regard dominance as a dirty business that's best left to the Republicans. But winning on dominance doesn't require fighting dirty, breaking the law, or deceiving voters. Nor is it a male thing. Women can engage in dominance politics every bit as effectively as men can. Liberals can overmatch opponents on dominance while remaining true to our own principles.

In a nutshell, high-dominance leadership is *reality-shaping* and *conflict-embracing,* and it *favors the language of the aggressor, the righteous, and the triumphant.* Low-dominance leadership is *reality-taking* and *conflict-averse,* and it inclines to the *language of the aggressed-upon and the endangered.*

Reality-shaping means striving to make opinion. The archetypal high-dominance leader crafts a narrative that casts himself, his allies, and his forebears as intrepid, successful protagonists. Even if the past includes darkness and defeats, he offers a vision of redemption, celebrating past victories as harbingers of still greater glories to come. He treats narratives and beliefs that oppose his own as falsehoods, not valid alternatives. He asks not "What do the people want to hear?" but rather "What do I want the people to believe?" His message does not shift in sync with opinion polls or in response to his opponent's reactions. He does not assume his audience knows the truth—*his* truth—without perpetual reminders. He stays on the case until his listeners get it—and then he keeps reminding them. A reality-shaping leader can earn a reputation for courage, staunchness, and trustworthiness. He may also inspire intense loyalty in followers and bend opinion to suit his aims.

In addition to being reality-shaping, the high-dominance leader is *conflict-embracing,* especially when facing aggressive opponents. She is happiest on the attack and chafes at playing defense. If she says something that causes controversy, she doubles down rather than qualify or apologize. In cases where she errs, she has the courage to correct course and move on. She prefers preemption to reaction. She seeks to win outright and big, not just avoid loss. She is risk-acceptant, not risk-averse. She grasps that membership is rewarding only if one's team is distinctive and morally superior to its opponents, so she knows that forging a strong in-group identity among her supporters *requires* us-versus-them framing.[2] In particularly contentious situations, she treats opponents as foes, not would-be collaborators. A conflict-embracing leader can establish a reputation as an implacable, all-weather fighter, thus arousing allies, intimidating enemies, and impressing neutral parties. She can also enable the formation of strong in-group identity, which deepens bonds among her supporters and potentially attracts leaners and the unaffiliated.

Finally, the high-dominance leader's *language* reflects her reality-shaping and conflict-embracing orientation. She uses the argot of onslaught and conquest. Embracing provocative parlance, she sometimes uses transgressive language. When dealing with extremists, her rhetoric may belittle and ridicule, turning opponents into objects of scorn and contempt. She creates an image of herself as mighty and her opponent as weak; herself as a victor and her opponent as a loser; herself as capable and her opponent as hapless; herself as patriotic and her opponent as disloyal; herself as protector and her opponent as vulnerable; herself as righteous and her opponent as immoral. Above all, everything she says and does conveys *confidence*, *optimism*, and *exuberance.*

What do these concepts and categories have to do with why liberals so often fail to trounce even adversaries who are morally and experientially unqualified for office?

Everyone is familiar with the Republican phrase "owning the libs." It even has its own *Wikipedia* page: "The phrase 'own the libs' comes from slang usage of the word *own*, meaning 'to dominate,' 'to defeat,' or, 'to humiliate'."[3] Liberals know they don't enjoy being "owned" but aren't sure what to do about it—or even whether anything should be done at all. The notion of turning the tables and *owning their opponents* instead rarely even occurs to them.

But nobody longs to be led by those who are dominated by others. If a leader can't get the best of his opponents, how can he be relied on to protect his followers—or the nation as a whole?

People want to be on the winning team. They favor leaders who project indomitability rather than vulnerability. They admire and trust leaders with stiff spines and strong principles. In a word, people gravitate toward high-dominance leaders.

This orientation is baked into our DNA. As psychologist Dan McAdams argues, the desire for dominant leaders is "very old, awesomely intuitive, and deeply ingrained." According to him, Trump prevailed in 2016 "because of a primal appeal that has generally gone unspoken. It is an appeal that derives ultimately from our human evolutionary heritage." Once in office, dominance remained Trump's trump card: "No U.S. president in recent memory, and perhaps none ever, has tapped so effectively into the primal psychology of dominance." McAdams suggests that Trump had little *but* dominance going for him.[4]

Political scientist Jeffrey Cohen has examined the concept of strength in the context of presidential leadership. While noting the shortage of studies on "strong leadership," Cohen proposed several key traits that the public might see as signs of strength, including being "resolute...not willing to back down...tough...in control of events." After examining public opinion polls between 1971 and 2008, he found: "No matter how the question is worded or the selections offered, strong leadership ranks as one of the most important traits that voters want in their ideal president."[5]

Some psychologists study what is known as "fearless dominance," which roughly means boldness. Psychologist Scott Lilienfeld and colleagues found that American presidents who score high on fearless dominance are more successful in elections, managing crises, and dealing with Congress.[6] As of 2012, the 20th- and 21st-century presidents who scored highest were Theodore Roosevelt, John Kennedy, Franklin Roosevelt, Ronald Reagan, Bill Clinton, George W. Bush, Dwight Eisenhower, and Lyndon Johnson. Other research suggests that the trait is positively associated with competence, ethical decision-making, persuasiveness, and heroism in leaders.[7]

High-dominance orientation isn't all that people seek in leaders. McAdams distinguishes between "dominance" leaders, who rely on shows of strength and mastery over others, and "prestige" leaders, who demonstrate "a degree of magnanimity, generosity, forbearance, and dignity in their leadership roles." Human evolution and growth in the complexity of communities led people to appreciate both qualities in their leaders.

These days, liberals almost always lead in the prestige department. This gives us an invaluable comparative advantage.

But prestige often isn't enough. As McAdams shows, people never quit seeking dominance in leaders. And there is no necessary contradiction between "dominance" and "prestige" qualities, as Presidents Roosevelt, Kennedy, Johnson, and Clinton showed. Among foreign leaders from the past, Africa's Nelson Mandela, India's Jawaharlal Nehru, and Britain's Winston Churchill and Margaret Thatcher were high on both qualities. Among contemporary leaders, Ukraine's Volodymyr Zelensky, Estonia's Kaja Kallas, Brazil's Luiz Inácio "Lula" da Silva, and Poland's Donald Tusk are high-prestige, high-dominance leaders.

There's no way to tell exactly how much of an advantage a high-dominance style provides compared to other assets a candidate might possess. Since this factor has been largely ignored in political science, the research needed has not yet been conducted. It's my hope that this book will prompt scholars to do a deeper dive into this question.

For preliminary insights, we can look at data on the qualities voters say matter in their leaders. During presidential election years, the American National Election Studies (ANES) research team asks respondents to assess candidates' traits. One question reads: "Think about the [Democratic/Republican] presidential candidate. In your opinion does the phrase 'provides strong leadership' describe the candidate extremely well, quite well, not too well, or not well at all?"[8] "Strong leadership" isn't exactly the same as high-dominance orientation, but it's as close as we'll get in available surveys.

Table 9.1 contains the candidate scores for each available year. They run from 0 to 1. In all five elections in which one candidate enjoyed an edge on perceptions of "strength," he won the election that November. In the remaining six elections, the candidates scored the same on strong leadership.

"How well does the phrase 'provides strong leadership' describe the Republican/Democratic presidential candidate?" (0 = not well at all, 1 = extremely well)					
Presidential election year	Republican candidate score	Democratic candidate score	Difference	Winner of election	Did the candidate rated as the stronger leader win?
1980	.5	.4	R +.1	R	Yes
1984	.6	.5	R +.1	R	Yes
1988	.5	.5	tie	R	--
1992	.5	.6	D +.1	D	Yes
1996	.5	.5	tie	D	--
2000	.6	.5	R +.1	R	Yes
2004	.6	.5	R +.1	R	Yes
2008	.6	.6	tie	D	--
2012	.5	.5	tie	D	--
2016	.4	.4	tie	R	--
2020	.4	.4	tie	D	--
The candidate who was seen as providing stronger leadership won 5 times and lost no times; 6 times the candidates had the same score on strong leadership.					

Table 9.1. Perceptions of Candidate's "Strength" as Leader

The survey also asks respondents whether they think each candidate "is knowledgeable." Table 9.2 presents the numbers. In five elections, the candidates tied on perceptions of knowledgeability; in three elections, the candidate seen as more knowledgeable prevailed; and in three, he or she lost the election. A reputation for knowledgeability might be a great thing, but it's not clear that it helps much in elections.

	"How well does the phrase 'is knowledgeable' describe the Republican/Democratic Presidential candidate?" (0 = not at all, 1 = extremely well)				
Presidential election year	Republican candidate score	Democratic candidate score	Difference	Winner of election	Did the candidate rated as more knowledgeable win?
1980	.6	.6	tie	R	--
1984	.7	.7	tie	R	--
1988	.7	.6	R +.1	R	Yes
1992	.7	.7	tie	D	--
1996	.7	.7	tie	D	--
2000	.6	.7	D +.1	R	No
2004	.5	.6	D +.1	R	No
2008	.6	.6	tie	D	--
2012	.5	.7	D +.2	D	Yes
2016	.3	.6	D +.2	R	No
2020	.3	.4	D +.1	D	Yes

The candidate who was seen as more knowledgeable won 3 times and lost 3 times; 5 times the candidates had the same score on knowledgeability.

Table 9.2. Perceptions of Whether Candidate Is "Knowledgeable"

What about perceptions of whether the candidate cares? It's hard to think of anything Democratic candidates spend more energy conveying. What's less clear is whether voters care about whether their leaders care. The candidate who was seen as more caring won five times and lost four times; one time the candidates were seen as equally caring. Table 9.3 provides the numbers.

"How well does the phrase 'really cares about people like you' describe the Republican/Democratic Presidential candidate?" (0 = not at all, 1 = extremely well)

Presidential election year	Republican candidate score	Democratic candidate score	Difference	Winner of election	Did the candidate rated as more caring win?
1984	.5	.6	D +.1	R	No
1988	.5	.6	D +.1	R	No
1992	.4	.6	D +.2	D	Yes
1996	.4	.5	D +.1	D	Yes
2000	.5	.5	tie	R	--
2004	.4	.5	D +.1	R	No
2008	.4	.6	D +.2	D	Yes
2012	.3	.5	D +.2	D	Yes
2016	.3	.4	D +.1	R	No
2020	.3	.4	D +.1	D	Yes

The candidate who was seen as caring more about people like the respondent won 5 times and lost 4 times; one time the candidates had the same score on caring about people like the respondent.

Table 9.3. Perceptions of Whether Candidate "Really Cares about People Like You"

In these studies, "strength" never loses. Knowledgeable and caring lose about half the time.

10. The Democrats' Dominance Deficit

T he Republicans assault democracy, celebrate incompetence, and abide criminality. They offer policies that are mostly at odds with majority opinion. The Democrats are committed to democracy, field more competent candidates, obey the law, and offer more popular policies. So how do the Republicans still beat the Democrats roughly half the time, and how have they brought democracy to the brink of disaster?

The Republicans' superior use of dominance is a key to their success. Let's look at how they do it, trait by trait.

Reality-shaping versus reality-taking. While the Republicans try to make opinion, the Democrats take it. When opinion doesn't move their way, Republicans double down; the Democrats back down. The Republicans pursue even unpopular policies with abandon. The Democrats often refrain from defending even popular policies lest the polls turn against them. The Republicans act as if their policies have more support than they do; the Democrats act as if theirs have less. The Republicans tell voters what they think; the Democrats tell voters what they think they want to hear. The Republicans pound their own truths—whether true or not—into listeners' heads. The Democrats present their case now and then and hope their audience will remember. Republicans connect the dots for voters; the Democrats expect voters will make the inferences on their own. The Republicans treat even petty wins as conquests. The Democrats are loath to trumpet even their transformational feats.

Conflict-embracing versus conflict-averse. The Republicans savor conflict. They don't hesitate to treat the Democrats like enemies. The Democrats dislike conflict and find us-versus-them politics distasteful. The Republicans play offense; the Democrats play defense. When the Republicans say something controversial, they push forward; when Democrats cause a stir, they walk it back. The Republicans attack; the Democrats react. The Republicans accept risk and play to win; the Democrats abhor risk and hope not to lose. The Republicans' messaging tries to stoke their base; the Democrats' messaging aims not to stoke the Republican base.

Language of the aggressor, the righteous, and the triumphant versus that of the aggressed-upon and the endangered. The Republicans use entertaining, aggressive, provocative language; the Democrats bore with bromides. The Republicans cast themselves as imposing, indomitable, menacing, and triumphant; the Democrats present themselves as imposed upon, vulnerable, menaced, and in danger of defeat. The Republicans call their opponents weak, lame, gutless, pathetic, disloyal, unpatriotic, disgraceful, immoral, and disgusting. Democrats cast their adversaries as callous, unfair, ruthless, terrifying, hurtful, heartless, scary, and offensive. The Democrats call the Republicans bullies but leave them in charge of the playground.

This assessment obviously ignores nuance and exceptions—and there are exceptions, as we will see later. For the most part, however, 21st-century Democrats, including party leaders Joe Biden, Al Gore, John Kerry, and Hillary Clinton, have fallen short on dominance.

When taken to extremes, high-dominance orientation can be a political liability. From one perspective, the Republicans' push for unpopular abortion bans showed temerity. Some Republicans may accept electoral losses as an acceptable trade-off for achieving a policy dream.[9] But by all accounts, their radical abortion laws prevented their takeover of the Senate in the 2022 midterm elections, and the issue continues to dog them in 2024. What is more, pressing the lie that Trump beat Biden in 2020, treating vaccines as deadly, and claiming climate change isn't happening go far beyond functional high-dominance reality-shaping and veer off into dysfunctional, delusional reality-rejection.

Authoritarians have fallen into this trap in other countries too, as with Vladimir Putin's invasion of Ukraine. Putin's belief that 200k Russian troops could easily conquer and annex an independence-minded nation of 44 million people is what hubris-driven high-dominance insanity looks like. Reality shaping, if untempered by a grasp of the reality one seeks to influence, can lead to disaster.

But high-dominance overreach isn't a danger for liberals these days. They have the opposite problem—which helps explain how high-dominance authoritarians like Trump and Putin have forced the world to accommodate their twisted visions.

The partisan dominance gap may have been decisive in Trump's 2016 win. In a Morning Consult/POLITICO exit poll conducted the day of Trump's election, more than twice as many voters said they wanted a "strong leader" as one who "shares my values" and "cares about people like me" combined.[10] People 65 and over—the demographic that votes at the highest rate and that put Trump over the top in Florida, Michigan, Ohio, and Pennsylvania—rated being "strong and decisive," "patriotic," and "able to command respect from other countries" as the qualities they most seek in a leader.[11] In the run-up to the election, while Clinton was seen as better prepared, more intelligent, and having higher moral standards, Trump was viewed as the stronger leader and as more honest and trustworthy.[12]

In the *New York Times* exit poll in the 2020 election, voters valued having a "strong leader" over all other qualities, including one who was a unifier, more caring, and had good judgment. Of those who valued having a strong leader the most, 72 percent voted for Trump.[13] As McAdams notes, it is Trump's "dominance strategy" that so many voters find appealing.[14]

For all his manifold defects, Trump is a reality-shaping leader—and transform reality he has. He embraces unpopular stances and says what he wants regardless of the audience. His political positions—from taxes to immigration to abortion—contradict most voters' preferences. But there is little evidence that the polls ever sway him. Therein lies his appeal—and therefore his ability to get away with cutting taxes for the rich, pursuing heinous immigration policies, and stacking the Supreme Court with anti-abortion justices.

Perceptions of his invincibility are reinforced by his refusal to walk back even his most controversial statements—critics and opponents be damned. Liberals characterize him as fear-driven. But even if childhood trauma propels his well-established narcissism, the way he manifests it in the public arena is an adaptation that builds a reputation for bravery. And while liberals claim that his followers are motivated by fear, he makes his minions feel more powerful in the listening.[15]

Liberals may not want to admit it, but Trump and his followers are so dauntless as to be dangerous and intimidating—a trait that has served them well against Democrats who *speak and act like* they are endangered and intimidated.

As Kamala Harris put it in January 2024 when an interviewer asked if she was scared by the prospect of a Trump second term: "I am scared as heck! Which is why I'm traveling our country. You know, there's an old saying that there's only two ways to run for office—either without an opponent or scared. So on all of those points, yes, we should all be scared."[16]

That's the ticket. I want my leaders to be *running scared* of Trump. In fact, if you have an opponent—any opponent, you know the old saying!—*scared* is the only way to run. And yes, I couldn't agree more; I should be *scared too*!

And thank gosh the vice president refrained from briny language in expressing how scared she was. "No h-e-double-toothpicks allowed!," as my second-grade teacher used to say.

Trump reaps the benefits of the reality-shaping leader. Liberals cannot comprehend how anyone could trust a man who lies about everything. But for many, Trump's mendacity about external reality says less about his trustworthiness as a leader than his stunning candor about his own internal world. Unlike most politicians, you always know what Trump is thinking—what you see is what you get.

The result is what Jonathan Allen and Amie Parnes noted in contrasting his messaging with Hillary Clinton's: "He could be genuine while lying; she came off as inauthentic even when she was telling the truth."[17]

Trump's habit of hammering his beliefs into listeners' heads reinforces his dominance. It helps him shape opinion—and possibly shape minds as well. Cognitive linguist George Lakoff explains: "Repetition of language has the power to change brains. When a word or phrase is repeated over and over for a long period of time...[It] physically changes your brain."[18] As Maria Ressa, the Nobel-Prize-winning crusader against disinformation, states: "When you say a lie a million times, it becomes a fact."[19]

Now consider the most absurd phrase in the English language: "Trump won" (with regard to the 2020 election). How can 3 in 10 Americans believe it?[20] Trump repeats the lie over and over, drilling it into listeners' heads. Try as he did, Trump couldn't void the election, but his relentless repetition of the lie might have changed brains.

His high-dominance approach enabled him to extinguish the classical conservative spirit of the Republican Party, turning the organization into a bastion of fanatics, profiteers, conspiracy mongers, vax-skeptics, Big Liars, Putin admirers, and sexual predators in search of public office. He became the Republican Party.

Trump is as conflict-embracing as he is reality-shaping, which deepens his dominance edge. He famously savors discord and is always on offense. Us-versus-them politics comes naturally to him. He has always intuited that there can be no strong sense of "us" without a separate "them" to which "we" are superior. Trump makes his supporters feel like part of a revolutionary movement, calls them together in raucous rallies, and forges a sense of solidarity that currently has no equivalent on the left.[21] In the absence of leaders with Trump's élan-inspiring, us-versus-them verve, the Democrats will struggle to create a similar sense of belonging.

Finally, Trump's language expresses his high-dominance orientation. He uses rhetoric that provokes and entertains. He calls opponents "low-energy," "weak," and "pathetic." He uses belittling nicknames (favorites include "Lyin' Ted" [Cruz], "Crooked Hillary" [Clinton], and "Ron DeSanctimonious" [DeSantis]). His speeches at rallies are peppered with easy profanity—just the kind of language many of us use in private conversation.

While liberals swoon with disapproval and stand above such childishness, neuroscience entrepreneur Spencer Gerrol found that Trump's style can be highly effective. Monitoring listeners' brain activity during televised debates, his team found that audiences—and not just Trump's followers—delighted in his boldness and provocations. By contrast, viewers were bored by Hillary Clinton's play-it-safe recitations of her policy stances and resumé. While Trump held audience attention at a 7 on a 10-point scale, higher than the most popular TV commercials, Clinton averaged a 4. Noting what Trump intuitively gets, and Democrats don't, Gerrol said: "The entertainment value of politics is actually really important."[22]

Across every aspect of dominance, Clinton could not have furnished a stronger contrast to Trump. Her every statement and position were transparently tailored to pollsters' advice. While Trump showed everyone the same glowering face, she said one thing to one audience and something else to another. On the eve of her 2016 campaign, after years of opposition and almost comical equivocations, she finally came out in favor of marriage equality—the moment the polls indicated it would serve her. She championed free-trade agreements such as NAFTA and the Trans-Pacific Partnership—except in leap years when she was running for president.[23]

She largely passed on turning Trump into the object of ridicule he was manifestly designed to be. He could get away with saying anything, knowing that indignation would be her strongest response.

She strove to avoid offending any organized interest. The only significant group whose opposition she openly welcomed was the NRA—but here, too, her opinion "evolved" in response to circumstances. In her 2008 race for the Democratic nomination, she tried to compete for voters in rural areas and small towns by questioning Obama's commitment to the Second Amendment.[24]

Trump was also conflict-embracing, while Clinton was perpetually on defense. By panicking over every hacked data dump by Trump (or his Russian allies), her campaign inadvertently blew trifling revelations into scandals. No, the DNC did *not* advantage Secretary Clinton unfairly; no, Secretary Clinton was *not* aware of DNC Chairwoman Debbie Wasserman Schultz's contacts with her staff during the primaries; no, Secretary Clinton's emails did *not* compromise national security! Instead of kicking Trump's ass for infractions far greater than anything her leaked emails revealed, she was ever covering her own—and keeping the media focused on her petty transgressions.

Clinton's language reflected her low-dominance style. While Trump expressed his lies provocatively, she told her truths vapidly. Trump entertained with colorful, transgressive language; she bored with forgettable banalities. She constantly called Trump out for his "insults" and "insinuations," while he insinuated and insulted away.[25] She never tired of indignantly pointing out all the groups Trump had presumably offended, but she rarely caused him much offense.

Instead, Clinton called Trump scary, frightening, and terrifying, thus reinforcing the narrative of the endangered, aggressed-upon victim. In a characteristic communique to her supporters, she lamented: "I think Donald Trump is terrifying, and I absolutely hate what he stands for. I hate how he insults women, people of color, and entire countries when it suits him. I hate his total lack of under-standing of complex issues that impact Americans."[26]

Do you want to be led by someone who finds Trump "terrify-ing"? Or would you prefer someone who terrifies *him*?

None of this means Hillary Clinton was a weak person. Nor is this critique meant to single her out since her political style reflected her party's—and it still does. She had so many other advantages that she won the popular vote by almost three million ballots. But a can-didate as unpopular, inexperienced, and unhinged as Trump should never have come within 10 million popular votes or 100 Electoral College votes of the White House.

The demand for dominance is felt across the political and de-mographic spectrum. In the 2022 Florida governor's race, Ron De-Santis scored a 19-point victory over Charlie Crist, the conflict-allergic Democratic former governor. Crist is a sweet fellow who ran on listening to voters' kitchen-table concerns and trying to heal partisan divisions. Hispanic voters were key: DeSantis won 58 per-cent of them, up from 44 percent in 2018. And despite what liberals characterized as his overtly racist policies, he even improved his standing among African Americans, from 14 to 17 percent.[27]

To explain the beating they took, Democrats predictably focused on their supposed failure to express the proper concern for voters' economic pain—ignoring the fact that Crist talked about little else.[28] One Republican strategist offered a different perspective: "The key takeaway that I hear from Hispanics over and over again, is some variation of 'he [DeSantis] has cojones'."[29]

Now, as it happens, those cojones aren't as heavy as many thought. The moment DeSantis faced Trump in the rough and tum-ble of the 2023-2024 Republican primaries his dominance act fell apart, delivering another lesson in the dynamics of dominance. When Trump attacked, DeSantis ducked. When Trump mocked him with insulting nicknames, DeSantis said he didn't want to "get in the gutter." Instead, he would stay focused on "the issues."[30] As he did, his shot at taking down Trump wilted.

DeSantis' timidity didn't go unnoticed. Pundits who had mar-veled at his unrelenting attacks on liberals, immigrants, schools, and businesses in Florida started calling him cowardly. Strategists piled on, bemused by his unwillingness to confront Trump.[31]

New York Times columnist Michelle Goldberg nails it: "Like Trump's 2016 rivals, DeSantis is making the mistake of believing that the primary race is about issues, while Trump instinctively un-derstands it's about dominance."[32]

Trump's critics-be-damned disdain for optics isn't a sign of courage. Instead, it's a manifestation of his narcissism combined with a lack of impulse control. But his congenital political gift is that he often makes these character defects look like bravery, at least to a substantial minority. It's what creates the perception that he's his own man (however sociopathic) and acts on his own convictions (even if they're nothing but ego-driven ambitions and resent-ments). It's what separates him from every other politician and ex-plains the fervor he elicits among those who thirst for strong leadership. It's what leads otherwise responsible people to debase themselves in his service. And it's what has enabled him to retain his grip on his party, even as he's proven to be a liability in elections. To many people, it makes him look indomitable—and other politicians like panderers by comparison.

Trump ignores the advice of consultants and pollsters—or of anyone else, save perhaps whatever sweet nothings Putin whispered in his ear during their many secret conversations. This is why Trump supporters will tell you their man doesn't sound like a politician. To them, he's Honest Donald, the only real leader in American politics.

Year after year, he furnishes his supporters with a most satisfy-ing spectacle: He says something insulting to trigger his detractors; a media frenzy ensues; the liberal social media bubble swells with indignation at his insensitivity; and just as his critics overcome the vapors, he dishes out the next outrage.

As president, he ruled the airwaves while channel-surfing in his pajamas, relishing every ruckus he stirred. He *owned* the people who disrespected him—the same people his supporters suspect also look down on *them.*

As Trump's fans watch us urbane sophisticates extend our elevated chins for the daily bitch-slap, their man never fails to deliver the blow.[33] He doesn't furnish much bread, but most folks figure they can provide that for themselves, and nobody offers half as good a circus.

Whether democracy survives hinges in part on overcoming the Republicans' dominance advantage. So far, that isn't happening. In a May 2022 survey, the term most frequently cited to describe the Democratic Party was "weak." Fifty-one percent ascribed that quality to it, while 41 percent said it applied to the Republicans. Thirty-eight percent saw the Democrats as "strong," compared to 46 percent for the Republicans.[34]

Jasmine Crockett, the high-dominance second-term Dallas congresswoman who's standing up to bigots and gun-nuts with audacity most Democrats lack, put it this way in May 2023: "I've been all over the state of Texas for various campaigns and I talk to people and ask them, why is it you don't want to vote? Honestly, I have heard more than once that Democrats are weak. We are not weak but there is this perception."[35]

11. Why Liberals Recoil from Dominance

H ow did it come to this?

Some requirements of high-dominance behavior may feel to liberals like violations of our ethics. A reality-shaping and con-flict-embracing orientation requires treating opponents' claims as dead wrong, not legitimate alternatives. It also involves expressing your own aggressive impulses, believing in and asserting your own superiority, and considering some opponents as incorrigible rather than misunderstood. Each of these requirements rubs many con-temporary liberals the wrong way.

Writing in the wake of Al Gore's and John Kerry's losses to George W. Bush, political psychologist Drew Westen argued: "Dem-ocrats tend to be conflicted about the appropriate use of aggression, and hence to hide their fear of confrontation behind the compassion, empathy, and tolerance that are central features of the morality of the left." Democrats have typically come to respond to opponents' attacks with a flurry of factual corrections, expressions of disap-pointment, and complaints of unfair play—all of which "reinforces the view of Democrats as weak and woosie" and as "the supplicant to the attacker."[36]

Shortly after Trump beat Hillary Clinton, psychologist John Jost and psychoanalyst Orsolya Hunyady penned a piece that should be required reading for all who seek to grasp liberals' difficulties in squaring off against the Trumpified Republicans.[37] The authors argue that the liberal "sees herself as driven by her own compassion and is therefore uncomfortable about her own competitive and aggressive impulses." Embracing one's superiority can also be problematic. Since liberals often attach supreme value to equality and open-mindedness, "[o]n some abstract level, liberals feel compelled to proclaim that conservative intuitions are equally acceptable, equally valuable, and equally valid to their own intuitions." Liberals, therefore, go to any lengths to sustain a good people/bad leaders picture of politics: "They struggle to separate Trump and his actions from the people who elevated him to power, and in doing so, they retain the ability to be empathetic. . . . Do conservatives engage in similar contortions of a political psychological nature? No, because their philosophy (and their psychology) does not require it."

Who, then, is to blame for the harms liberals see multiplying all around them? According to Jost and Hunyady, liberals' "psychological discomfort with placing blame squarely onto 'the other'" drives them to "introspection or 'self-examination'," a move that rarely happens among authoritarian right-wingers.

The liberals' mindsets are inconsistent with an us-versus-them mentality, which requires seeing adversaries as fully responsible for their own actions. It means "othering" them—and for many liberals there is no higher crime. If the MAGA crowd are decent folks who are just duped by a bad leader, how can they be enemies?

The impulse to affirm everyone's needs and engage in introspection is, in proportion, a virtue. It is central to the liberal ethic of empathy and understanding and gives liberals a comparative advantage.

But like all virtues, it can become dysfunctional if taken to extremes. A no-enemies mindset is laudable when reality justifies it, but it can prevent us from defending ourselves when others really are out to destroy us. Psychologists distinguish between healthy empathy and codependence. Having compassion for an addict in your life is fine, but that doesn't mean you should feel responsible for his behavior, still less tolerate his abuse. The cornerstone of addiction programs is that addicts must be held accountable for their actions.

Critical self-examination is necessary to make tactical adjustments when needed. But it can also lock us into cycles of self-recrimination that enable us to avoid open conflict with those who are actually to blame. We assure ourselves that if we just make peoples' lives better, play by the rules, and show how much we care, we can achieve our goals without ever going to war.

But this is the mindset of counselors and HR representatives, not leaders tasked with safeguarding the nation against dire threats.

Differences in political leaders' professional backgrounds might explain some of the growing partisan disparity in dominance orientations. Specifically, Democratic leaders tend to hail from helping professions where intense competition isn't necessarily central to accomplishment, while Republicans' backgrounds lie in fields where it is.

Members of Congress complete a survey on their professional backgrounds. Let's look at the trends in recent decades.[38]

We'll start with the helping professions. During the 1980s, roughly the same percentage of Democrats and Republicans had backgrounds in education—between 10 and 12 percent. Since then, the number of Democrats with such backgrounds has trended up while the number of Republicans hasn't. As of 2021, the Democrats' percentage of members with an education background was double that of Republicans—20 versus 10 percent.

A similar difference can be seen in the number of members with public service backgrounds. After starting at about the same level in the 1980s, the numbers trended up for members of both parties, but the Democrats' increased more. As of 2021, almost half of Democrats, versus about one third of Republicans, had public service backgrounds.

Now let's look at the data for the profit-seeking professions, where the ability to prevail over rivals determines success and even survival. Republican members who have a background in business have consistently outnumbered the Democrats who do, and the gap has grown since the 1980s. In 2021, 48 percent of Republicans, versus 29 percent of Democrats, said they worked as businesspeople before arriving in Congress. In related fields, such as farming and real estate, the Republicans are similarly better represented than the Democrats.

Now, I, like most liberals, would like to see more legislators who spent their careers teaching students, conducting research, and serving the public. But in an increasingly polarized and even vicious political environment, those who hail from lines of work in which getting ahead means routing rivals might be at a competitive advantage.

My friends in the corporate world tend to say much the same thing. As a successful tech entrepreneur with an unfortunate party affiliation put it to me in conversation: "Dominating your competitors is the key to winning? Duh. Everyone in corporate knows that. Maybe the reason you liberals can't handle Trump is that the people you put up for office are schoolteachers and social workers."

That's obviously an exaggeration, but it's hard not to see her point.

Other life experiences can shape one's mentality toward competition as well. Service in the military is one of them. Until the 1990s, most members from both parties had served in the armed forces, and the partisan difference was slight. As World War II veterans passed from the scene, the proportion of members from both parties who had served fell off sharply and mostly in tandem. In 2005, 26 percent of Republicans and 20 percent of Democrats were veterans. But as of 2021, the numbers had fallen to 24 percent of Republicans and just 10 percent of Democrats.

None of this means that Democrats should start favoring real estate moguls over academics for office. But the numbers we've seen help make sociological sense of the partisan dominance deficit undermining the Democrats.

In normal times, when all parties respect the rules and norms of fair play, leaders from professions that cultivate soul-searching, sensitivity, and personal connection may be at a comparative advantage. But today's Democrats face adversaries who think rules are for suckers and winning is all that counts.

In 2018, former Secretary of State Madeline Albright, a distinctively high-dominance liberal, wrote in her book, *Fascism: A Warning*: "Decades ago, George Orwell suggested that the best one-word description of a fascist was bully."[39] So let's try a thought experiment. Consider how you might respond to your kid being tormented on the playground. Do you warn your child against rallying the other kids and striking back lest he antagonize the bully? Do you tell him that fighting back would reduce him to the bully's level?

I do know some parents (I live in the San Francisco Bay Area) who would answer yes to those questions. I know because I asked them. They basically said that they'd hope the bully would evolve, given the proper counseling and understanding. They would also encourage school administrators to step in.

But it may take years for the bully to "evolve," if he ever does. And the school administrators can't be around all the time. What then?

As Chris Rock put it in his inimitable assessment of Trump's rise, "We got rid of bullies, a real bully showed up, and nobody knew how to handle him."[40]

So how should bullies be dealt with in the real world? Therapist and mediator Bill Eddy says: "Bullies don't negotiate; they make demands, they make threats, and they fight for them. They generally lack the modern skills of win-win. . . . So don't think of their demands as a form of true negotiation. It's more like warfare. And you don't want to give in to that."[41] More specifically, according to psychologist Shawn Smith, "[B]ullies and predators...scan for vulnerability. When they do, responding quickly is more important than responding perfectly."[42]

Whether confronting bullies on the playground or in the political arena, there's no substitute for hitting back fast and hard. The response must be persistent because bullies are always looking for weakness. The last thing they want is to take on someone who fights back. And this, of course, is their Achilles heel. *Persistently and aggressively* defeating their dominance is the name of the game. Until liberals internalize this truth, authoritarians will control the political playground.

In sum, the drive to affirm the needs and desires of others and to engage in self-examination can be laudable—but only to the extent that they suit reality. When opponents are willing to lie, cheat, steal, and incite violence to win, these otherwise praiseworthy habits can lead to a cycle of demoralization and futility.

Liberals' billowing spirit of pity and introspection also feeds a swelling current in 21st-century liberal political culture: a well-intentioned but politically maladaptive cult of empathy that regards celebration of progress as tantamount to insensitivity to those who still suffer. We also may worry that it will breed complacency or make us sound arrogant, just like our opponents. Then there's the purported political hazard: Feting progress could leave still-suffering people feeling unloved and therefore more vulnerable to the appeal of Trumpism. For some on the left, acknowledging that things are far better than they used to be practically marks you as an ally of plutocrats and bigots.

Let's look at one example. Most Americans have no idea that thanks to the Democrats, child poverty plummeted by more than two-and-a-half times between 1993 and 2019. When Bill Clinton took office in 1993, 28 percent of American children lived in poverty; in 2019, 11 percent did. Poverty plunged in every state, and improvement was especially dramatic among kids of color. In 1993, half of all Black children in America lived in poverty; in 2019, 18 percent did. In 1993, 52 percent of Hispanic children were poor; in 2019, it was 19 percent. Poverty among white children fell from 18 to 8 percent.

There's still a gap between children of color and white kids, but it has narrowed, and children in every group made stunning gains.

And as if all that isn't good enough, in 2021 the overall child poverty rate fell to five percent.[43]

What is more, most of the drop is due to government action. Economic growth hasn't been fast enough to account for the spectacular gains. The improvements are largely the result of a gaggle of programs that Democrats championed over Republican resistance.

Why do liberals fail to tell this extraordinary success story?

A writer at the *New York Times* inadvertently revealed the reason. Shortly after the *Times* reported the data—earlier versions of which had been publicly available for years—David Leonhardt wrote: "I am guessing that many readers are surprised to hear about the big drop in child poverty since the 1990s. I'll confess that I was—and I have been covering economics for the past two decades." Leonhardt speculated about the reason: "Journalists and academic experts...worry that we will come off as blasé or Pollyannaish when we report good news...I understand why many people are reluctant to focus on the poverty decline. The U.S. has not solved poverty."[44]

Leonhardt's reflections help us grasp why liberals don't broadcast one of the greatest stories never told—and one that reflects magnificently on the Democrats. We do fear seeming blasé and Pollyannaish. Beyond that, we (usually subconsciously) reason, if people knew the good news, they might think we've come far enough. Perhaps worst of all, we fear sounding callous to those who are still poor.

But that approach undercuts liberals' messaging and fails to tell the truth.

Liberals could brandish the news to shape public opinion on poverty and how to conquer it. We could also bolster our reputation for efficacy.

Instead, we essentially *hide* the glad tidings—even from ourselves.

It wasn't until I started doing research for this book that I began to see the pattern and how damaging it can be to liberal causes and candidates. So I have made a point of getting the word out when I come across good news.

The disincentives for doing so soon became apparent. Case in point: When I mention the fall in child poverty to fellow liberals, neither fist-pumps nor fist-bumps typically ensue. Instead, my interlocutors typically pass through what we might call the Four Stages of Good-News Denial (the Four Ds):

Stage 1: *disbelieve* the data

My friend: "*What?* Child poverty has fallen *how* far? Wait, you mean in *Finland*, right?"

Me: "No, right here at home. It's fallen more than two-and-a-half times since 1993, when Clinton took office."

Stage 2: *dispute* the data

My friend: "Well, then, they must have used the wrong indicators."

Me: "Nope, they used the standard Census Bureau indicator, the Supplemental Poverty Measure, see?"

I show him the website on my phone.

Stage 3: *deflect* to other data (a.k.a. "whataboutisms")

My friend: "Well, maybe the *kids* are all right, but what about *overall* poverty rates?"

Me: "Actually, in 2021, eight percent of Americans lived in poverty, and that's the lowest rate on record."[45]

After a few more whataboutisms, he grows quiet, then shrugs and hurries off to an appointment.

Stage 4: *debug* the data

A few months later, my friend flags me down in the hallway, waving his phone.

Here it is, he proclaims, pointing to the latest *New York Times* piece by Paul Krugman, titled "America Betrays Its Children Again." In September 2023, new data showed that child poverty rose in 2022 from 5 to 12 percent.[46]

There you have it, worldview restored. America is no Finland after all.

And this brings us to another critical point. Krugman was right about the data but wrong about the culprit. The disaster was the direct result of the Republicans blocking renewal of the child tax credit; the Democrats fought tenaciously to sustain it.

So did "America" betray its children, as Krugman claims? Or did the *congressional Republicans* do it?

Why do liberals parrot Republican talking points by accepting blame—or, worse yet, placing it on "America"? Senator Ted Cruz declares, "The left's attack is on America. The left hates America"— and liberals just keep loading him up with ammunition.[47]

Liberals' stunning reticence—and even denial of progress for which we are responsible—leaves even normally well-informed people in the dark about the domestic equivalent of whipping Hitler in World War II. It also leaves voters unaware that, as with the war against the Nazis, liberal leaders did most of the whipping.

Our refusal to take the win undermines us in eight ways:

First, it may be especially damaging among those most likely to vote for the Democrats but least likely to turn out: under-30 voters. I hear it from my (mostly progressive, idealistic) students all the time: Why should I organize—or even get out to vote—for a party that never does much for what I care about anyway? These kids are anything but apathetic. Some would be sporting tees and toting bags emblazed with donkeys if they knew the squeeze the Democrats put on poverty. And if they had an inkling of Biden's role, they'd see him as the chillest old dude alive rather than a fossil they can't relate to.

Second, it makes liberals look like ungrateful whiners to non-progressive but swayable voters. Touting gains isn't a substitute for fighting injustice; it's a vital part of the effort. It's surely a better way to soften up these voters than conveying that nothing these folks have done or could do—like paying higher taxes to fund food stamps and Medicare—ever makes much of a difference.

Third, it undermines our reputation for effectiveness. Everyone knows that poverty reduction is a paramount goal for the Democrats. But in the absence of a drumbeat of good news, people can be forgiven for regarding liberals as hapless dreamers rather than the daring doers we actually are.

Fourth, we fail to bring forth another piece of evidence for the greatest provocative truth we have to tell. Namely, that for the past century, practically all of what has made America the envy and light of the world is the product of striving by ordinary, forward-looking Americans under the leadership of progressive politicians.

Fifth, it dishonors the sacrifices of those who lived and died for justice. How are the lives of Jane Addams, Ida B. Wells, and A. Philip Randolph—or the countless thousands of activists whose names we will never know—exalted by tacit denials that they ever made a difference?

Sixth, it might dampen liberal activism and slant policy to the right. Political scientists David Broockman and Christopher Skovron find that state legislators from both parties grossly overestimate their constituents' support for conservative positions, resulting in legislation that is out of sync with public opinion. The authors note: "[W]hile voter turnout for conservatives and liberals differs only slightly, conservatives have recently been significantly more likely to participate in the public sphere in other ways, such as by contacting their legislators or attending town hall meetings."[48] Is it possible that Republicans' habit of ceaselessly publicizing their wins might inspire political engagement more than liberals' bashfulness does? Where do we find evidence that ignoring progress spurs activism?

Seventh, it can undermine substantive progressive aspirations. The breakthrough on poverty is just one source of remarkable progress that we typically fail to shout about or even reveal. Another is the march toward gender equality—one of the many areas in which the United States has long been an international leader. When I ask students to estimate the number of women in the Senate today compared to when I entered college in 1980, most say it has pretty much stayed the same or has risen moderately.

The reveal? In 1980, there was one woman Senator. Today, there are 25 times more. Do we still have work to do to achieve full parity? Of course! But it's also undeniable that leaps have already been made and should be celebrated as such.

Now, these are political science majors studying at the best university in the world. The fact that so many get this wrong shows how little we do to keep them abreast of news that reflects brilliantly on the liberals' performance. The Democrats, after all, are responsible for the reforms and struggles that made such progress possible. What's more, over 70 percent of female members of Congress are Democrats.

In a landmark study published in 2016, political scientists Danny Hayes and Jennifer Lawless found that most Americans believe women face much higher barriers than men when competing for public office. In-depth analysis of the 2010 and 2014 congressional elections, however, revealed that "male and female House candidates communicate similar messages on the campaign trail, receive similar coverage in the local press, and garner similar evaluations from voters in their districts. When they run for office, male and female candidates not only perform equally well on Election Day—they also face a very similar electoral landscape."

Then comes the bombshell: Hayes and Lawless find that the widespread, erroneous *belief* that women face higher obstacles discourages women from running for office. Thus, overcoming conventional pessimism is critical to boosting women's representtation.[49]

Eighth, failing to tout gains may undermine the reputation of democracy itself. According to some surveys, faith in democracy has waned in America and worldwide since the beginning of the 21st century.[50] Those who have noted the trend typically attribute it to democracy's supposed failure to deliver prosperity, justice, and good governance. But whether the goal is ensuring political stability,[51] bolstering economic growth,[52] fostering human development,[53] promoting innovation,[54] reducing corruption,[55] enhancing quality of public administration,[56] advancing gender equality,[57] enabling dignified treatment for LGBTQ people,[58] or allowing the human spirit to flourish more generally,[59] democracy is the superior regime.

A more plausible explanation for democracy's declining reputation, particularly among the young, may be that liberal elites fail to trumpet its advantages. Even acknowledging democracy's proven superiority often comes hard.

The generations that came of age after World War II grew up in poorer, less just societies than their more fortunate offspring inhabit today. But they had little doubt that their democracy was hardwon, precious, and superior to the alternatives. They knew it because that is what their parents, schoolteachers, professors, media, and political leaders told them.

So why, in the 21st century, have so many become disillusioned—or just plain bored—with democracy? Why do they take it for granted—indeed, to such an extent that democracy itself is endangered? Why have shockingly large portions of the electorate fallen for chumps like Trump, who tell them that democracy isn't any better than authoritarianism? How can we explain the recent findings of political scientist Kristian Frederisksen, who reports that young people are less likely than their elders to punish politicians' undemocratic behavior? The author finds "comprehensive evidence for the proposition that young people are less committed to democracy than older people" in the United States as well as other major democracies.[60]

In response, we might ask ourselves how much liberal opinion-shaping elites are doing to instill an appreciation for the glittering promise of democracy and the vast detriments of its alternatives. We might consider how our fondness for pessimistic—and often false—

narratives about relentlessly escalating insecurity and injustice and "democracy's failure to deliver" might be playing out on the ground. Beyond a certain point, has our allergy to "triumphalism" encouraged a generation to forget—or never learn—about the immense comparative advantages of democracy? Could it have dulled our awareness of the urgent need to defend free government?

In a July 2023 article, Paul Krugman struck again. After reviewing a raft of data showing that the American economy is cooking and extending its lead over Europe, he warned: "I've been sensing a mood swing in how the United States sees itself in the world. American triumphalism—we're No. 1!—is making a comeback. As always, we should curb our enthusiasm." He concludes: "The U.S. economy has been doing pretty well lately, but we shouldn't let it go to our heads."[61]

There you have it. With an election pending that will determine the fate of democracy, half of Americans are still convinced that the economy is getting worse despite robust growth, rock-bottom unemployment, and falling inflation. The Democratic incumbent struggles to stay even with Donald Trump in the polls. Clearly, the last thing we want is for voters to feel "enthusiasm" about how well things are going.

This mindset, while forged by good intentions, is more conducive to languor than prudent restraint. It sees fearlessness as foolishness and dauntlessness as a prelude to rashness. It confuses the self-assurance required to inspire followers and overpower foes with insolence and conceit. It takes blame for problems opponents caused, blurring the essential distinction between a competent, virtuous "us" and a bungling, immoral "them."

As Nicholas Kristof noted in his 2023 end-of-year roundup, "This Was a Terrible Year, and Also Maybe the Best One Yet for Humanity": "[O]ne thing I learned long ago as a journalist is that when our coverage is unremittingly negative, people tune out and give up. If we want to tackle problems—from the war in Gaza to climate change—then it helps to know that progress is possible."[62]

12. Profiles in Low-Dominance Leadership

The Democrats' low-dominance aversion to "triumphalism" was on display in the 2022 midterm elections. Let's have a look at how it manifested in their political campaigns.

Profile in low-dominance leadership #1: Failure to demolish the Big Lie. Like enemies of democracy everywhere, the Republicans cultivate the notion that any elections they don't win are fixed. They do so to suck the legitimacy out of any contest they lose and to create the impression that any actions they might take—fixing or annulling elections, even staging violent insurrections—just intend to undo injustice.

Since losing in 2020, Trump has pounded away at the lie that he won. For congressional Republicans, the price of challenging his Big Lie has been dismissal from leadership positions. For many, it has also been the end of their political careers, as they have gone down in primaries to Big Lying Republicans.

The 2020 presidential election wasn't even close. Biden won by over seven million popular votes and 74 Electoral College votes. The Big Liars don't even have a *theory* of Trump's victory. After the comedy of MAGA Arizonans' post-election "audit," the Republicans gave up on even trying to concoct a plausible tale. Instead, they just intone "Trump won!"[63]

For a shocking number of Americans, saying that is enough. In a May 2023 Monmouth University poll, 30 percent of respondents, including 68 percent of Republicans, believed Biden's victory was "due to voter fraud." *Just 59 percent agreed that Biden "won fair and square."* That leaves an astounding 41 percent—perhaps twice the number of those who can rightly be labeled deplorables—either sure Biden lost or saying they didn't know.[64]

The truth-tellers have failed to do what it takes to bury the Big Lie. And one of those who has refrained from pushing the Big Truth with adequate force is the man who beat Trump.

On November 2, six days before the 2022 midterm elections, Biden gave a speech that some Democrats considered the high-water mark in his defense of democracy. The fact that this address was seen as a strong statement speaks volumes about how low the standard for dominance has sunk among liberals.[65]

A hammer-wielding MAGA fanatic had just invaded the home of Nancy Pelosi and punched holes in her husband's skull. Around the country, Trump followers continued to threaten the safety, lives, and children of anyone who defied their cult master. Violent threats against members of Congress rose tenfold in 2021.[66] Meanwhile, most Republicans running for office in the midterms still claimed Trump beat Biden in 2020, and many refused to commit to honoring the results this time if they lost.[67]

What did Biden have to say in this, his most muscular speech of the midterm season? On political violence and intimidation, the president declared:

> There is an alarming rise in the number of people in this country condoning political violence or simply remaining silent because silence is complicity. The disturbing rise in voter intimidation. The pernicious tendency to excuse political violence or at least try to explain it away. We can't allow this sentiment to grow. We must confront it head-on now. It has to stop now.

Of the Big Liars who threaten to destroy democracy, the president opined:

Wherever fact or evidence have been demanded, the Big Lie has been proven to be just that, a big lie, every single time. Yet, now, extreme MAGA Republicans aim to question not only the legitimacy of past elections but elections being held now and into the future. The extreme MAGA element of the Republican Party...is trying to succeed where they failed in 2020 to suppress the rights of voters and subvert the electoral system itself...It's estimated that there are more than 300 election deniers on the ballot all across America this year. We can't ignore the impact this is having on our country. It's damaging, it's corrosive, and it's destructive...As I stand here today, there are candidates running for every level of office in America—for governor, Congress, attorney general, secretary of state—who won't commit—they will not commit to accepting the results of elections that they're running in. That's a path to chaos in America. It's unprecedented, it's unlawful, and it's un-American. As I've said before, you can't love your country only when you win.

What was missing? What would a high-dominance statement include that this one didn't?

First, it would *declare victory*, not just admonish those who refuse to acknowledge it. Then, it would drill the reality of Biden's 2020 romp into people's consciousness and treat it as an omen of greater victories to come.

All Biden says in his speech is that Trump didn't win. Fair enough, but *who did?* And did the victor just squeak through? Is there any room for doubt?

Biden doesn't say.

Second, a high-dominance speech would promise presidential action, not just urge voters to care. More to the point, it would *threaten* democracy's enemies, not just *critique* them. Time and again in his speech, Biden mentions intimidation and violence against voters and elections officials. But what is he doing about it?

He offers two and only two prescriptions. First, he insists that "we must, with an overwhelming voice, stand against political violence and voter intimidation. Period. Stand up and speak against it." Second, he declares that "all of us must unite to make it absolutely clear that violence and intimidation have no place in America."

Okay, we can do that. I just did it three times today: once in a conversation with a friend over coffee, then in an irate Facebook post, and again in a heartfelt soliloquy to two carpoolers who *so* wanted me to shut up and go back to reading the news on my phone.

But what about the commander of the armed forces and every federal agency of investigation and coercion in the land? What is *he* doing to save our democracy from lying, violence, and intimidation?

He doesn't say.

In fact, at the time Biden spoke, the Justice Department was pursuing indictments of January 6 insurrectionists. Some had already been charged, and several of the ringleaders have since been sent to prison. Those actions have powerfully bolstered the rule of law. While those investigations and prosecutions are best left to Justice Department lawyers, the president would be very much within his rights to read the riot act to those who would destroy democracy. A high-dominance president would emphasize the powers at his disposal and resolve to exercise them to protect lives and the law.

Such an approach would also allow him to declare the defense of democracy a matter of public order, thereby seizing the law-and-order issue from the goons on the right who have used it to devastating effect. The president could present himself as a wrathful scourge of the lawless, not merely an importuning cheerleader for the well-intentioned.

Such rhetoric and behavior came naturally to past presidents facing misfits who threatened democracy and civil peace. When Governor Orval Faubus defied the Supreme Court and used the Arkansas National Guard to block the doors of Little Rock Central High School to Black students in 1957, President Dwight Eisenhower told him: "The only assurance I can give you is that the Federal Constitution will be upheld by me by every legal means at my command."[68]

When Faubus failed to get the point, Eisenhower deployed the elite 101st Airborne Division to take up positions around the school and make sure Black students were admitted, free from violence and intimidation.

Biden also passed on doing the third thing that any high-dominance leader would: rallying allies rather than defending adversaries. He mentions the Republicans seven times, each time either to call them victims of violence or to say that "only a minority" of them accept the Big Lie—which itself is a falsehood. Democrats are mentioned twice, both times as targets of intimidation and violence. Biden *not once* extols the Democrats—his own political troops and now the bulwark of American democracy.

It's hard to imagine any Republican leader—or, for that matter, any leader who understands how to mobilize her own troops—defending opponents while neglecting her own partisans, but that is what Biden does. Little wonder he stirs so little enthusiasm among the party's base despite his outstanding record of progressive accomplishments.

The fourth high-dominance move Biden doesn't make is to square off against his enemies. He mentions "extreme MAGA Republicans" who are undermining democracy, but not once does he address them directly. The best Biden can manage is his anodyne, confusing stock phrase: "As I've said before, you can't love your country only when you win."

He warns of no barbarians at the gates and hails no heroic defenders barricading the doors. Biden directs his remarks into the ether, gazing over the crowd and assuming somebody out there will realize how unprecedentedly unacceptable things have gotten—and then go do something about it themselves.

Where is the bold leader we need to direct defenders of the besieged city and let the intruders know what lies in store if they dare breach its walls? Biden never enters his own speech except as a supplicant and purveyor of opinion. He uses "I" 18 times—but not once is it followed by a pledge, a declaration, a challenge, a threat, or an order. Instead, we hear phrases like "I appeal to all Americans"; "I know it isn't easy"; "I wish—I wish I could say the assault on our democracy had ended that day, but I cannot"; "So I ask you"; "I hope you"; and "And I believe we will."

All we hear is the pathos of a petitioner. There is no hint of the vitality of a commander in his speech.

Thus speaks the unifier of the world's democracies, subduer of Putin and Xi, the guardian against nuclear obliteration. So says the man who routed Trump and who is the chief figure now standing between liberty's survival and extinction in the world's most powerful free country.

Biden is, in fact, all those things. But who would know?

Biden's language more generally constitutes the fifth low-dominance feature of his speech. Nowhere do we find potent, novel, or provocative parlance. To describe the assault on democracy, Biden relies on a raft of bland, hackneyed adjectives—"alarming" "unlawful," and "disturbing" among them—that better characterize my 17-year-old's disquieting driving habits than the greatest crime against America since the Civil War. And the president directs none of these words against an actual person or party. Each is aimed *solely* at *conditions* that are, well, "disturbing."

Low-intensity banality is audible at every turn. Here's how Biden describes Republicans' explicit threats to miscount ballots to steal elections: "Well, I think, first, we believe the vote in America is sacred—to be honored, not denied; respected, not dismissed; counted not ignored. A vote is not a partisan tool to be counted when it helps your candidates and tossed aside when it doesn't."

That's nice. But does his statement intensify your outrage and harden your resolve to thwart the highest crime that can be committed in a self-governing polity? Does it bolster your confidence in the chief executive's determination to guarantee your vote is counted no matter what?

And what exactly will our president do if democracy's saboteurs try their hand at trashing votes for their opponents?

Again, crickets.

What, then, are the consequences of Biden's low-dominance approach?

First, the Big Lie is fairly easy for the Republicans to sustain. While liberals marvel at how anyone could believe that Biden lost, we must acknowledge that Biden never really tells the story of his win. And while we lack data on the matter, it's a safe bet that not one in a hundred Americans remember the numbers from 2020, even within a few percentage points.

We never quit hearing about Trump's 2016 win during his time in office. If Biden regularly declared victory, ground his margins into our minds, wielded them to predict an even bigger romp in 2024, and threw in a healthy dose of ridicule for the Big Lying losers, the lie would be harder to sustain. The Democrats, moreover, would get a regular, morale-boosting reminder of our decisive win. And while Trump's hardcore loons still wouldn't believe it, even *they'd* have the numbers on Biden's margins memorized.

It's hard to avoid the impression, fair or not, that Biden is intimidated by democracy's enemies. He fears they'll become even more mobilized, vociferous, and perhaps even violent if he takes them on. He's also almost certainly averse—as overeducated liberals tend to be—to repeating what he regards as obvious truths over and over again. For us, that's just tacky.

But we would be wise to recall George Lakoff's and Maria Ressa's insight: Repetition is essential to making something feel true. Truth-tellers had better repeat themselves at least as much as the liars do, especially on a matter as crucial as saving democracy.

Biden's blasé attitude toward his own party faithful leaves the Democrats feeling uninspired and unled. His refusal to play us-versus-them politics may blunt followers' ferocity and block the development of strong party identity. When the head of the party neglects his own voters and fails to aggressively take on his opponents, we might expect organizational identity and enthusiasm to be a problem.

And it is: During Biden's first year in office, as the economy roared ahead, the Democrats' edge in party identification evaporated. It shifted from a 49-40 lead to a 47-42 Republican advantage.[69] In June 2023, Democratic pollster John Della Volpe reported that fewer young people identify as Democrats—even as increasing numbers support progressive policies and Biden vigorously pursues such measures. A stunningly small 49 percent of Blacks under 30 called themselves Democrats, down from 64 percent in 2019. Given that party identification is now the best predictor of voting behavior—even more than race—Democratic Party leaders should treat this trend as a five-alarm fire.[70]

How could Biden rally the troops and vex democracy's enemies? Here's some language he could use to declare victory for a change and begin telling the Big Truth, all in Bidenesque jargon:

So I keep hearing from some badly misinformed folks that Trump beat me in the last election. Well, I've got news for you MAGA Big Liars and the hysterical whiner you worship: I beat Trump 51 to 47 percent. I won seven million more votes. I got 74 more Electoral votes. You got that? 51-47, seven million votes, 74 Electoral votes.

I won Pennsylvania, Georgia, and Arizona. I beat Trump in Wisconsin, Minnesota, Michigan, and Virginia, too. All the swing states swung to me—and they're going to do it again. But this time I'm going to make it even bigger. Mark my words and your calendars, folks: On November 5, 2024, the Democrats are going to ride my coattails and their own great talents to take back the House and expand our Senate majority.

Then we're going to get on with saving our nation's democracy from the snivelers who are trying to snuff it out. We'll make sure that our will, the people's will, and not some shady MAGA guys or state party bosses, *always* decides who wins. We're going to do what it takes to ensure every American's right to vote for all eternity. We're going to prosecute the cheaters, the hate-mailers, the death-threateners, and everybody else who menaces law and order. And for the clowns who think you can lose your elections and install yourself in office anyway—well, Make. My. Day.

Imagine Biden saying something like this—and repeating it every Tuesday and Thursday afternoon. Not outsourcing it to surrogates—though the more other Democrats amplify it, the better. As much as we would like to think that Stephen Colbert and John Stewart can do the job, surrogates can't own your opponents for you. You have to do that yourself.

And that's the kind of language that earns media coverage. Trump's main talent is his ability to draw attention, usually because he makes provocative statements. They earn clicks—and revenue— for the outlets that report them.

If Biden uttered anything like the words offered here, Trump would have trouble getting airtime for anything other than his indictments. Did you ever notice how nobody seems to care about how old high-dominance politicians like Trump and Bernie Sanders are?

Profile in low-dominance leadership #2: Failure to tout even popular policies for fear of opponents' reactions. Under Biden, manufacturing has boomed. Labor power has escalated. Unions are growing, and strikes are proliferating for the first time in half a century. As voters went to the polls in November 2022, unemployment had not been lower at the time of a national election since 1968.

Yet the Democrats rarely dwelt on any of this during the 2022 midterm campaign for Congress. As if taking their cues from the Republicans, their economic message for the midterms focused on the one piece of bad news: inflation.

As the *New York Times's* Jim Tankersley noted three weeks before the election: "Democratic candidates in competitive Senate races this fall have spent little time on the trail or the airwaves touting the centerpiece provisions of their party's $1.9 trillion economic rescue package, which party leaders had hoped would help stave off losses in the House and Senate in midterm elections." Why this strategic retreat? According to Tankersley: "In part, that is because the rescue plan has become fodder for Republicans to attack Democrats over rapidly rising prices, accusing them of overstimulating the economy with too much cash." As a result, "Some Democrats worry that voters have been swayed by the persistent Republican argument that the aid was the driving factor behind rapidly rising prices of food, rent, and other daily staples."[71]

Inflation was indeed a top concern for voters. But rather than seizing control of the narrative, the Democrats stuck largely with channeling the anguish voters must have felt over the price of a tankful for their Dodge Ram 3500s.

Rep. Tim Ryan, the Democratic candidate for Ohio's open Senate seat, couldn't even bring himself to deny Biden's culpability for inflation. No serious economist believes Biden's programs accounted for more than a negligible part of the rise in consumer prices. But in his first debate with Trump-endorsed charlatan J. D. Vance, this was Ryan's response when the moderator asked if Biden was to blame for the inflation crisis. "I think we're all to blame—I mean, we're coming out of a pandemic."[72]

"We're all to blame" indeed. Just as "America" has abandoned its children and "America" botched the COVID response. Given the way the liberals frame culpability, it's not hard to see how the Republicans get away with claiming that we're weak-kneed, unpatriotic doomsters.

Ryan also abandoned Biden during his campaign. The fact that no president in modern times has been more pro-worker than Biden didn't matter to Ryan, even though his whole campaign aimed to cast himself as the blue-collar Buckeye's greatest champion. Biden was down in the polls in Ohio, so Ryan said he wanted to see him replaced as the Democrats' nominee for president in 2024.

This story merits attention not because Ryan is an especially low-dominance Democrat. In fact, his attacks on Vance for being Trump's "ass-kisser" and a weak foe of Putin displayed higher-than-average dominance orientation for a Democratic politician.

But periodic feints in the direction of dominance politics weren't enough. His relatable personality and relentless focus on working-class kitchen-table issues didn't pay off either. Nor did his opponent's total lack of ethics or experience. Ryan, whose campaign bus was emblazoned with PUT WORKERS FIRST, won 43 percent of non-college voters, including 34 percent of non-college whites. In the overall count, he fell to Vance 53-47. These were precisely the same margins by which Trump bested Biden in Ohio two years earlier.[73]

A more accurate, high-dominance answer might have sounded something like this:

> Inflation is a plague and Democrats hate it. For our high gas and food prices, we can thank the dictators of Russia and Saudi Arabia, who are Trump's favorite foreign buddies. He keeps sucking up to them while they drive prices through the roof with their wars and their production cuts. No wonder Trump loves these goons: Putin helped put him in the White House and the Saudi dictator paid Jared Kushner a cool $2 billion for his father-in-law's services. Biden's already got inflation lower here than in Europe. Of course it's still too high, but nobody in the world is doing a better job than Biden at fighting inflation and our adversaries who stoke it—and with him at the helm, we will beat this thing.

The Democrats' angst-and-anxiety approach represents a pattern: The Democrats post a hard-won policy achievement over Republican opposition. The Republicans concoct a story about the policy's dreadful consequences. The Democrats rock back on their heels, afraid of provoking still stronger attacks. The Republican narrative takes hold—or just seems like it might. The Democrats conduct a poll to assess the damage. Upon finding that two (or four or whatever) percent of voters have moved toward the Republicans' position, they treat Republican-swayed opinion as a *fait accompli.* Or, even without the poll, to borrow Tankersley's phrase, they just "worry that voters have been swayed by the persistent Republican argument." Finally, the Democrats move on to their next policy fix.

Until the Republicans attack it, that is.

Profile in low-dominance leadership #3: Damsel-in-distress messaging. Georgia Senator Raphael Warnock is the Senior Pastor of Ebenezer Baptist Church in Atlanta. His predecessors in the post include Martin Luther King. No one can step into those shoes, but it would be hard to find a more worthy successor. Warnock is the author of two brilliant, bestselling books on Christian faith.[74] Whether delivering from the pulpit, his books, or the Senate floor, Warnock can be an effective communicator. He's also an exemplary human being.

Warnock's opponent in 2022 was Herschel Walker, a Trump-endorsed former football star whose claim to fame was the Heisman Trophy, which he won almost 40 years ago. He went pro in 1983 and left the Peach State, only to return for the 2022 campaign. He is a resident of Texas who never established legal residence in the state he aspired to represent in the Senate. Nor had he ever held public office.

Walker is, to put it mildly, an intellectual nonentity with some notable ethical deficiencies. During the campaign, it emerged that he had abused former romantic partners and prevailed upon one to have an abortion when she became pregnant by him. Walker initially favored banning abortion with no exceptions. Besides being "hypocritical"—how to say it? the term doesn't exactly capture it—his stance on abortion was a detriment in the Peach State, where two-thirds opposed the repeal of *Roe v. Wade*. For his part, Warnock is pro-choice.[75]

One would think that Walker's nomination would have sealed the deal for the Democrats, even in a purple state. But Warnock eked out a win by less than a percentage point in the first round. In the run-off, which Georgia law requires in the absence of a majority first-round winner, Warnock won 51-49 after an eleventh-hour intervention by Obama (more on that later).

Why didn't Warnock do better?

His low-dominance campaign didn't help. He retreated from his signature issue, progressive spending policies, as soon as his opponent started calling them inflationary. Comparing Warnock's first run for the Senate in the 2020 by-election with his current 2022 run, Tankersley reported: "In the midst of a critical runoff campaign that would determine control of the Senate [in 2020], the Rev. Raphael Warnock promised Georgia voters that, if elected, he would help President-elect Biden send checks to people digging out of the pandemic recession. Mr. Warnock won. The Democrats delivered up to $1400 per person. But this year, as Mr. Warnock is locked in a tight re-election campaign, he barely talks about these checks."[76]

To be sure, Warnock's not a weak man. But that's the point. Even Democrats who are strong, upstanding people—and that would certainly include Biden—fall back on low-dominance messaging in the political palestra. Warnock saved his sharpest jabs at Walker for an empty lectern when the Republican didn't show up for their second debate.[77]

Warnock's main pitch to would-be donors compounded his low-dominance profile. His schtick was based less on challenging Walker's attacks on core American values than on Warnock's own supposedly insurmountable *vulnerability.* Meanwhile, Warnock's supporters were characterized as falling apart at the horror unfolding around them.

This was the pitch on his behalf sent out by End Citizens United in the waning weeks of the campaign:[78]

> This is hard to write.
>
> If we can't fund our ads, Rev. Raphael Warnock could lose re-election. He's vulnerable! Almost NO ONE is donating. Please chip in.

Then, emblazoned on a photo of the Senator's none-too-happy-looking face were the words:

EMERGENCY REQUEST
RAPHAEL WARNOCK:
MOST VULNERABLE SENATE DEMOCRAT
CHIP IN $5 NOW

Secure.actblue.com
We're PANICKING   Donate now

What's wrong? Not stoked about being one of the rare chumps who shells out for a flailing campaign? Don't find your fist pumping in the air as you move your cursor to the link that reads "We're PANICKING"?

Yes, you had to hit the panic button to donate.

But wait! As it turns out, competition for the title of "MOST VULNERABLE SENATE DEMOCRAT" was stiff that year. This text was sent from the campaign of Nevada Senator Catherine Cortez Masto:

BREAKING: The New York Times just called me "the most endangered Democratic incumbent in the country!" And they're not alone: All of these news outlets say I'm the most vulnerable Democratic senator in America:

➔CNN
➔The Cook Political Report
➔Nate Silver from FiveThirtyEight
➔National Journal
➔Roll Call

That's some seriously *unrivaled vulnerability*—and no fewer than FIVE major sources confirmed it!

Cortez Masto managed to turn back her Republican opponent—but like Warnock, just barely. She beat Adam Laxalt by 0.8 percent. Nevada has been won handily by every Democratic presidential candidate since 2008. And Laxalt, who had been defeated in his run for governor four years earlier, called *Roe v. Wade* a "joke" in a state where 69 percent call themselves pro-choice.[79]

While the tone of these pitches for donations may differ from those made to the electorate as a whole, they are often just exaggerated versions of what Democrats show voters more broadly.

Markos Moulitsas, founder of *Daily Kos*, a leading progressive blog, calls it out: "Constantly screaming about doom, how we're going to lose—it may raise money for them. Clearly they do it because it raises money for them, but it does not create an environment where Democrats are eager to fight and win, because nobody wants to fight for a team they know is going to lose."[80]

Los Angeles Times opinion writer David Ulin said this about the barrage of desperate messages he received from Tim Ryan's 2022 Senate campaign: "[T]repidation is a lousy selling point, especially for someone who aspires to lead. I'm not looking for false bravado—we had enough of that during the last administration—but I wouldn't mind a bit of fortitude." He concluded: "I'd like to make a plea for resilience over fear . . . I can't be alone in wanting to vote—and donate—*for* something rather than reacting, from a defensive crouch, to apocalyptic fears. . . . [W]hat I'm really starting to worry about is that fear won't sow support as much as it will wear us out" (emphasis in the original).[81]

Historian Lara Putnam and journalist Micah Sifry noted that the Trump presidency seemed to stimulate a new era of Democratic activism. But, as they wrote in a *New York Times* op-ed before the 2022 midterms, less than two years after Trump left office "national progressive organizations seem to have done very little to translate that energy into a lasting movement. What happened?"[82]

According to Putnam and Sifry, "The core role of supporters is to be whipped into panicked giving by messages like this from Nancy Pelosi on April 28: 'I asked—several times. Barack Obama told you the stakes. Joe Biden made an urgent plea'." Pelosi proceeded to issue a confusing, frantic plea that ended with a call "to rush $15, and help me close the fund-raising gap before the End of Month Deadline in 48 hours." As Putnam and Sifry write, this is "a way of squeezing money out of individual donors that reliably produces brief spikes in donations but over the course of an election cycle overwhelms their willingness to keep giving."

But donor fatigue isn't the biggest problem. According to the authors, "Democrats receiving apocalyptic messages can feel more battered than activated, leading to demoralization and despair." Indeed, they argue that the Democrats' detached, dispiriting the-sky-will-fall-unless-you-send-us-$15-now messaging has become a *substitute* for—even an impediment to—the kind of spirited organization that's vital to defeating MAGA.

The Republicans' abortion bans, along with their nomination of atrocious candidates in swing states, saved the Democrats from a rout in 2022. Had Trump's party been savvier, the Senate would have fallen to Republican control, just as the House did.[83]

As I was finishing the final review of this book, I received a text from the Save Democracy Pac, a national group working to defeat Republican extremism and protect democracy. It read:

Joe Biden is BEGGING.
Do you approve of Joe Biden?
YES: gosavedemocracypac.com/121412
NO: gosavedemocracypac.com/121412
**Respond by 11:59PM

For some reason, I missed that 11:59 pm deadline.

13. Bridling the Boss

U ntil the final days of the 2022 campaign, Barack Obama was rarely seen or heard from. A few weeks before the election, a CNN report explained why: "More than a dozen advisers and others who have spoken with Obama say the former president's approach in the fall campaign will remain limited and careful. That cautious approach comes as Obama tells people his presence fires up GOP opposition just as much as it lights up supporters."[84] *Politico* reported, "Obama, who in his post-presidency remains a political lightning rod, has been wary that his campaigning may serve to turn out more voters on his right than on the left."[85]

Obama did have another big project in the works, though. It was his Democracy Forum, a meeting of experts at Stanford University to be held two weeks after the midterms. Of the gathering, Obama wrote, "We'll explore a range of issues—from strengthening institutions and fighting disinformation, to promoting inclusive capitalism and expanded pluralism—that will shape democracies for generations to come."[86]

Obama's powwow no doubt provided a stimulating think-in on important issues. But there's plenty of reason to question why Obama funneled his singular talents into an academic conversation about saving democracy rather than hitting the campaign trail to save democracy instead.

How justifiable is the fear that Obama will turn out more voters on the right than the left?

President Obama is the most popular national politician in America. He was the first person since Dwight Eisenhower to be elected and reelected with 51+ percent of the popular vote both times he ran, and he left office with an approval-disapproval rating of 59-37 percent. Since then, his stock has risen even further. As of spring 2024, 63 percent of Americans said they liked him versus 24 percent who didn't. The only other living political figures with 90+ percent name recognition who were at least as well-liked were former California Governor Arnold Schwarzenegger (60-13 percent) and Jimmy Carter (58-15 percent).[87]

Obama's popularity, moreover, is highest among under-30 voters. He captured two thirds of this group in 2008, a feat matched neither before nor since by any presidential candidate. If this group voted at the same rate as seniors do, a Democrat would always be president and the Democrats would hold roughly three fifths of seats in both houses of Congress. Democracy would be safe, we might not spend twice as much on healthcare as the Europeans, the planet would have a better shot at survival, and Trump, having been exiled from New York by his erstwhile friends, would be working as a carnival barker at the Oklahoma State Fair.[88]

Let's be honest: Democratic Party operatives don't think of Obama as a "lightning rod" because he pushed radical policies or has such a provocative personality. He governed as a moderate liberal. He saved global capitalism from ruin in 2009, gave the people healthcare in 2010, and is practically as personable as Tom Hanks. Instead, liberals fret that the worst of Trump's MAGA base can't get over having had an African American in the Oval Office. God forbid we stoke their memories of *that* nightmare and drive them, pitchforks in hand, to defeat our oh-so-very *endangered* and *vulnerable* candidates.

This is what cowering before racists looks like.

Eventually, Obama did enter the fray, but only in the last 10 days of the campaign. And he really jumped in only *after* November 8 to help Raphael Warnock beat Herschel Walker in the run-off.

Georgia has plenty of deplorables to worry about inflaming, but Obama finally threw foolish caution to the wind. He barnstormed the state, stirring up raucous crowds thick with young Black, Brown, and white Peach State voters. At Pullman Yards in Atlanta, he took the stage at a Warnock rally, bellowing into the microphone, "Hello Atlanta, I'm back! I am back! Si se puede! [Yes we can!]. I am back! Yes we can!" He proceeded to shred Trump and Walker with withering wit. He never used mean or vindictive language—an Obama trademark. He delivered a powerful vision of redemption that felt more like a religious revival than anything the Democrats have staged in years—in fact, since Obama left office.

Gone was the angst over being a "lightning rod"; Obama was having a blast.

Democrats—and probably many Independents and even some anti-Trump Republicans—were elated and relieved to finally see him back on the campaign trail (I know I was). In the second round of voting, Warnock tripled his first-round margin, and the Democrats retained their wafer-thin Senate majority.[89]

Obama has his own brand of dominance, which is rooted in profound self-confidence and unflappable wit. When he combines that with ebullience on the campaign trail, his dominance can fly off the charts.

The Nation correspondent John Nichols wrote about it in an article titled "Barack Obama's Politics 101: Ridiculing the Republicans Works." He noted: "If there was any doubt that Barack Obama remains the Democratic Party's ablest campaigner, it was removed last week when the former president swept into Georgia for the final push of U.S. Senator Raphael Warnock's reelection bid."[90]

Yet the hesitation remains.

Obama's absence from all but the tail end of the campaign, together with his effectiveness when he did step up, raises questions about why other anti-MAGA political heroes weren't out on the hustings as well. "Bubba" Bill Clinton would no doubt be willing. He's the guy who won the white working-class vote twice, was beloved of

African Americans, and won the Hispanic vote by the largest margin in history. He also left office with the highest approval rating of any president since polling started in the late 1940s.

Ah, yes, but what about the blow-job in the Oval Office? Just imagine the fodder *that* would give the Republicans to attack us!

Yes, and Obama's Black, too, you know.

And why not enthusiastically enlist the Terminator in the campaign? Arnold Schwarzenegger is a Republican who won the governorship of deep-blue California twice. He's not a Democrat, but he is a passionate democrat. He can't stand Trump. Listen to his recent message on anti-Semitism and ethnic bigotry, where he explicitly addresses MAGA folks with relatability, grit, and grace that no Democrat can match. Listen to him talk about how his "loser" father lost his way by joining the Nazis.[91]

Yes, he's kind of uncouth, what with all the muscles and those B-level shoot-'em-up films. And yes, he's a Republican.

That's the point.

If Democrats could stop worrying about what Republicans and other critics will say if they call on these and other strong, popular messengers to get out and rally our voters, maybe the media would start talking about our raucous crowds instead of obsessing over the Front Row Joes at Trump's rallies.

Obama's ambivalence about stepping out front during the midterms—and party leaders' skittishness about turning him loose—was nothing new. David Axelrod, his political strategist, advised him against "dancing in the endzone" during his time in office. In a keen postmortem on the administration's messaging strategy, *Politico* senior staff writer Michael Grunwald revealed how this worked.[92] As Grunwald reported, Axelrod never tired of warning his boss that crowing about a better economy would backfire as long as some people were still hurting.

So Obama rarely exalted publicly in the great things that were happening on his watch—and there were many. On the campaign trail, he was freer to display his genius for conveying a sense of hope and forward movement. But between elections, his White House was so worried about sounding too jaunty that they never quite managed to overcome the Republicans' mendacity machine.

Obama saved America and the world from a depression during his first year in office. "But the message the White House spent the most time debating," notes Grunwald,

> was the simple question of how things were going, and it struggled to crack that code too. By late 2009 and early 2010, America had escaped the Great Recession much faster than other advanced economies, converting massive job losses into modest job gains. Still, Obama's strategists warned that celebratory rhetoric was politically untenable since their polls suggested the public wasn't feeling the recovery. Phrases like "America is back" were banned from speeches.

As a result, "Typically, Obama split the difference with on-the-one-hand messaging that satisfied no one. We're making progress, but not enough, but better days are ahead, but people are hurting, but less than they would be if we hadn't acted, but there's so much left to do, and so on."

But the president couldn't *always* be bridled. One time, in the run-up to the 2014 midterm election, Grunwald recounts, Obama "got sick of the narrative of gloom hovering over his White House. Unemployment was dropping and troops were coming home, yet only one in four Americans thought the nation was on the right track—and Democrats worried about the midterm elections were sprinting away from him. He wanted to break through the noise."

So on October 2, 2014, Obama stepped out. He used a speech at Northwestern University to make his case.[93]

Like Bill Clinton's messaging on the economy, Obama repeatedly laid out what his naysayer opponents might argue and then took them down with incisive, upbeat responses. He closed his talk with a vigorous defense of the pro-business effects of his progressive policies, drawing appreciative laughter as he noted that even business leaders who "don't like to admit it because they don't like me that much" liked his policies' sweet effects on balance sheets. He closed with a word about the forthcoming election: "Now, I am not on the ballot this fall. Michelle's pretty happy about that (laughter). But make no mistake, these policies are on the agenda—every single one of them. This isn't some official campaign speech or political speech, and I'm not going to tell you who to vote for—although I suppose it's kind of implied (laughter and applause)."

Doesn't sound that bad to me. But Grunwald reported:

> The only line that made news came near the end of his 54-minute address, an observation that while he wouldn't be on the ballot in the fall midterms, "these policies are on the ballot—every single one of them." When Obama boarded Air Force One after his speech, his speechwriter, Cody Keenan, told him the Internet had already flagged that line as an idiotic political gaffe. "What was untrue about it?" Obama asked, a bit incredulous.
>
> Nothing, but Obama's words couldn't change the narrative of his unpopularity; they just gave Republicans a new opening to exploit it. They quickly became a staple of campaign ads and stump speeches tying Democrats ball-and-chain to their leader.

Three days later, instead of pressing Obama and the Democrats to double down and regain control of the narrative, Axelrod hung his boss out to dry before two million viewers on *Meet the Press*. With the midterms a month away, he also had a scintillating proposal for his fellow Democrats. Speaking of the speech and how to recover from the supposed disaster, he argued:

> It was a mistake. But you know, fundamentally, the issue that he should be driving and the Democratic Party should be driving is forward looking, because the problem is how are middle class people going to make a living in this country, and what policies can we implement that can help? We ought to have that debate.[94]

Maybe we should organize a conference. Hillary Clinton could launch the event with a discussion on the struggles of the working person to make a living in America. Sean Hannity could moderate, because, you know, fair and balanced. Then the talking heads could all nod along in grim agreement as the full scale of the catastrophe that befell the middle class during the Obama years was laid bare. Obama, of course, would have to go into hiding. But Axelrod would be on hand to make sure no one cracks a premature smile.

Meanwhile, no matter what, *do not* try to control the conversation. And never, ever think that you can shape the narrative. Polling is polling, and there's nothing you can do about that. So just lie back and think of England instead.

Axelrod served as Obama's political director in his successful presidential runs. But when it came to messaging between elections, he failed to grasp that the endzone dance is the money shot in every football game. It's the part that makes the highlights everyone sees on the evening news. In politics it's the shot in the arm that rouses supporters. And regardless of which team scored, everyone gets the exhilaration of the touchdown celebration.

Reveling in accomplishments and weaving them into a story that projects future feats is central to high-dominance leadership. It's indispensable to bending public consciousness and opinion to your advantage.

But a reined-in Obama rarely got to revel and rouse in office. As a result, Americans never fully appreciated what he'd done for us— or how well the economy was doing as a result. Little wonder, then, that even as median personal household incomes rose faster in his second term than during any other presidential term on record, Gallup's Economic Confidence Index remained in negative territory for most of Obama's years in office.[95]

In any event, the Republicans pounded the Democrats in the 2014 midterms, picking up *nine* Senate seats. Much the same thing had happened four years earlier, when the Republicans gained six Senate seats. That happened just after Obama had rescued the country from the hapless hands of George W. Bush, who left the economy hemorrhaging over half a million jobs a month. Then, too, as Grunwald notes, "strategists warned that celebratory rhetoric was politically untenable since their polls suggested the public wasn't feeling the recovery."

Is this leadership?

Not everybody around Obama saw things like Axelrod did. Remarkably, Grunwald reports that Vice President Biden, more than any other top figure, thought it was a mistake to allow the punditry and the Republicans to define Obama's message. The vice president told Grunwald: "Even my own folks say 'Jeez, Joe, you got 60-70 percent of the American people [who] think we're going in the wrong direction. 'What do you mean, don't try to buck it? If everybody doesn't buck it, guess what, it's gospel, man. We must have really screwed the pooch'."

Vice President Biden got it—does President Biden?

There are signs that he does. In the summer of 2023, the president started touting "Bidenomics"—a laudable step toward the credit-claiming that's a crucial part of muscular messaging. His March 2024 State of the Union Address also exuded optimism, confidence, and dominance—and the numbers on his policies' ability to "move the U.S. in the right direction" soared among those who watched the speech.[96]

But it's not yet clear he will stick with it—or that the Democrats will let him do so even if he wants to follow through.

According to Lora Kelly of *The Atlantic,* "The economy is notoriously hard to control, so an individual's attempt to associate themselves with it can be risky." Says political scientist Lori Cox Han, "I'm not sure a lot of people are feeling as enthusiastic about the economy as the Biden team wants them to be." For that reason, Han is "not confident that a clever slogan will change people's minds."[97]

Rep. Steven Horsford dislikes a term that focuses on the president. He says: "With all due respect to the president, to the White

House . . . [w]e have to do a better job framing this not so much for one person—for the office of the presidency—but for the people."[98]

In fact, Congressional Democrats are mostly running away from Bidenomics; as *Axios* reports, "The term was seen as tone-deaf to voters still struggling economically."[99]

Will Marshall, president of the centrist Progressive Policy Institute, calls for more contemplation before stepping out with a message: "There ought to be a lot of thinking in the White House now about changes in the way they present their case for the economic good this administration has done." After all, he says, "At this point, Bidenomics doesn't really have strong answers to people's biggest worries."[100]

So who *does* have those "strong answers"?

The Republicans are happy to offer an opinion.

Michael LaRosa, a former spokesman for First Lady Jill Biden, also can't believe how dumb it is to claim credit for gains until everything's turning up roses: "I've never understood why you would brand an economy in your name when the economy hasn't fully recovered yet."[101]

Hmmm, let's see: Combining robust growth, rock-bottom unemployment, and declining inflation is often said to be impossible, yet that's what Biden is delivering. For the first time in forever, America's economy is even outpacing China's. The Dow can't quit setting records.[102]

Is it a "full recovery" yet?

The Republicans certainly don't think so.

And Biden's *so old*. Panicked Democrats can only concur.[103]

But the two parties' leaders don't always agree. One year before Ronald Reagan's reelection, unemployment ran at nine percent. The inflation-adjusted price of a gallon of gasoline was higher than it is today. Throughout 1983, Reagan's approval ran between the high 30s and the mid-40s, about the same as Biden's rate now.

But Reagan and his messaging team touted "Reaganomics" anyway, and his party backed him to the hilt. When Reagan seemed befuddled—far worse than anything Biden has ever shown—during practically his entire first debate with Walter Mondale, his age shot to the top of the news cycle, he dropped seven points in the polls, and the Democrats pounded away at what they claimed was the septuagenarian president's weariness and mental decline. But Reagan laughed it off in the second debate and never appeared defensive, and nary a Republican could be seen fretting in public, come what may.[104]

Reagan's speeches throughout his presidency, moreover, were so laced with tales of America's greatness and limitless promise that people *wanted* to believe him. He earned the nickname "The Great Communicator" but stated at the end of his presidency: "I wasn't a great communicator, but I communicated great things, and they didn't spring full bloom from my brow, they came from the heart of a great nation—from our experience, our wisdom and our belief in the principles that have guided us for two centuries."[105]

That's the way he often spoke—and the Republicans always stuck with him.

Who'd have thought it, but Reagan's message broke through. As Jim Tankersley reported in November 2023, "At this point in [Reagan's] presidency, Americans were far more likely to report hearing positive news about the economy and prices than they do under President Biden. They even reported hearing better news on unemployment, at a time when the rate was near 9 percent. It is 4 percent today."[106] Reagan went on to win everywhere but the District of Columbia and Mondale's home state of Minnesota a year later.

Now back to the Democrats today. *Politico*'s Adam Cancryn and Holly Otterbein report that Democratic leaders they interviewed worry that running on Biden's achievements "asks voters to buy into an overarching economic philosophy they may not be totally sold on...And crucially, [Democratic leaders] worry that christening Biden's legacy well before it's finished is plain old risky."[107]

Plain old risky.

Maybe it's time the Democrats surmount our prodigious risk-aversion and diffidence, get our twitchy noses out of last week's focus-group data, and fall in behind our leader with abandon.

Bill Clinton's messaging guru, "Ragin' Cajun" James Carville, nails it in his recent conversation with Maureen Dowd: "When the polls are not good, you don't believe in polls. If the polls are good, you believe in polls."[108]

Worked pretty good for Bubba.

14. How the Democrats Can Win with Dominance

Let's return to the theory of dominance leadership. This time, we'll specify how to apply the lessons we've learned so far.

It's important to remember that a high-dominance style can be expressed in many ways, depending on a leader's skill set and personality. Some own their opponents with sharp humor (Abraham Lincoln), badass bulldozing (Lyndon Johnson), intellectual brilliance and mastery of policy (Bill Clinton), ineffable cool (Barack Obama), or all of the above (Franklin Roosevelt and John Kennedy). While styles may differ, the most effective leaders rely on some combination of the practices we'll spell out below. They also practice them *habitually and across the board—every chance they get, and their allies follow suit.*

Biden has what it takes. By the accounts of many of his colleagues, he's got a wicked sense of humor. It's just a matter of showing it in public.

His half-century in public office made him a master of policy—and his remarkable policy achievements despite Republican intransigence prove the point.

If you question his grit, check out his medical history. In 1988, at the age of 45, Biden suffered two brain aneurysms. Half of people who have just one die within three months, and of those who survive, two-thirds experience permanent brain damage. Wearing a baseball cap to cover his surgery scars and what seemed like a permanent ear-to-ear grin, Biden roared back.

If you're still unsure of his resilience, consult his family history. It includes losing his wife and infant daughter in a car crash when the Senator from Delaware was 30 years old. Their two other children, Beau and Hunter, almost died with them. Beau died at 46, after a grueling struggle with brain cancer in 2015.

And Biden perseveres.

If you don't think he's a hard-driving hard-ass, speak with his staffers.

If you doubt his fortitude and resolve, have a word with Putin or Xi.

And Kamala Harris had a reputation as a badass during her time as a public prosecutor and then attorney general of California. Why not bring it now?

Biden is not a *naturally* high-dominance leader like Kennedy, Johnson, or Trump. He's an incurably nice guy. He fully recognizes the Republican turn toward antidemocratic darkness, but his decades of close across-the-aisle friendships in the Senate prevent him from really *experiencing* these people as enemies. All of that just makes it still more important that he pursue an effective rhetorical strategy. He can *say* the right things in the right way—and that's what really counts. The same, of course, is true of other leading Democrats.

The overall tone in which effective leaders express their dominance is one of *confidence*, *optimism*, and *exuberance*. That means demonstrably *having fun* while *owning opponents*. There will be times when opponents' transgressions call for anger, disdain, or derision, and in such instances there can be no hesitation to go there. But in practice, that will be the spice rather than the staple for high-dominance *liberal* leaders.

Let's take stock of what a politician does to up her dominance game. No 10-point list for us; like Spinal Tap guitarist Nigel Tufnel's beloved amplifier, ours goes to 11:

1. Relentlessly embrace and tout your victories. Cast yourself, your allies, and your predecessors as intrepid, successful protagonists.

2. If the battle hasn't yet been won, promise victory. Stop pleading and *vow* to succeed. Don't say *we should* or even *we must*. Say we *will* prevail. Make your supporters feel like winners who are part of a thrilling revolutionary movement that will surely succeed.

3. Never shift your positions or walk back your statements in response to polling numbers or controversy.

4. Stay on the offensive. Quit acting offended when opponents transgress, which is a weak, defensive display. When dealing with belligerent, toxic, or extreme opponents, kick it up a notch to belittle and humiliate them. Use humor every chance you get.

5. Embrace us-versus-them framing. Name the enemy and attack the enemy directly.

6. Aim to rouse your own; forget about the ostensible danger of rousing your opponents. Doing otherwise is pure cowardice and will be felt as such by your supporters, opponents, and fence-sitters alike.

7. Relentlessly defend your own people, and don't make excuses for opponents. Implacable foes are to be offended, not defended.

8. Where appropriate, reclaim the issues on which your opponent scores dominance points (such as safeguarding "law and order").

9. Embrace provocative—even transgressive—language that outrages adversaries, delights your base, impresses swing voters, and generates maximum media coverage.

10. Never cast yourself as faltering, vulnerable, scared, or endangered. Define your opponents in such terms instead.

11. Repeat the above *ad nauseam*, without embarrassment over being repetitive. Recite your message so often that the media has no choice but to adopt your frame. Repeat it so insistently and frequently that even your most diehard detractors have it burned into their brains.

15. Why Liberals Need Not Shun Dominance

As we've seen, 21st-century liberals look askance at dominance politics. Many tend to regard it as bellicose (and even violent), exclusively (and even toxically) masculine, personalist (and anti-pluralistic), dictatorial (and therefore undemocratic), hubristic (and thus prone to calamity), selfish (and disdainful of others' needs), uncivilized (and thereby regressive), and rightist (and ergo anti-progressive). Trump's over-the-top dominance style has only deepened liberals' suspicions of high-dominance leadership.

Mostly, we liberals avert our eyes from dominance and turn our noses up at it, much like when we speed past a Hooters in Bakersfield on our drive from LA to San Francisco or encounter a big bowl of pork rinds at the party of (someone we thought was) a friend. To the extent that we intuit the mass appeal of high-dominance leadership, we view it in the same light as nationalism: an atavism that we hope will fade as humanity matures. As noted by Dan McAdams, however, we shouldn't hold our breath.[109]

This distaste for dominance comes at a hefty political price. Given the importance of dominance in political struggles, if liberals were right to disdain dominance as they do, arresting authoritarianism's march would be a hollow hope, and democracy's prospects would be grim.

But high-dominance leadership need be none of the things we rightly detest.

Contemporary world history knows no expression of higher dominance orientation than the Freedom Riders.[110] They were the young Black, white, and Asian–American activists who electrified the world by riding buses into the Deep South to protest segregation of public transportation. They encountered vicious mobs along their 1961 journey. But even when the police would not protect them, and hospitals would not treat their wounds, they pushed ahead anyway.

John Lewis, Diane Nash, James Farmer, and their fellow Riders were high–dominance archetypes. They sought to refashion reality, not accommodate themselves to it. They scorned public opinion in the states into which they rode. They forged a spectacular heroic narrative that inspired generations thereafter.

They were brazenly conflict–embracing. They barged into areas where they were hated and attended church services surrounded by mobs wielding baseball bats and bicycle chains. They were shunned, whipped, jeered, and jailed, but they just kept going. Playing defense was not for them.

They spoke the language of winning and redemption. One searches in vain for doubt, complaint, defeatism, or defensiveness in their public statements.

They were led collectively, in part by women. They were anti–authoritarian, lacking in hubris. They were other–regarding, nonviolent, and militantly progressive.

And they were *stronger* than the racists as well. Following their audacious sojourns, the nation's laws and opinions on voting rights, interracial marriage, and integrated housing underwent radical liberalization.

The American civil rights movement was replete with high–dominance progressives, not least Fannie Lou Hamer, Robert F. Kennedy, Pauli Murray and, of course, Martin Luther King. It would be hard to find a leader who was less solicitous of public opinion and more intent on transforming it than King. At the height of his fame and influence, his conscience compelled him to take up the yoke of opposing the Vietnam War. The shift dimmed his reputation, including among some middle-class Blacks. Like his Galilean lord, he was murdered amidst a diminishing band of supporters. Only a half-decade after his assassination—and many thousands of dead Americans and Vietnamese later—would public opinion finally converge with his own.[111]

King's language was always that of a victor holding the moral high ground—while also being devoid of arrogance. His rhetoric brimmed with the promise of deliverance, building heroic narratives of national struggle.

His Speech on the Civil Rights Movement in the United States and the Anti-Apartheid Movement in South Africa, delivered in London en route to receive the Nobel Peace Prize in 1964, is one of his lesser-known public addresses. But it models the power of the redemptive story for inspiring democrats and dispiriting democracy's antagonists—and should be required reading for Democrats today.[112]

The structure of the address contains a distinctive sequence found in many of King's speeches: past injustice—triumph over past injustice—current injustice—call to action—vision of redemption. For each obstacle the civil rights movement faced, King began with a bracing story of past gains, which he used to portend future victories. Time and again he asserted that America had come "a long, long way" in its pursuit of justice, and he punctuated his statements with references to "our great nation." Only then did he delve into the injustices that remained to be conquered if America was to "move on toward its greatness." Along the way, he built a pantheon of heroes, from the Hebrew Prophet Amos to Jesus and from Thomas Jefferson to Abraham Lincoln.

The address is replete with smooth but stiff jabs at the opponents of civil rights. They include his words for Barry Goldwater, the 1964 Republican presidential nominee. King said he was ready "to at least go halfway with Brother Goldwater" on the notion that legislation can't solve racism, and that "you've got to change the heart." With tongue planted firmly in cheek, he lauded Goldwater's honesty, saying "I think Mr. Goldwater sincerely believed that you couldn't do anything through legislation, because he voted against everything in the Senate, including the civil rights bill." But he then took apart the notion that legislation isn't necessary: "It may be true that morality cannot be legislated, but behavior can be regulated. It may be true that the law can't change the heart, but it can restrain the heartless. It may be true that the law can't make a man love me, but it can restrain him from lynching me. And I think that's pretty important also."

King's reference to "Brother Goldwater" bore no hint of sarcasm. But he also knew that he was *owning* his opponent by wielding what he always called "the weapon of love" to establish moral superiority, since Goldwater would never have the good grace to address him as "Brother King." With his uncompromising, high-dominance eloquence, King never gave his opponents a chance.

As was ever his wont, King concluded with a burst of buoyancy and a stark vision of deliverance from darkness. His call to "adjourn the counsels of despair" too often goes unheeded by liberal leaders today:

> I believe that mankind will overcome, and I believe that the forces of evil will be defeated. With this faith, we will be able to adjourn the counsels of despair and bring new light into the dark chambers of pessimism. With this faith, we will be able to transform this pending cosmic elegy into a creative psalm of peace and brotherhood. With this faith, we will be able to speed up the day when all of God's children—black men and white men, Jews and Gentiles, Protestants and Catholics, Hindus and Muslims, theists and atheists—will be able to join hands and sing in the words of the old Negro spiritual, "Free at last! Free at last! Thank God Almighty, we are free at last!"

King showed what liberal, truth-telling high-dominance talk sounds like. Many current-day Democratic leaders ask. They plead. They implore their opponents and the nation as a whole to do the right thing. They resist good-versus-evil framing. King didn't implore; he *told* those who resisted his call that they would be defeated. In his own polite way, he told them to *get over it and get with the program*, showing a measure of self-assurance and faith in the nation that is sorely needed if the partisans of progress are to regain the upper hand. And he never shrank from framing the contest as what it was: a showdown between the forces of light and darkness.

Current-day Democratic leaders also often act as if they themselves have little role in the fight. As we saw earlier, in Biden's vague call to Americans to reject Trumpism, the president seemed to forget that he's the nation's commander-in-chief, with a bully pulpit and the might of the federal government at his disposal. King, armed only with his powers as a private citizen, is explicit about his own agency and that of the movement he leads in taking down the adversary.

And King's way of touting past wins and predicting future victories, of course, couldn't differ more dramatically from that of deceitful high-dominance authoritarians like Trump. Their brand of dominance is self-aggrandizing, hubristic, egotistical, and boorish—in a word, everything that many contemporary liberals have unfortunately come to associate with high-dominance leaders.

King was the anti-Trump. For him, small was the gate and narrow the road that led to salvation, and no unaided human power— still less a single leader—could serve as the guiding agent. Still, Providence itself, if buttressed by a justice-seeking people, would triumph over evil. They would push the Barry Goldwaters and George Wallaces to the margins of history to stew in their festering resentments.

Or maybe even reexamine and rectify their ways. After some self-reappraisal and a healthy dose of political calculation, both Goldwater and Wallace came around in their dotage and transcended their illiberal pasts. Goldwater became an early advocate for gay rights. During the last of his five terms in the Senate, the retired Air Force major general advocated for lifting the ban on gays in the military. At age 84, he told a newly elected Bill Clinton to cut the coy compromise of his "don't-ask-don't-tell policy" and just sign an order lifting the ban. About members of his own party, he said: "To see the party that fought communism and big government now fighting the gays, well, that's just plain dumb." When asked what else he would say to the party that he led three decades prior, then as an opponent of civil rights, he stated: "Don't raise hell about the gays, the blacks and the Mexicans. Free people have a right to do as they damn please."[113]

Wallace came around, too. After three terms as Alabama's segregationist governor, he took a term off, asked Blacks for forgiveness, and returned to the governor's mansion in 1983 as a born-again Christian and advocate of racial reconciliation. In Birmingham they still luved the guvner—but the last time around "they" included Black Alabamans, over 90 percent of whom cast their ballots to send him back to do things differently than he'd done the first three times around. Wallace did what he could do, appointing a record number of African Americans to government positions.[114]

Getting licked by high-dominance liberals has a way of changing a bigoted politician's calculations—and maybe even his heart to boot. Depolarizing politics isn't about playing nice with illiberal enemies. It's about defeating them and thereby forcing them to get out or reform—and then welcoming those who mend their ways back into the family.

King's message could also help account for why no leader since has so thoroughly held the national imagination. Today, he tops the list of Americans' most esteemed historical figures.[115]

Reality-shaping defiance of prevailing opinion, conflict-embracing behavior, clear good-versus-evil distinctions, and opponent-owning parlance of triumph also defined the approach of Eugene Debs. He was America's preeminent labor organizer and socialist leader of the early 20th century.[116] His activism earned him extended spells in prison, but no amount of pushback or punishment ever affected his course. The statement he offered at his sentencing for sedition in 1918 encapsulates his contempt for prevailing opinion, exuberant embrace of struggle, harsh indictment of injustice, and invincible faith in the ultimate victory of his cause:

> Your honor ... I am thinking this morning of the men in the mills and factories; I am thinking of the women who, for a paltry wage, are compelled to work out their lives; of the little children who, in this system, are robbed of their childhood, and in their early, tender years, are seized in the remorseless grasp of Mammon, and forced into the industrial dungeons, there to feed the machines while they themselves are being starved body and soul.
>
> Your honor, I ask no mercy, I plead for no immunity. I realize that finally the right must prevail. I never more fully comprehended than now the great struggle between the powers of greed on the one hand and upon the other the rising hosts of freedom. I can see the dawn of a better day of humanity. The people are awakening. In due course of time they will come into their own.
>
> When the mariner, sailing over tropic seas, looks for relief from his weary watch, he turns his eyes toward the Southern Cross, burning luridly above the tempest-vexed ocean. As the midnight approaches the Southern Cross begins to bend, and the whirling worlds change their places, and with starry finger-points the Almighty marks the passage of Time upon the dial of the universe; and though no bell may beat the glad tidings, the look-out knows that the midnight is passing—that relief and rest are close at hand.
>
> Let the people take heart and hope everywhere, for the cross is bending, midnight is passing, and joy cometh with the morning.

Debs's indomitability and talent for telling a stirring redemptive narrative made his followers true believers. Said one: "That old man with the burning eyes actually believes that there can be such a thing as the brotherhood of man. And that's not the funniest part of it. As long as he's around I believe it myself."[117] They also earned him the respect of his detractors. President Warren G. Harding, a defender of the plutocrats Debs devoted his life to defeating, commuted the socialist leader's ten-year sentence after he had served three years of it and then received him with delight at the White House.

High-dominance liberal leadership is by no means distinctly male, as the women leading the push against Putin in Europe demonstrate. Chief among them is the president of the European Commission, Ursula von der Leyen. Another is the Czech minister of defense, Jana Černochová, who has posted pictures of herself sporting a t-shirt emblazoned with FUCK YOU PUTIN over an image of a skeleton's hand flipping off the Russian tyrant.[118] Sviatlana Tsikhanouskaya, the Belarusian opposition leader who beat Aleksandr Lukashenko in the 2020 election but had her victory annulled and was driven into exile, shows what courage in the face of a bloodthirsty dictator looks like. The widow of Alexey Navalny, Yulia Navalnaya, does as well.

Sanna Marin, the former Finnish prime minister, helped direct her country's accession to NATO. Her response to a reporter's question on whether Putin might require a face-saving "off-ramp" after his disastrous invasion of Ukraine shows how she deals with the tyrant next door. She answered with an acerbic quip: "The way out of the conflict is for Russia to leave Ukraine, that's the way out of the conflict." With a derisive chuckle at the ridiculous premise that Putin could ever be appeased, she dismissed the follow-up questions shouted by the reporters and walked away. The glamorous 36-year-old furnished a 10-second display of the kind of leadership that delights as well as inspires: Two days after Marin made her statement, it had been viewed online over four million times.[119]

These women, together with the Swedish prime minister, Magdalena Andersson, the Lithuanian prime minister, Ingrida Šimonytė, the Estonian prime minister, Kaja Kallas, the Danish prime minister, Mette Frederiksen, and the president of Moldova, Maia Sandu, have erected a democracy-defending wall of feminine steel along Russia's western edge. They represent a mix of Greens, social democrats, and classical center-right conservatives. Their leadership has been instrumental in defending Europe from the monster next door.

Their rise and success bear out a slew of studies that focus on American politics. Nancy Cohen, founder and president of the Gender Equity Policy Institute, documents a wave of recent research showing that women can and do project dominance and are rewarded for it at the polls. She reports: "Voters did not view female candidates who demonstrated toughness to be uncaring or unlikable. Nor did they penalize them for being tough. Indeed, acting tough outside the bounds of conventional femininity boosted women's favorability ratings, and tough women were viewed as more likely to be effective presidents."[120] Cohen's findings reinforce those of political scientist Deborah Jordan Brooks. Her 2013 book, *He Runs, She Runs: Why Gender Stereotypes Do Not Harm Women Candidates*, concluded: "The bottom line from my analysis is that I do not find any evidence that women face a gendered double bind. In fact, to the extent that any of the results are related to candidate gender, it is that women *benefit* from toughness more than their male counterparts on a couple of key measures" (emphasis in the original).[121]

There is nothing necessarily masculine, still less toxically masculine, about high-dominance leadership. Ovarian fortitude can overmatch the testicular variety in politics no less than in all other realms of social interaction.

Dominance isn't just for hotheads, imperialists, illiberals, sexists, egomaniacs, boors, and reactionaries. Liberals can be for dominance, and it can be for us. Given the political costs of a low-dominance approach, especially in a struggle with high-dominance authoritarians, the lack of necessary contradiction between liberalism and dominance is great news for democracy's prospects.

One last question: Doesn't a robust dominance strategy risk *deepening* polarization? Perhaps paradoxically, the answer is no—all the more under the circumstances that prevail in American politics right now.

When neither party focuses on polarizing the electorate as a central electoral strategy, a high-dominance approach might be less necessary. But when one party intentionally deepens social and political cleavages as a political tactic, as the Trumpified G.O.P. does today, pursuit of anything other than a high-dominance response by their opponents risks making them look defensive, irresolute and lacking in principle—even if they are just trying to avoid polarization.

So while it may seem counterintuitive, it is under conditions of acute polarization—or, more specifically, intense polarization driven principally by one side—that a high-dominance strategy by the party that seeks to *reduce* division is the best hope for depolarization. Under such circumstances, the only way to overcome divisions is to decisively and repeatedly defeat the polarizers, thereby forcing them to reconsider their strategies.

Still more is this the case when the polarizing party doesn't even respect the rules. Trump and his party don't just seek to inflame rancor over political opinion and identity. That's bad enough, but they also seek to *open a new cleavage based on political regime*—that is, to create a divide based on whether democracy is the right way to govern. They contest the very ideas that the victors in elections have the right to take office, that voting should be easy for all citizens, and that the votes should be counted by neutral parties. They further question whether the rulers should have to obey the rules.

Under such circumstances, for the non-polarizing, prodemocratic party to refrain from a high-dominance strategy affords its opponents the chance to legitimate polarization as a political strategy. It makes democracy's polarizing assailants appear to be tougher and more committed to their own ends. As such, it threatens to make democracy look *weaker* than the authoritarian alternatives—and playing by the rules for chumps.

This, of course, is precisely what all autocrats and would-be autocrats do. After all, convincing the people on this score is more than half the road to discrediting democracy and consolidating their hold on power indefinitely.

"Uniting not dividing" is a nice-sounding slogan, but for the Democrats to plead for unity and peace now serves themselves and democracy poorly. When facing the Trumpified Republicans, the only smart strategy is to win the fight and *then* offer unity—*if* we win, and then on our own terms.

Our own terms, of course, are that democracy be respected— nothing more or less.

16. When Liberals Grasp Dominance

L iberals yearn for dominance as much as anyone, even if we are often uncomfortable admitting it. We show as much when one of our own breaks the low-dominance norm. At the conclusion of Trump's 2020 State of the Union address, then-House Speaker Nancy Pelosi ostentatiously tore up her hard copy of the speech as the cameras rolled—and the image instantly went viral.[122]

In 2022, California Governor Gavin Newsom picked a fight with his Sunshine State counterpart, Ron DeSantis. Admonishing his co-partisans to take on DeSantis's attack on textbook bans and assaults on LGBTQ rights, he asked: "Where is the Democratic Party? Why aren't we standing up more firmly, more resolutely? . . . We need to stand up, where's the counteroffensive?"—and Democrats nationwide broke into speculation about him replacing Biden in 2024.[123]

After years of mostly taking the "high road" while listening to Trump call him "Slow Joe," "Basement Biden," "Beijing Biden," "crooked," and "senile," in early 2024 Biden finally let it rip when White House aides leaked that in private, the president describes Trump as a "sick fuck" who revels in other people's misfortunes.

At long last, it was time for the *Republicans* to recoil with wounded umbrage. A senior Trump campaign adviser sniffed: "It's a shame the Crooked Joe Biden disrespects the presidency both publicly and privately. But then again, it's no surprise that he disrespects the 45th president the same way he disrespects the American people with his failed policies."[124] For his own part, the 45th president himself screeched "Biden Just Called Me a Sick-F Word!," moaning to his supporters that "Biden will spit on us & call us every curse word in the dictionary."[125]

Poor baby!

Biden was finally controlling the conversation, and by all accounts his supporters were delighted. Some Republicans were impressed as well. G.O.P. strategist Doug Heye commented that while such language isn't "presidential," "it works … It also shows a vigor that we often say Joe Biden doesn't have in his advanced years."[126]

Liberals often say we want our leaders to "be fighters" or "stand up for us." What we really mean is that we thirst for them to *own* the Republicans for a change. Still, as Newsom's remarks suggest, high-dominance acts aren't standard fare for Democratic Party leaders.

Some liberal leaders bear marks of high-dominance leadership but fail to deliver the complete package. Bernie Sanders is one. In some ways, he resembles Debs and King, the two figures he cites as his heroes. He's an opinion-maker, not an opinion-taker. He tells every audience the same thing—and unlike most Democratic leaders, he's as happy going on FOX News as MSNBC to share his message. His views don't shift with public opinion; he waits for opinion to evolve to meet his own (and over the decades, in some ways it has). He hammers home his own truth at every turn, never assuming his audiences have heard enough.

He is also conflict-embracing rather than conflict-averse. Us-versus-them framing comes naturally to him. He is comfortable with the language of combat. Consequently, he has established a reputation as an unyielding, all-weather fighter. He inspires fierce loyalty in his followers and has the respect of his enemies.

But for all these laudable high-dominance traits, Sanders lacks a redemptive story. Much the same can be said of the otherwise high-dominance New York congresswoman, Alexandria Ocasio-Cortez. Both rail against the plutocracy and have no fear of taking on their opponents, but they provide no portrait of the promised land. What's more, they too rarely seem like they're *having fun* (though AOC did seem to do so during her first few years in office). Their absence of a celebratory style and failure to convey faith in ultimate victory can make them seem more scolding than uplifting, at least outside their progressive base. Consequently, while their voices enthuse followers, they don't remake the political field.

Some liberal leaders present a mix of low- and high-dominance styles. Nancy Pelosi, arguably the highest dominance major Democratic Party leader of the 21st century, is an example. She was one of the few Democrats who sometimes *owned* Trump. She didn't limit herself to protesting Trump's hardheartedness; she ridiculed and emasculated him as well. She still does.

One such event occurred during a White House meeting between leading congressional Democrats and Trump and his national security team. The gathering focused on Trump's decision to allow Turkish troops to decimate Kurdish forces in Syria. According to his one-time National Security Advisor, John Bolton, Trump's policy was driven by his personal commercial interests.[127] Recep Tayyip Erdoğan wished to eliminate Kurdish troops stationed in Syria, and there's a Trump Tower in Istanbul, so Trump cozied up to the Turkish ruler by abandoning the Kurds, long America's most effective allies against ISIS. Putin also wanted Americans to withdraw, so Trump got a twofer.

Russian forces working in Syria to prop up the homicidal regime of Bashar al-Assad soon overran the areas where American troops had been stationed. Russian TV broadcast images of them ransacking the emptied bases and mocking the American troops who had been stationed there. Trump was good with that.[128]

Pelosi's meeting with Trump was heated and intense. Trump's tweet afterward featured a picture of Pelosi standing, her finger wagging at him across the table. The brass flanking Trump were staring down at their hands, visibly humiliated by what Trump had made them do in Syria—and now by Pelosi's righteous attack. Trump is pictured with his mouth agape, clearly trying to talk over her. Above the picture, Trump tweeted, "Nervous Nancy's unhinged meltdown!"[129]

Yet Pelosi looked anything but nervous. Instead, what came across was her—the lone person standing, all of 5-feet-2, and the only woman at the table—treating Trump like the whining toddler he is.

The photo went viral and prompted a flurry of press coverage. CNN commentator and Republican strategist Ana Navarro retweeted the image under the statement: "I hope this picture of Nancy Pelosi, the sole woman at the table, standing up and speaking-up, inspires more bad-ass women to run for office." Pelosi's daughter Christine retweeted Trump's picture under the caption "Looks like she owned you on #NationalBossDay. Been there. Don't mess with mama!"[130]

Pelosi ground it in. She made the photo her Twitter cover image and told reporters, "We have to pray for his health." Asked what she was saying the moment the picture was taken, she replied: "I was probably saying all roads lead to Putin."[131]

This is how to turn the tables on Trump.

Since relinquishing the speakership, Pelosi has kept on dishing. In August 2023, remarking on the criminal charges against Trump for trying to overturn the 2020 election, she said Trump looked like a "scared puppy" as he appeared to face the charges. And she'll have none of the defeatist talk about a Trump second term. If Trump beats Biden, "It would be a criminal enterprise in the White House. . . . It cannot happen, or we will not be the United States of America."

Trump's response made it clear how much blood she drew. The former president of the United States called Pelosi "really quite vicious . . . a Wicked Witch . . . a sick and demented psycho who will someday live in HELL!"[132]

Insert guffawing smiley here.

But Pelosi wasn't adequately relentless in pressing her high-dominance messaging in the House. Her flashes of dominance exhilarated Democrats and humbled her foes. But intermittent action isn't enough; it's required on a weekly and daily basis. Unfortunately, Pelosi had to contend with a House full of Democrats who didn't share her high-dominance inclinations. The party and movement she led were generally uncomfortable celebrating triumphs, provoking opponents, ignoring polls, embracing us-versus-them framing, and telling their truths provocatively. This meant that she too sometimes fell back on low-dominance style. But it's clear that her natural inclination is towards high-dominance.

If Pelosi's personality had become her party's to the same extent that Trump's did with the Republicans, the dominance gap might have narrowed. But the Democrats, to our credit, will never become anybody's cult-party, so closing the gap will have to be the work of the many rather than the few.

That said, presidential leadership is critical. Liberals tend to dislike personalism, preferring to place policies before personalities. But even liberals like having *a* leader. Who doesn't? People naturally seek the person in charge. So when one of your own occupies the chief executive office, his voice matters more than everybody else's in your tribe. His mode of messaging has an enormous bearing on the organization's morale. It will also largely determine how it's perceived by the electorate as a whole.

On the global stage, Joe Biden is no stranger to high-dominance leadership. He's got Putin's number and shows no sign of playing nice. He doesn't react to his enemies' moves; he heads them off. As he defends Ukraine, he weaponizes intelligence by publicizing Putin's plans in advance, often preempting Russian attacks. He can be faulted for slowness in responding to some of Ukraine's military needs, but no one doubts his commitment to expelling Putin's forces. He also keeps China from going much beyond rhetoric in its support of Russia's invasion.

He states that America will respond with force if China invades Taiwan. He slaps stiff controls on American exports of technology to China at the very moment Xi declares himself dictator for life. He sticks up for freedom rhetorically and militarily, framing the conflict between democracies and autocracies in appropriately black-and-white terms. Little wonder, then, that in a 2021 Pew study, 62 percent of people across countries regarded Biden as a "strong leader," compared to 46 percent for Trump during his first year in office.[133] Most countries in the survey depend on the United States for their security, and unlike in America, there's no contest over which American president is made of sterner stuff.

The fruits of Biden's high-dominance ways abroad are an invigorated Western alliance; restoration of American prestige and transformation of global opinion on American leadership; a Ukraine that is standing firm against Putin's marauders; the absence of nuclear war; and despots who thought democracies were dissolute learning the hard way to respect people who govern themselves.[134]

Biden's brand of dominance on the world stage is distinctly liberal. He doesn't seek conflict for its own sake or use it to divert attention from domestic problems. He tells the truth, including in his public assessments of the war in Ukraine. He plays hard and plays to win, but anger doesn't drive the tone of his messaging. His language is tough and straightforward, but it's never shot through with resentment.

In short, when it comes to foreign affairs, Biden shows a face that he less often reveals at home. He shapes reality rather than just taking it. He acts boldly, regardless of opponents' reactions. He embraces conflict rather than avoiding it. He welcomes risk and prefers playing offense. He doesn't shrink from the language of righteousness and wickedness.

America's allies never seem to have lost much sleep about Biden's age—except, that is, insofar as Americans care, thereby stoking the nightmare of Trump's return.

But Biden and the Democrats don't deal with Trump and the Republicans like they deal with Putin and the Russians. Nor do they skillfully sport their manifold achievements abroad to build support at home. They treat their delivery of the world from Putin's clutches like they treat the delivery of millions of children from poverty: They leave the good news untold. They neglect to hammer home what would have happened had Putin's man won in 2020—a rudderless

West, an enslaved Ukraine, a panicked Europe, and an America left to Putin's and Xi's predations.

When Biden ups his dominance game, even just a little, it boosts him like no policy achievement can. Public response to his February 7, 2023, State of the Union address illustrates the effect. A CNN/SSRS survey showed that 71 percent of those who watched the speech felt Biden's policies would move the country in the right direction, versus 52 percent among the same group before the speech. That was an unusually large increase, tying the speech for the third-biggest bump from a State of the Union address since 1994. The most significant improvement came among those who disapproved of Biden's handling of the presidency before the speech. Among that group, 45 percent said afterward that Biden's policies would move the country in the right direction, compared to seven percent who expressed such confidence before the address. Among Independents, that number rose from 40 to 66 percent.[135]

Navigator Research provided no less remarkable numbers. Using a live-reaction dial group, it gauged audience reaction among soft partisans and swing voters. Navigator also took polls before and after the speech. When asked if Biden "is up for the job of President," 35 percent said he was before the speech, compared to 55 percent after it. Confidence in his ability to handle Social Security and Medicare climbed from 38 to 69 percent. Astronomical jumps were found in assessments of the president's ability to handle other issues as well.[136]

How did Biden pull this off?

First, on the content of the address: Gone was the handwringing about the supposedly straitened working person and the blame-taking for his plight. Biden spelled out the good news with brio: "800,000 good-paying manufacturing jobs, the fastest growth in 40 years"; "unemployment at 3.4 percent, a 50-year low." When dealing with the biggest remaining economic woe, Biden put the blame where it belonged and created a sense of movement: "Inflation has been a global problem because the pandemic disrupted our supply chains, and Putin's unfair and brutal war in Ukraine disrupted energy supplies as well as food supplies, blocking all that grain in Ukraine. But we're better positioned than any country on Earth right now." "Gas prices are down $1.50 from their peak"; "a record 10 million Americans applied to start new businesses. And by the way, every time—every time someone starts a small business it's an act of hope." The speech conveyed optimism and a sense of better things to come: "We're going to create hundreds of thousands of new jobs across the country. . . . That's going to come from companies that have announced more than $300 billion in investment in American manufacturing over the next few years"; "Outside of Columbus, Ohio, Intel is building semiconductor factories on thousands of acres—literally a field of dreams."[137]

To be sure, the address contained its fair share of platitudes delivered in yawn-worthy language. What is more, some of its high-dominance features are found in all State of the Union addresses, which invariably convey news about what the president is accomplishing and how great the country is. But at least Biden didn't fail to do these things.

Beyond that—and most importantly—Biden looked and sounded *strong*. Old, to be sure. But this time, he seemed more like a stern grandfather whose years lent him authority, wisdom, and self-assurance. He baited the Republicans on Social Security. When the usual suspects heckled him, Biden allowed them to make fools of themselves. He then maneuvered the Republicans into a standing ovation for his defense of Social Security—and quipped with a wry smile that the threat to the program seemed to have suddenly passed. He touted his 15-percent minimum tax on billion-dollar companies with aplomb. That left the Republicans sitting stone-faced with their hands in their laps as the Democrats cheered his requirement that these firms pay the same rate as nurses. He took credit for stopping Putin and standing up to China. He raised his voice and waved his finger as he thundered that no one in the world would want to be Xi anymore, given the fix the dictator was in.[138]

In a word, Biden *owned* the Republicans with his delivery. He appeared in command while the Republicans looked like impetuous children in need of a time-out. And though he didn't smile much, he seemed to be *enjoying* himself.

He exerted dominance in a liberal way. There was none of the "only I can do it and only I'm to credit" that Trump and other authoritarians dish out. Biden always shared the credit ("I stand here tonight after we have created, with the help of many people in this room, 12 million new jobs—more jobs created in two years than any president has created in four years, because of you all, because of the American people").

Biden's speech was a bright spot, but such behavior must shine through *all the time* to reshape the political arena, and it decidedly has not in Biden's day-to-day messaging. The task is both more pressing and easier to execute than many liberals imagine. The contrast between the good man Biden, strong of heart and character, standing toe-to-toe with the likes of Mitch McConnell and Marjorie Taylor Greene, need not be hard to project. Biden's State of the Union address provided a glimpse of how to do it.

After all, high-dominance authoritarians are at bottom mostly a cowardly lot. Ego-driven fears, resentments, and insecurities are usually what makes someone an authoritarian in the first place. The high-dominance authoritarian's power often depends not on internal fortitude but on bluster and the reluctance of others to take him on.

Hitler was a bundle of contamination fears, sexual complexes, and Oedipal obsessions. Self-pitying tantrums and tears, accusatory indignation, and emotional collapses filled his days. His public behavior, including his hysterical speeches about the insufferable wrongs he had allegedly endured, bore the marks of his pathologies.[139]

Putin is Hitler redux. Bottomless oceans of grievance and victimhood drive his every action. In meetings with his foreign counterparts, he rails for hours against imagined slights. His entire approach to war centers on slaughtering, torturing, and stealing from civilians.[140] His speech to the Russian elite announcing the "annexation" of four Ukrainian provinces on September 30, 2022, distilled the world according to Putin. The address is 37 minutes and 24 seconds of hysterical whining about illusory Western plots to deprive Russia of its due. Resentment is his *Weltanschauung*: "The collective West wants to see us as a colony; they want to see us not as a free society, but a crowd of soulless slaves; they pose a direct threat to our thought, they even seek to suffocate our philosophers." The West "has no need for Russia"; it does not respect Russia; it ignores Russia; it slights Russia. There is no end to Western power and Russian helplessness.[141]

Putin used to be the battering ram of authoritarians across the globe. He brazenly manipulated cyber tools to help elect an American president, sent mercenary forces to plunder African countries, and united autocrats around the world under the banner of a twisted but compelling narrative of grievance and aggression.

How quickly the mighty have fallen. Since the invasion of Ukraine and the disasters that followed for Russia, Putin has become what pathetic looks like—though the Republicans are trying to save him.

Scratch the highest-dominance, most influential enemy of democracy, and you will find little but self-pitying pathos. You don't even need to scratch him anymore; he wears it on his tear-and-snot-soaked sleeve.

Trump follows his mentor's lead. In his January 15, 2023, announcement of his presidential candidacy, he cried: "I'm a victim. I will tell you, I'm a victim . . . We will be attacked. We will be slandered. We will be persecuted just as I have been." Of his time at home with Melania, Trump said: "I go home and she says, 'You look angry and upset.' I say, 'Just leave me alone'."[142]

You would think that all this petulant wailing would erode Trump's tough guy image, and there are signs that, on occasion, it does. But until the liberals leverage these lapses to humiliate Trump the way he has degraded so many others, he—or his wannabes—will bounce back.

On the strength of his dominance orientation, this pathetic Putin-owned stooge owns the Republican Party. Even his 2020 defeat and demonstrably dampening effect on Republicans' performance has generated no serious anti-Trump faction. Republican leaders continue to live in terror of him. Senator Lindsay Graham says he misses Trump in the White House since he enjoyed how Trump frightened him. Even when Trump slanders Mitch McConnell's wife, Elaine Chao, with racist slurs, McConnell refuses to object.[143]

And the Democrats leave all this material, all these opportunities to dominate the dominator, untapped.

Anti-Trump former Republican strategist Rick Wilson gets right to the point:

> I want to encourage people in the pro-democracy fight ahead to keep a key fact close to their hearts. Donald Trump is a coward. A chickenshit. He's a yellow cur, running from, not to, the sound of guns. . . . Behind it all is a man scared of his ferocious father and controlling mother, a man who has never taken or delivered a punch, a man who knows he's a fraud and a fake, but dreams of one more con before he's caught. Remember, America. Trump wants you to be afraid of him . . . because he's petrified you'll see him for precisely the coward he is.[144]

The question for Biden and other Democratic leaders is: Why does it take a Republican to say that?

The underlying cravenness of our opponents hands the liberals a priceless opportunity. But seizing it requires attacking our opponents' *smallness* rather than just their cruelty, unfairness, or incompetence.[145] It means ridiculing, belittling, and diminishing the worst of them, not just critiquing their policies. Above all, it means shutting down the umbrage factory, going on the attack—and enjoying every minute of it.

Beating opponents in their areas of greatest strength is a powerful way to establish lasting advantage. As we've seen, dominance is an area of authoritarian advantage, but there's no reason that need be the case.

Besides their dominance game, the authoritarians have established another area of strength. Beating them in that realm as well would leave them without a leg to stand on. That second source of their power and how Democrats can seize it from them is the subject of the pages that follow.

PART THREE

SEIZING THE FLAG AND RECLAIMING THE AMERICAN STORY

17. The Liberals' Nationalism Challenge

W ho are we as a nation, and what do we intend to become? Claiming the nation—defining who's part of it, what its values are, and what it seeks to be—is the ultimate high-dominance move. But it's not just a feature of high-dominance politics; it's also an indispensable part of tapping nationalism, the world's most powerful political force.

That reality is no mystery to authoritarian demagogues. Adolph Hitler, Josef Stalin, and Benito Mussolini sold themselves as the ultimate enthusiasts and guardians of the nation. From Putin to Trump and India's Narendra Modi to Hungary's Viktor Orbán, today's enemies of democracy also strive to seize the flag and tell national stories that connect.

But the authoritarians' narratives are narrow fables that glorify the leader and obliterate core tenets of their countries' identities and traditions. Nowhere is that truer than in the United States, where Trump exalts his own greatness while trashing America's most sacred values. He shreds democracy, stokes racism, vilifies immigrants, breeds corruption, and abandons democratic allies in favor of anti-American despots.

Before we go any further, let's clarify the terms we will use. *Nationalism* is often confused with *ethnonationalism*, which means privileging one ethnic or religious group over others. Some also identify nationalism with looking down on or seeking to dominate other countries. Thus, some writings distinguish between nationalism, which is seen as bad, and patriotism, which may be viewed as good.

But many scholars define nationalism in a broader way, to mean feelings of attachment to the whole country, including all its inhabitants. I conceive of nationalism in this "whole-country" sense and use the term interchangeably with patriotism.

In her masterful book on the vital importance of wielding a national narrative for protecting democracy, political scientist Aram Hur clarifies the concept:

> Nationalism refers to the deep psychological and emotional attachment to one's national community. . . . When pundits or policy experts say that "nationalism" is a threat to democracy—from Narendra Modi's revival of exclusionary Hindu nationalism in India to Donald Trump's stoking of American white supremacist nationalism—what they are actually referring to are the effects of oppositional national stories. In such cases, demagogues have married national attachments with stories of exclusion and inferior treatment by the state . . . to destabilize the establishment and justify their own rule. These are consequences of opportunistic politics, not nationalism per se.[1]

It's easy to make the case—and liberals *should* make the case—that a true nationalist can't be an ethnonationalist since *nation*alism requires the inclusion of *all* members of the *nation*. Another way of thinking about it is that a patriot can't be an ethnonationalist because real *patriot*ism, by definition, encompasses all who reside in the *patria* (homeland).

Trump's exclusionary, nativist story should be easy for the Democrats to beat. But 21st-century liberals have become squeamish about nationalism. Many have come to see it much as they regard dominance politics: an unfortunate throwback that is best left to authoritarians.

But most people long to be part of a great nation, and that will not change any time soon. They are grateful for and proud of their membership in their national community. They respond to leaders who convey their aspirations in a compelling narrative of national glory and promise. If the Democrats fail to arm themselves with such a story, Republicans—despite their betrayal of America's core values—will continue to be widely seen as the more patriotic party.

Liberals' skepticism about nationalism is one reason for our failure to articulate an inspiring national narrative. Another may be that our premier 21st-century leader seemed to get by so well without one. Half-Kenyan and half-Kansan, committed to liberal values, wide awake but not woke, social-democratic but pro-market, firm in defense of democratic allies abroad, and incurably optimistic about the nation's promise, Barack Obama *was* the national story. The fact that he embodied it meant he rarely had to spell it out.

To be sure, he sometimes articulated his own American story, which laudably included a notion of national exceptionalism. As he said, "In no other country on earth is my story even possible."[2]

But Obama's evidence that America was special was himself. And since it was America's dreadful history of racial oppression that made his presidency remarkable, his line could conjure thoughts of national disgrace as well as redemption. It also lacked the guts-and-glory edge found in the national narratives of figures like John Kennedy, Martin Luther King, and Ronald Reagan.

Obama himself was appealing enough to boost the Democrats and make America—and democracy—cool again after the era of the bungling, war-mongering George W. Bush and Dick Cheney. But as George Packer noted, "Obama was always better at explaining the meaning of democracy than at fighting its opponents. Other than 'Yes, we can' and a few other phrases, it's hard to remember any lines from his speeches."[3] He left little for his successors to work with after his departure from office.

Unfortunately, what all this means is that the Republicans have a compelling story, while Democrats do not. Trump tells it all too well. It's a bigoted, misleading yarn, to be sure, and it's appealing only to a diminishing minority. But in the absence of a potent countervailing liberal narrative, it's often all we get.

Democratic operatives sometimes recognize that something is missing. After heavy losses in the 2014 midterm elections, the party convened a special task force. Topping their list of concerns was the widespread perception that their party's message was little more than a "long list of policy statements." To develop a unifying message for future elections, the task force proposed a "National Narrative Project." That was a decade ago, and the project's fruits—or even evidence that anybody's paying attention to the problem— have yet to surface.[4]

Nationalism and high-dominance style often go hand in hand. Indeed, nationalism may appeal most strongly to people who value a high-dominance style in their leaders. They include working-class people, residents of rural areas and small towns, and recent immigrants. That is to say, nationalism may be particularly important to the voters who liberals need to win more of to turn back Trumpism. And that group definitely isn't limited to whites. "Americans are starved for a meaningful politics of what it means to be an American," writes historian Jefferson Cowie. While the left is mired in debates over "socialism," he says, "the full mosaic of the American working class" is "looking to recapture a sense of nation."[5]

Some of America's most perceptive commentators have offered incisive takes on the liberals' nationalism problem and how it prevents them from successfully confronting Trumpism. *New York Times* columnist David Brooks did so in a pair of op-eds on the eve of the 2018 midterm elections. In "Do Democrats Know What Unites Us?," he writes:

National identity is the most powerful force in world politics today. Most of the strong leaders around the world were swept to power with a strong nationalist story and govern in nationalist ways. This is true in Russia, China, India, the U.S., Israel, Turkey,

Britain, Brazil and on and on. It's hard to see how any party could appeal or govern these days without a strong national story.

In this country, Donald Trump has almost nothing but a national story, which he returned to with a vengeance in the closing days of this year's campaigns. It happens to be a cramped, reactionary and racial story ... Trump's blood-and-soil nationalism overturns the historical ideal of American nationalism, which was pluralistic—that we are united by creed, not blood; that our common culture is defined by a shared American dream—pioneers settling the West, immigrants crossing an ocean in search of opportunity, African-Americans rising from slavery toward equality.

The Republicans have flocked to Trump's cramped nationalism and abandoned their creedal story. That's left the Democrats with a remarkable opportunity. They could seize the traditional American national story, or expand it to gather in the unheard voices, while providing a coherent, unifying vehicle to celebrate the American dream.

And yet what have we heard from the Democrats? Crickets.

What is the Democratic national story? A void.[6]

Given the urgency of formulating a story that can bury the MAGA narrative, why have the Democrats failed to generate it?

Brooks has a few ideas. One is that the Democratic Party has become what he calls, in a column by that name, "The Materialist Party." While the Trumpian challenge is essentially cultural and moral, the Democrats' "basic political instinct is that you win votes by offering material benefits." According to Brooks, "Democrats missed the Trumpian upsurge because while society was dividing into cultural tribes, they spent 2008 through 2016 focusing on health care. Now that the upsurge has happened, they are still pinioned to health care."

The second is that when the Democrats do make a moral argument, "it tends to be of the social justice warrior variety. The core argument in this mode is that the oppressive structures of society marginalize women, minorities and members of the L.G.B.T.Q. communities." There's everything right with advocating for justice, writes Brooks, but the Democrats' way of doing it can preclude a unifying national message that can beat Trump's clear, firm—if essentially anti-American—narrative:

> It turns out that if your basic logic is that distinct identity groups are under threat from an oppressive society, it's very hard to then turn around and defend that society from authoritarian attack, or to articulate any notion of what even unites that society. You can appeal to women as women and to ethnic groups as ethnic groups, but it's very hard to make a universal appeal to Americans as Americans, or defend the basic American norms that Trump calls into question. It's a messaging vulnerability that Democrats have imposed upon themselves.[7]

The upshot is a Democratic Party that has undermined its own ability to counter the Trumpian narrative—and a Trumpian party that has usurped the national story. In "Do Democrats Know What Unites Us?," Brooks writes:

> Here's the central challenge of our age: Over the next few decades, America will become a majority-minority country. It is hard to think of other major nations, down through history, that have managed such a transition and still held together.
>
> It seems that the Democratic Party is going to lead us through this transition. The Republicans have decided to pretend it's not happening. Trump had a chance to build a pan-ethnic nationalist coalition but went with white identity politics instead. Republicans have rendered themselves irrelevant to the great generational challenge before us.
>
> But if the Democrats are going to lead this transition, they'll need not just a mind-set that celebrates diversity, but also a mind-set that creates unity. . . .

If you don't offer people a positive, uplifting nationalism, they will grab the nasty one. History and recent events have shown us that.

Historian Jill Lepore also perceives the problem. In the absence of a compelling national counternarrative to the Trumpian fable, Lepore writes that the new crop of far-right leaders will "lament 'American carnage.' They'll call immigrants 'animals' and other states 'shithole countries.' They'll adopt the slogan 'America First.' They'll say they can 'make America great again.' They'll call themselves 'nationalists.' Their history will be a fiction. They will say that they alone love this country. They will be wrong."[8]

Oh yeah? Who says they aren't nationalists? Who says we're better nationalists than they are?

Somebody's going to have to say it—and liberal leaders are failing to do so.

Indifference to nationalism—or even feelings that the nation doesn't deserve to be defended due to its historic moral failings—can be found among some who constitute the Democratic Party's base. In his analysis of the "four Americas," George Packer offers a penetrating look at the problem.[9] Packer divides the country into four groups: "Free America," "Real America," "Smart America," and "Just America." Nationalism is embraced by people in the first two groups, who also make up the base of the Republican Party. To some in the second two categories, however, nationalism can seem pointless or even repellent.

In Packer's view, some "Smart Americans"—mostly winners in the meritocracy who figure prominently among liberal elites—"are uneasy with patriotism. It's an unpleasant relic of a more primitive time, like cigarette smoke or dog racing. It stirs emotions that can have ugly consequences. The winners in Smart America—connected by airplane, internet, and investments to the rest of the globe—have lost the capacity and the need for a national identity, which is why they can't grasp its importance for others." These overachievers often fail to recognize what they owe their country for the bounty they enjoy. As a result, "Their passionate loyalty, the one that gives them a particular identity, goes to their family. The rest is diversity and efficiency, heirloom tomatoes and self-driving cars. They don't see the point of patriotism."

"Just Americans"—often the progressive children or students of "Smart Americans"—may even regard the country as unworthy of allegiance. On the one hand, Just America performs the great service of doing what the other narratives don't. Namely, it "forces us to see the straight line that runs from slavery and segregation to the second-class life so many Black Americans live today—the betrayal of equality that has always been the country's great moral shame, the heart of its social problems." But it fails to put forth a vision of a better nation that most Americans can relate to: "Just America has a dissonant sound, for in its narrative, justice and America never rhyme. A more accurate name would be Unjust America, in a spirit of attack rather than aspiration. For Just Americans, the country is less a project of self-government to be improved than a site of continuous wrong to be battled. In some versions of the narrative, the country has no positive value at all—it can never be made better."

Packer then puts his finger on two problems with the rejection of patriotism. First, "abandoning patriotism to the other narratives guarantees that the worst of them will claim it." Here Packer has in mind the unsavory aspects of the Republican base.

The second drawback of Just America's approach is that patriotism is critical to achieving great tasks: "If your goal is to slow climate change, reverse inequality, stop racism, or rebuild democracy, you will need the national solidarity that comes from patriotism."

To these we may add a third problem: It puts liberals at a disadvantage in winning voters' allegiance as long as the Republicans can claim patriotic superiority.

Those who shun patriotism start any discussion about the nation's future—as well as their political campaigns—with one strike against them. The patriotic majority includes most working-class people and first-generation Americans, who often made enormous sacrifices to join the American nation. They and their children tend to be profoundly grateful for and proud of their American citizenship. To win their support, liberals must ever and openly show that we share their faith in the nation's inexhaustible promise—with absolutely no reservations.

Yet tapping and stoking nationalism doesn't come naturally to even many deeply patriotic liberal leaders. Given the ambivalence of parts of the Democratic party's base toward nationalism, perhaps it's understandable that some Democratic leaders hesitate to wave the flag without apology. But the key to energizing all segments of the party while also reaching beyond it isn't laying off the patriotism, which just plays into the Republicans' hands. It's offering an uncompromisingly inclusive portrait of the nation that even social justice warriors can buy into. The patriotism deficit among some in this group, after all, might be due less to dislike of country than to the fact that the only national narrative they hear is the Republicans' repulsive ethnonational story, and the only people they see waving the star-spangled banner are MAGA enthusiasts.

Democrats are paying a price for their lackluster approach to nationalism. In a 2022 poll, 56 percent of respondents chose the term "patriotic" to describe the Republican Party, while 46 percent said the term describes the Democrats.[10] This, even as Republicans line up behind a man who shreds America's most sacred traditions, jeopardizes national security for profit, and sucks up to Vladimir Putin. As political analysts Aliza Astrow and Rachel Reh noted after reviewing these data, "Democrats should be outraged...[they] disdain or ignore patriotism at their peril."

18. Why Liberals Need Not Fear Nationalism

W hy is nationalism essential, and how does it comport with liberal values? It might seem that feelings of attachment to the nation must be waning as globalization deepens and modernization advances, particularly in rich countries. Or perhaps tribalism within countries is loosening the hold of nationalism as feelings of allegiance to ethnic, religious, or other subnational groups are growing stronger.

The evidence shows otherwise. Political scientists Gina Gustavsson and David Miller find that while "globalization and international migration have connected people across national boundaries to an unprecedented extent" since the 1990s, feelings of attachment to country have actually grown stronger in most Western countries, including the United States. The average percentage of those who say they feel "very close" or "close" to their countries rose from 84 percent in 1995 to 88 percent in 2013, the last year covered by the survey.[12]

Pride and gratitude accompany national attachment. In a 2014 GSS survey, 84 percent of Americans said they "strongly agreed" or "agreed" that they "would rather be a citizen of America than of any other country in the world."[13] In a 2022 Gallup survey, 65 percent said they were "extremely" or "very" proud to be Americans, while another 22 percent said they were "moderately proud." There was no substantial difference between Republicans and Democrats.[14]

Do ethnic minorities identify less closely with the whole nation, and does patriotism offend them? In the 2020 ANES survey, 80 percent of Blacks said their ethnic identity was extremely or very important to them, compared to just 20 percent of whites. But 72 percent of Blacks, versus 64 percent of whites, also said their American identity was extremely or very important to them. Nationalism and strong group identity can go together, and there should be little reason to fear that red-white-and-blue messaging would alienate minorities.[15]

Americans prize patriotism. In 2023, 73 percent said patriotism is important to them—more than who feel that way about marriage, belief in God, religion, or having children. Sixty-four percent of American adults own an American flag.[16]

Nationalism is strong and here to stay. People can't be expected to get over it any more than they can be expected to get over their instinctive desire for high-dominance qualities in their political leaders.

Another misconception that affects liberal thinking is that nationalism is destructive. But a spate of recent research shows that nationalism's persistence isn't bad news for democracy or justice. Nationalism can strengthen opposition to antidemocratic action, enhance political trust, encourage generosity toward other groups, and reinforce liberal values.

Political scientists Gregory A. Petrow, John Transue, and Manuel Gutierrez conducted an experiment to assess whether prompting Americans to think about their patriotism would affect their view of Trump's efforts to overturn the 2020 election. The authors reported: "When we reminded Trump supporters of their commitment to patriotism, they were less likely to say he should remain in office if he lost the election. Interestingly, patriotic symbols had stronger effects among those who approved more of Trump's presidency." They concluded: "Our results suggest that one way to defuse Trump's false claims of election fraud could be to appeal to American patriotism, reminding people that false claims run counter to the U.S. tradition of democracy and freedom."[17]

Sociologists Jan Voelkel, Joseph Mernyk, and Robb Willer showed that policy positions matter less than the language in which they are embedded, and patriotic rhetoric is key. They carried out an experiment that gauged people's support for a hypothetical 2020 Democratic presidential nominee. They found that people were largely indifferent to whether the nominee proposed moderate or progressive economic policies. But the candidate who used the rhetoric of patriotism, family, and the American Dream consistently fared better among moderates and conservatives—and no worse among liberals—than the one who spoke the Democrats' usual language of compassion and justice.[18]

In separate experiments, Voelkel and Matthew Feinberg found that attacking Trump's patriotism ("he has repeatedly behaved disloyally towards our country") reduced his appeal to conservatives, while liberals' typical framing ("his unfair statements are a breeding ground for prejudice") did not.[19]

Nationalism can also be an ally in the liberal battle against destructive forms of ethnic tribalism. Political scientists Gina Gustavsson and Ludvig Stendahl studied how nationalism affects political trust. Trust is often thought to boost democracy since people who have faith in their compatriots might be more likely to feel the people are fit to govern. Examining the United States and the Netherlands, they found "[N]ational attachment does indeed have a strong positive relationship to trust...We find little evidence, moreover, to support the worry that this comes at the cost of excluding out-groups...National pride, moreover, is not the villain it is often made out to be . . . [S]coring high on national pride is remarkably strongly and robustly related to higher levels of political trust."[20]

Nationalism may ease ethnic tensions and promote magnanimous action toward other groups. Political scientists Volha Charnysh, Christopher Lucas, and Prerna Singh found that prompting Indian Hindus to think about their national identity as Indians made them more likely to be generous toward Indian Muslims.[21] In a follow-up article, Singh lauded the tactics of Indian Muslims who had recently sung the national anthem and carried the national flag and placards with quotes from the Indian Constitution in their street demonstrations against Prime Minister Narendra Modi's anti-Muslim politics. According to Singh, such actions give the lie to Modi's characterization of Indian Muslims as outsiders who are more loyal to Pakistan than to their homeland.[22]

In light of this research, it's unsurprising that identification with the nation can be associated with liberal values. In a survey of citizens of the United States and nine European countries, Gustavsson and Miller found that the extent to which people agreed with the statement "I see myself as part of the (____) nation" was positively correlated with their support for civil rights and sexual and religious tolerance.[23]

Does nationalism encourage an aggressive foreign policy? Appeals to nationalism have sometimes been used to justify imperialism and national belligerence. But many opponents of foreign misadventures have effectively argued that imperial wars degrade their country's values and international status. In his 1967 speech, "Beyond Vietnam: A Time to Break Silence," Martin Luther King excoriated America's policy because it prevented the United States from realizing its vast potential for global leadership: "[M]y beloved nation...America, the richest and most powerful nation in the world, can well lead the way in the revolution of values" that he said was vital to overcoming "deadly Western arrogance."[24] King, the moral conscience of mid-20th-century progressive patriotism, declared: "I criticize America because I love her. I want her to stand as a moral example to the world."[25]

What's more, nagging feelings of national inferiority can actually stoke belligerence and expansionism. As a longtime specialist in Russian politics and society, I can confirm that Putin's bullying of neighbors and invasion of Ukraine, as well as many Russians' support of his horrid behavior, are rooted less in the certainty that Russia is great than in fears that it decidedly is not.

Nor does patriotism necessarily promote an uncritical spirit. While a large majority of Americans from both major parties express pride in and attachment to the nation, 60 percent also "strongly agreed" or "agreed" that "There are some things about America today that make me feel ashamed of America." A remarkable 70 percent strongly agreed or agreed that "The world would be a better place if Americans acknowledged America's shortcomings," while just eight percent strongly disagreed. Virtually equal percentages of Democrats, Republicans, and Independents answered the questions this way. As the *Washington Post* headline stated in its report on the survey, "Americans Love Their Country, but It's a Surprisingly Tough Love."[26]

Nationalism doesn't equate to hubris. In a 2022 Pew survey, just 23 percent of Americans said they think the United States "stands above all other countries in the world," while an equal number said "there are other countries that are better than the United States." Fifty-two percent held that their country is "one of the greatest countries in the world, along with some others."[27]

Liberals who would harness nationalism to counter Trumpism need not worry that it will encourage their compatriots to abandon the critical self-examination necessary to confronting injustice. Whole-country nationalism is part of the democratic project, and it can propel values and sentiments that underpin liberty and justice for all.

Still, telling a national story that most liberal members of "Smart America" and "Just America" will be happy to embrace—and that also appeals to members of other political tribes—poses a challenge. We'll turn to that task now.

19. Grappling with Race in the Nation's Story

U nder Republican Governor Ron DeSantis, the Florida Department of Education rejected a college-level advanced-place-
ment course on Black history, describing it as "woke indoctrination
masquerading as education." DeSantis has also enacted laws that
have led to the removal of books, including *The Life of Rosa Parks*,
from school libraries.[28] And there's more: The state's guidelines now
require that the Sunshine State's middle school kids learn that enslaved Blacks acquired skills that "could be applied for their personal
development." Once they get to high school, they'll learn about "violence perpetrated against and by African Americans" during 20th-
century race massacres of Blacks perpetrated by whites.[29]

That's the MAGA story on race. It minimizes the evils of white
racism and denies the need for a national effort to address the legacies of slavery and Jim Crow. Republican officeholders, candidates,
spokespeople, and media personalities echo this story with clarity
and consistency.

What's the Democratic story? Unfortunately, it is much less
clear and consistent—and therefore easy for the opposition to caricature and distort.

According to the Republicans, the Democrats are trying to strip
the names of George Washington and Abraham Lincoln off our
schools because we think they were racists. They say we want to in-
doctrinate white kids into believing they are guilty of the crimes of

their ancestors. They claim the only story we have about America is a tale of woe about racial injustice that divides the country into white victimizers and victimized people of color. That narrative, they say, is demoralizing our children, undermining patriotism, and leading the youth to hate America.

In other words, they portray every Democrat as being on the far edge of what George Packer calls "Just America"—the people who consider the nation irredeemably unjust.

In fact, as we saw above, the vast majority of Democrats are proud to be Americans and do regard the country as worthy of allegiance. But that reality is lost on many—perhaps most—non-Democrats.

In 2022, the group More in Common published a survey on what people from each party felt about teachings on race in schools and compared the results to the views members of the other party *thought* their political opponents held. The findings should give Democrats pause.

The survey found that the vast majority of Democrats do not hold radical views on race and racism. Eighty-seven percent agreed that "students should not be made to feel personally responsible for the actions of earlier generations." The same percentage endorsed the statement, "In learning about past injustices in American history and their impact on the present day, students should not be made to feel disempowered or helpless." And the same number agreed that "George Washington and Abraham Lincoln should be admired for their roles in American history."

Yet when Republicans were asked what Democrats believed, less than half got it right, ranging between 42 and 46 percent. And here's the worst news: *Independents'* estimates of Democrats' views hardly differed from those of the Republicans, with only between 44 and 50 percent rightly answering the questions on how Democrats think. In other words, most non-Democrats think Democrats hold much more extreme views on race and racism than they actually do.[30]

But partisan misunderstanding is mutual. A 2019 More in Common survey found that while 79 percent of Republicans agreed that "racism still exists in America," just 51 percent of Democrats thought Republicans held that view. Seventy percent of Republicans agreed that "Many Muslims are good Americans," but only 41 percent of Democrats believed Republicans thought that way. And here's the twist: "[W]hile Republicans' misperceptions of Democrats do not improve with higher levels of education, the Democrats' understanding of Republicans actually gets worse with every additional degree they earn. This effect is so strong that Democrats without a high school diploma are three times more accurate than those with a postgraduate degree." The basis for the difference, the authors believe, is that highly educated Democrats report having few Republican friends while their Republican counterparts have about equal numbers of friends in each party.[31]

Highly educated liberals grossly overestimate how intolerant most non-liberals are, which means we're basing our political decisions on misconceptions. This is a big problem—but it also creates a major opportunity.

When it comes to telling a compelling national story that grapples with race, the Democrats face what might seem to be an impossible dual task. The first part of the problem is to disabuse non-liberal but persuadable voters of the erroneous notion that we regard America as a hall of injustice that hasn't improved since the days of slavery. The second is to do so without alienating core constituencies on the left. They include African Americans, whose turnout helps determine our party's—and now democracy's—fate.

Yet this isn't the conundrum it appears to be to many liberal analysts. If we get the story right, we can discredit the Republicans' false narrative about us in the minds of centrists and persuadable non-deplorable (meaning real) conservatives, while mobilizing—not disenchanting—our core progressive constituencies. But doing that requires a more compelling national story on race than we have been offering. How can we tell a story that cuts *all* people of goodwill in on the struggle for justice?

Let's start by recognizing that only a quarter of Americans consider themselves liberals. In 2022, 37 percent labeled themselves moderates, 36 percent conservatives, and 25 percent liberals.[32] So it's key that we understand what our current messaging sounds like to people outside the liberal tribe.

Consider the writings of *New York Times* columnist Charles Blow. Millions read his articles; they have influence. As a guide to effective political messaging, however, Blow's approach is the path to oblivion. It feeds the distorted story the MAGAmen tell about us.

In his May 2021 piece, "Is America a Racist Country?," Blow quotes a remark Lincoln made in one of his famous debates with segregationist Stephen Douglas in 1858 that indeed sounds racist by today's standards.[33] Based on this, Blow dismisses Lincoln as a white supremacist. He disregards everything else in Lincoln's story, from the Emancipation Proclamation to his remarkable friendship with Frederick Douglass, who lauded Lincoln as "one of the very few white Americans who could converse with a Negro without anything like condescension, and without in anywise reminding him of the unpopularity of his color."[34] Nor, apparently, does Lincoln's leading the war against the Southern slaveholding states or being assassinated for his efforts by a white supremacist count, either.

Blow goes on to claim that America might have made little progress since the Civil War. He writes some will argue "that was then and this is now, that racism simply doesn't exist now as it did then." But he adds: "I would agree. American racism has evolved and become less blunt, but it has not become less effective. The knife has simply been sharpened. Now systems do the work that once required the overt actions of masses of individual racists."

This is a perfect expression of what baffles so many people about the notion of "systemic" or "institutional" racism. Apparently, the "systems" of the current age are just sharper and more effective than the slavers' whips—not to mention the Jim Crow regime, which had some pretty sharp "systems" of its own.

In Blow's accounts, "America" is ever to blame. In his column on the savage beating-to-death of a young African American man by five police officers in Tennessee, entitled "Tyre Nichols's Death Is America's Shame," Blow called the tragedy "a damning indictment of American perversion...America should be ashamed."[35]

Blow acknowledged that the officers involved were aggressively charged, then added: "But instead of leaping to my feet to applaud a system working as it should, rather than as it was designed, I am stuck on the fact that there should have been federal legislation to prevent such killings. But there wasn't, and there isn't, because America has once again failed Black people." He ignored the fact that in 2020, and then again in 2021, House Democrats passed the federal George Floyd Justice in Policing Act with zero Republican votes. Senate Democrats worked hard to strike a deal with Senate Republicans, but none would support the bill in any form, and the measure died twice in the Senate.[36]

So is "America" to blame for the lack of federal legislation? Or are Republican politicians?

There's no doubt that too little has been done to counter police violence against African Americans. But instead of a call to further action, Blow all but throws in the towel, declaring the project dead. He even dismisses many of the Black Lives Matter protesters as "evanescent allies, poll-chasing politicians and cooped-up Covid kids who had used the protests as an opportunity to congregate. Even Black people's support for the Black Lives Matter movement eventually began to fall."

What are liberal activists to do with that? And how could any aspect of this story open the door to moderate and conservative voters?

The irony here is that while Blow's patriotism is beyond question and his intentions are light-years ahead of Trump's, his tale of America is only a little less narrow. It mischaracterizes the country as a house of wrong and its ethnic majority as shivering with hatred and fear. As such, it creates the impression that the Trumpians are the real owners of the nation. It hands the country to the Republicans.

If Blow were right about America's racist essence and incapacity for improvement, perhaps we could sadly concur in his analysis, even while recognizing that America-is-to-blame messaging hurts us at the polls. But is he right?

Earlier, we saw how Americans' attitudes on race have liberalized in recent decades. Now, let's look at a bit more data that are important to understanding where we stand today.

Recently, liberal discourse has been awash with speculation that whites, particularly those who lack a higher education, not only believe that anti-Black racism has disappeared but also that racism against whites has become a major problem. This possibility understandably creates angst among liberals. How can racism be confronted if whites don't even acknowledge it exists? How can a party that places racial justice at the top of its agenda, as the Democrats should and do, make inroads among people who think *they* are the victims of more discrimination than Blacks?

Perhaps in response to these concerns, in 2012, ANES started asking: "How much discrimination is there in the United States against [name of racial group]?" The response categories are "a great deal," "a lot," "a moderate amount," "a little," and "none at all." For each ethnic group, we combine the first three responses to show the total percentage who think there is a significant amount of racism.

	Percent saying there is substantial anti-Black racism	Percent saying there is little or no anti-Black racism	Percent saying there is substantial anti-Hispanic racism	Percent saying there is little or no anti-Hispanic racism	Percent saying there is substantial anti-white racism	Percent saying there is little or no anti-white racism
All	81	19	71	29	25	75
Non-college whites	78	22	69	31	32	68
Non-college Blacks	88	12	76	24	25	75
Non-college Hispanics	83	17	82	18	20	80

Table 19.1. Perceptions of Racism, Whole Sample and by Ethnic Group, 2016

Table 19.1 has the numbers for the year Trump was elected. Non-college whites, like all respondents, overwhelmingly see racism against Blacks and Hispanics as a problem and do *not* see racism against whites as a problem. Seventy-eight percent of non-college whites believe there is substantial anti-Black racism in American society, versus 32 percent who perceive racism against their own group—a 46-point spread. Notably, a quarter of non-college African Americans perceive the existence of anti-white racism, just seven points lower than the number of their non-college white compatriots who think the same thing.

Non-college whites also believe that anti-Hispanic racism is a thing. Sixty-nine percent hold that it is—again, versus 32 percent who perceive the presence of anti-white racism.

The data contradict three ideas that are widely held by well-educated liberals: That most working-class whites fail to appreciate racism against people of color; that most working-class whites regard anti-white racism as worse than racism against people of color; and that most working-class whites' views on racism are out of step with those of other Americans. Declarations by the Proud Boys that the only racism that remains in America is directed against whites are alarming and understandably garner press attention. But theirs are marginal, not mainstream opinions.

Nor do most Americans think racism should be ignored in their kids' history courses. In a 2021 Pew survey, 53 percent said that increased public attention to the history of slavery and racism is very or somewhat good for society, over twice the number (26 percent) who said it is somewhat or very bad. Those numbers are especially remarkable since the question doesn't ask if paying attention to slavery and racism is a good thing; instead, it asks whether *increased* attention is desirable.

And Americans don't just want more discussion of racial problems; they want action, too. When asked how much needs to be done "to ensure equal rights for all Americans regardless of their racial or ethnic backgrounds," 50 percent said a lot, 34 percent said a little, and 15 percent said nothing at all. The constituency for reform is obviously immense, and fewer than one in six Americans think nothing more needs to be done to advance racial equality.[37]

But it's also important to understand people's perceptions of progress. Even as large majorities believe that racism remains a problem, they also believe substantial headway has been made. A 2021 Gallup survey asked: "Thinking back over your lifetime, how do you feel civil rights for Black adults have changed in this country?" Seventy percent—including 57 percent of African Americans—said they thought the situation for Blacks has greatly or somewhat improved during their lifetimes.[38]

That progress is visible at the highest reaches of power. Obama's presidency, Kamala Harris's vice presidency, and Lloyd Austin's secretaryship of defense, none of which would have seemed likely or even possible during the adolescence of anyone over 60 today, are perhaps the starkest symbols of progress. In 1960, Congress included four African Americans—0.7 percent of members. In 2024, there are 60, or 11 percent of members.

All this evidence sheds light on why most people might regard the "Just America" narrative, which largely ignores the country's colossal strides, as more than a little off-putting.

Imagine what the Democrats could do with a public this liberal if only we grasped the reality that the data reveal and had the political will to capitalize on it. Consider the potential pay-off if we always told our story in a way that embeds the struggle for justice in a narrative that raucously celebrates past progress.

American history is shot through with racism. But too often progressives tend to blame "America" rather than racists. American history is in large part a story of haltingly and incompletely—but nevertheless significantly—overcoming racism, from the Emancipation Proclamation to civil rights legislation to the election and reelection of Barack Obama. If the Democrats fail to place that splendid tale at the center of our narrative of the nation, we stand to lose our compatriots who are more than willing to acknowledge the reality of racism but still long to feel proud of their country.

That leads us back to how we communicate with our fellow Americans on race, again with an eye to understanding what kind of messaging does and does not work.

Since the U.S. Census Bureau projected in 2015 that whites would lose their majority status within 30 years, news of the impending "majority-minority" shift has become a staple in press reports and classrooms. Social scientists have found that exposure to the news has been associated with white fears of anti-white discrimination, more significant opposition to immigration, and increased support for Donald Trump.[39]

Does that mean demographic change must leave whites veering toward Trumpism? In a breakthrough study, political scientists Morris Levy and Dowell Myers show that the answer is no. Using a battery of survey experiments, the authors find that whites' negative reactions are "byproducts of a *narrative* about the country's racial future that dominates political rhetoric and media coverage" (emphasis in the original). The authors note that the dominant narrative isn't even consistent with contemporary realities: "The irony is that this prevailing narrative depicts future racial change in the twenty-first century through the lens of nineteenth-century stereotypes of racial identity and classification. In the face of a rising tide of mixed-race marriage and racial fluidity and pluralism among America's young—one multiplied forward in the Census Bureau's own fore-casts—the dominant narrative of racial change assumes the contin-uation of a strict white-nonwhite binary decades into the future."

The good news is that while the standard majority-minority story evokes a sense of threat among whites, "[a]lternative accounts that highlight multiracialism elicit decidedly positive reactions re-gardless of whether they foretell the persistence of a more diverse white majority." Such alternative narratives, which in any event more accurately capture 21st-century demographic realities and self-identification, aren't off-putting to people of color: "Non-white groups respond favorably to all narratives about rising diver-sity, irrespective of whether they include the conventional majority-minority framing."[40]

So *narrative* is everything. The way our leaders *talk* about the na-tion can shape how people feel about demographic change. Perhaps telling a story that casts the nation as a coherent, rising, superb whole rather than as a collection of racially distinct groups vying for status can alleviate white anxieties—and whites' perceptions of the party that seeks to help non-whites. It can also appeal to people of color. It can resonate much more broadly with the vast majority than Trump's panicked, ethnonational tale.

What about taking whites to task for failing to understand their own privilege? In a recent study, political scientist Rachel Lienesch started by noting: "Prominent Democratic politicians in recent years have challenged White Americans for not doing enough to under-stand their own privilege and the racism still faced by nonwhites in America." But Lienesch's experiments showed that approach didn't endear leaders to hypothetical voters: "White Democrats and Inde-pendents express less support for a candidate who is critical of

Whites, regardless of the candidate's race." She concluded that "threats to self-esteem can undermine White support for pro-racial equity candidates and their messaging."[41]

It's important to note that Lienesch doesn't find that *promoting racial equality* reduced a politician's support. Instead, *criticizing whites for not appreciating their privilege* was problematic. That's a matter of messaging, not policy. It's also noteworthy that she focused on white *Democrats and Independents*; even *they* were put off by such messaging.

Evidence produced by social psychologist Nyla Branscombe further shows how efforts to convince people of their privilege can backfire.[42] In a paper with fellow psychologists Michael Schmitt and Kristin Schiffhauer, she tested how prompting whites to think about white privilege affected their attitudes toward race. The authors found: "White Americans randomly assigned to think about White privilege expressed greater modern racism compared to those assigned to think about White disadvantage or a race-irrelevant topic."

Still, the authors don't recommend dropping the discussion of racial privilege altogether. Instead, they concluded that emphasizing "superordinate identities"—which may be national identities— may prevent whites from responding to reminders of their racial privilege by becoming more racist. "Indeed," the authors note, "Martin Luther King Jr. employed this strategy in his attempts to influence White Americans by emphasizing the American identity that they share with Black Americans."

The reference to King is especially apt. He not only emphasized all Americans' common national identity as he crusaded for racial justice. He also never tired of declaring that everyone suffers when one group oppresses another. Nor did he cast the oppressors as beneficiaries of racial discrimination. "For it is a fact of life that you cannot keep a man down in the valley without staying down there with him" was one of his favorite lines and themes. He told audiences of all colors that racial injustice held *everyone* back, and that America could fulfill its dazzling promise only to the extent that it embraced liberty and justice for all.[43]

Upon reflection, it becomes clear that telling whites that what they have is due to their race unintentionally suggests that every gain for people of color comes at their expense. That risks reinforcing the divisive MAGA message that many liberals blame for the white working-class drift toward Trump.

Let's look at this from another perspective. How does a message of "systemic," "structural," or "institutional" racism resonate with *people of color*? A 2023 survey asked respondents which viewpoint better represented their own: Is racism "built into our society, including into its policies and institutions" or does it "come from individuals who hold racist views, not from our society and institutions"? Among non-white respondents who did not graduate from college and who classified themselves as moderate or conservative, 61 percent said individuals are to blame, versus 39 percent who faulted society and institutions. This contrasts dramatically with the views of college-educated whites who classify themselves as liberals, 82 percent of whom faulted society and institutions rather than people who hold racist views.

These numbers are all the more arresting since over three quarters of non-white Americans who lack a college degree classify themselves as moderate or conservative, and only about one quarter of non-white Americans have a college degree. The data reveal a yawning gap between the mindsets of people of color and the well-educated white progressives who predominate in educational institutions and among Democratic Party operatives.

In his report on these findings, political scientist Ruy Teixeira argued that the institutional racism perspective "held by current Democratic Party orthodoxy" helps account for the alarming slippage in support for the Democrats among people of color in recent years. According to Teixeira, that trend "is a direct threat to the massive margins Democrats need to maintain among nonwhite voters to achieve victory."[44]

The danger Teixeira flags is real. In a November 2023 CNN/SSRS poll, 46 percent of Hispanics and 23 percent of Blacks said they intended to vote for Trump; men of color overall split 49-46 for the Republican. Neither rising African American and Hispanic incomes nor Biden's exemplary record on civil rights is arresting the movement of non-whites to the Republicans.[45]

There are institutions, such as unfair sentencing guidelines, that lead to racist outcomes regardless of the intent of the people charged with enforcing the rules. But enlisting more whites—and non-whites—in the struggle for justice and boosting the popularity of anti-racist politicians may require laying blame squarely on those who deserve it—not on "America," structures that can't be readily comprehended and changed, or dark forces that supposedly lurk in the hearts of the ethnic majority.

A more effective approach—whether we're talking about politicians in search of votes or teachers forming kids' hearts and minds in the classroom—would treat the nation as a majestic whole rather than a patchwork of contending ethnic groups. It would cast all Americans as the inheritors of a splendid tradition of fighting injustice, an effort that has wrought untold progress even as its work remains woefully incomplete. It would characterize people of color as authors rather than casualties of the American story. It would portray the fight for justice as a heroic task to be joined with relish in pursuit of a still greater nation rather than a chore to be taken up as penance for past crimes.

It would *elevate*, not *chastise*. It would aim to *improve*, not *redress*.

It would be aggressively inclusive—just what liberals *say* we wish to be. To that end, it would offer a pantheon of enticing white anti-racist heroes along with the heroes of color with whom they fought and continue to labor today.

There is no end of candidate characters to be featured in that story. Why shouldn't they figure prominently in schools' curricula as well as liberal politicians' speeches?

Alongside titans like Frederick Douglass and Rosa Parks, we could include an inspiring character like Cassius Clay, the crusading 19th-century planter, politician, and publisher of the perfectly named *True American*, a radical abolitionist newspaper. Clay grew up on the sprawling Whitehall Plantation in Kentucky. But after attending a speech as a student at Yale by the abolitionist William Lloyd Garrison, Clay resolved to attack the institution that had made his father rich.

After freeing the enslaved people on his plantation and setting about his work as an abolitionist, he suffered multiple attacks by racists and always came out on top. While Clay engaged in a political debate in 1843, a hired assassin shot him in the chest. Clay pulled out his Bowie knife and sliced off his assailant's nose before tossing him into a nearby embankment. Six years later, while making a speech urging abolition, he was set upon by six brothers who stabbed, beat, and shot him. Somehow, he fought off the entire bunch and, brandishing his trusted Bowie knife, slayed one of the would-be assassins.

Lincoln made Clay ambassador to Russia, but before he could take up his post the Civil War started, and the president needed him at home. There were no federal troops in Washington, D.C. at the time, so Clay organized 300 volunteers to guard the White House in the event of Confederate attack. After federal troops arrived, Clay set sail for Russia.

Once in St. Petersburg, Clay secured Tsar Alexander II's agreement to aid the Union in case the British or French entered the war on the Confederate side. The tsar sent a fleet to New York harbor, which might have dissuaded the French from siding with the Confederacy.

Lincoln recalled Clay in 1862 to command Union armies, but Clay said he would take the job only if Lincoln freed the slaves. Shortly thereafter, Lincoln issued the Emancipation Proclamation.

After the war, President Ulysses S. Grant sent Clay back to Russia, where he negotiated the purchase of Alaska. Upon returning home, Clay attacked the power of the railroad magnates and other robber barons and installed cannons in his home and office for protection. In 1890, at 80 years old, he was elected president of Kentucky's Constitutional Convention. He finally gave up the ghost 12 years later and was said to have expired of "general exhaustion." He left behind two daughters, each a pioneering activist for women's rights.[46]

If you've never heard of him but his name sounds familiar, it's because his fellow Kentuckian, Odessa Clay, named her boy after him. He later came to call himself Muhammad Ali.

Here's another interesting set of facts: Nearly 100k white Southerners volunteered for the Union Army. The First Alabama Cavalry subverted Confederate communications, marched with William Tecumseh Sherman's Union Armies throughout the South, and flanked him as he seized Atlanta.[47]

These are stories that inspire and sway. They're not about abstract, impersonal "structures," "systems," or "institutions," which leave just about everybody but Marxist sociologists cold. They have flesh-and-blood heroes and villains. Consistently weaving such stories into our political messaging and school curricula would undermine the MAGA narrative that casts liberals as disuniters of the nation who are bent on breaking the country into antagonistic racial groups.

To be sure, Joe Biden doesn't tell the forlorn story of white supremacy ruling America. Nor does he talk of intergenerational guilt. When asked shortly after arriving in office if he thought America is a racist country, Biden replied: "I don't think America's racist, but I think the overhang from all of the Jim Crow, and before that slavery, have had a cost, and we have to deal with it." Striking the same tone in response to a similar question, Vice President Harris stated: "No, I don't think America is a racist country. But we also do have to speak truth about the history of racism in our country and its existence today...These are issues that we must confront, and it doesn't—it does not help to heal our country to unify us as a people to ignore the realities of that."[48]

Those statements are fine as far as they go, and they might seem to strike the right balance. Yet questions remain: Are Democratic leaders wrapping their aspirations in a narrative that forcefully conveys both their contempt for those who would block Black advancement and their own unqualified love of country? Are they consistently justifying their calls for progress by spelling out how overcoming racism is imperative to *American greatness*? Doing so is vital to maximizing Black enthusiasm and turnout for the Democrats, undermining Trump's ethnonational narrative, giving all Americans a role in the effort, and convincing voters outside the progressive base of the Democrats' unconditional patriotism.

Given what we've learned about public sentiment and the liberals' political assets and liabilities, how may we answer the question posed by Thomas Edsall of the *New York Times*: "How should Democrats deal with the [Republicans'] 'weaponization' of critical race theory?"[49]

At the root of the problem with Democratic messaging is party leaders' apparent—and mistaken—belief that the Republicans hold the advantage in the culture wars and that the best thing liberals can do is steer the conversation to the economy. They are also driven by an obsessive risk aversion that marks low-dominance behavior. As we saw earlier, fixation on not rousing the MAGA base guides the Democrats' strategy. It leaves the progressive base uninspired and voters more generally unimpressed with Democratic leaders' courage and commitment to principle.

Let's look at how these dynamics played out in the responses of two prominent Democrats to Glenn Youngkin's victory over Democrat Terry McAuliffe in Virginia's November 2021 governor's race. Virginia went for Biden by 10 points in 2020 and is normally solid blue, so Youngkin's win over a successful former Democratic governor rightly set off alarm bells among Democrats. Youngkin had pulled ahead of McAuliffe in the race after the Democrat said, "I don't think parents should be telling schools what they should teach" in a debate. Youngkin spent the rest of the campaign capitalizing on that gaffe, and the data showed that he won on his promise to give parents more say in school curricula and his criticism of teaching critical race theory (CRT) in the schools.[50]

We'll start with Rep. Pramila Jayapal, the Seattle congresswoman who chairs the Congressional Progressive Caucus. In her explanation for the election's outcome, she stated:

> Every attack that I saw against Terry McAuliffe did not say, Congress hasn't passed the infrastructure bill. It has to do with education and parents. And I think what we have to do is, we have to get real relief to parents who are struggling, to families who are struggling. And that is the best case for why we have to pass both of these bills, the infrastructure bill and the Build Back Better bill. And that's what I'm hearing from all my colleagues as well.[51]

So there you have it: The stalled spending bills had nothing to do with the Democrats' defeat, so the key to winning is for the Democrats to—you guessed it—pass said spending bills. And as usual among Democratic leaders, Jayapal assumed that the party would be rewarded for delivering "relief" to those ever-"struggling" families.

Jayapal was no doubt right to say her colleagues shared her view. Democratic leaders typically treat cultural controversy like kryptonite and dive for cover in economic-policy pablum—even when it's obvious that people are voting on culture and not economic policy. If you're afraid to engage on culture and all you know how to do is offer material benefits, doing the same thing over and over again and expecting a different result—the definition of insanity—is all that's left as a course of action.

Now to President Biden. What did he have to say about the Democrats' abysmal performance?[52] At a press conference the day after Youngkin won, a reporter asked: "As leader of the Democratic Party, how much responsibility do you take for the dismal results in Virginia and beyond last night?" Biden responded:

> What I do know is—I do know that people want us to get things done. They want us to get things done. And that's why I'm continuing to push very hard for the Democratic Party to move along and pass my infrastructure bill and my Build Back Better bill. I think if we—look, think about what we—what we're talking about here. People are upset and uncertain about a lot of things—from COVID, to school, to jobs, to a whole range of things, and the cost of a gallon of gasoline. And so, if I'm able to pass—sign into law my Build Back Better initiative, I'm in a position where you're going to see a lot of those things ameliorated quickly and swiftly. And so that has to be done.

Another reporter followed up: "What should Democrats possibly do differently to avoid similar losses in November [2022], especially as Republicans are now successfully running on culture-war issues and false claims about critical race theory?" Biden responded:

> Well, I think that we should produce for the American people. Look, one of the things that is important to understand: If—if they pass my legislation, we're going to be able to reduce the price—people are going to see a reduction in the price of the drugs they—they have to get because Medicare will be able to negotiate and lower the price of drugs...They're going to see that, you know, they'll get tax breaks—I mean, genuine tax breaks. Look, people—people need a little breathing room. They're overwhelmed. And what happened was—think we have to just produce results for them to change their standard of living and give them a little more breathing room.

Undaunted by the president's stonewalling, still another reporter pressed the question: "Can you just—what's your message, though, for Democratic voters, especially Black voters who see

Republicans running on race, education—lying about critical race theory—and they're worried that Democrats don't have an effective way to push back on that?" Again ignoring the question, Biden nattered on about his legislative program and finished with:

> Look, I just think people are at a point—and it's understandable—where there's a whole lot of confusion. Everything from, "Are you going to ever get COVID under control?" to "Are my kids going to be in school? Are they going to be able to stay in school?"; to "Whether or not I'm going to get a tax break that allows me to be able to pay for the needs of my kids and my family?" And they're all things that we're—that we're going to—that I'm running on—that we'll run on. And I think we'll do fine.

Values? Inspiration? Confidence? Let 'em eat asphalt instead.

Top Democrats have been nothing if not consistent, skirting CRT and practically every other hot-button cultural issue except abortion. They think they're dodging bullets, but they're being shot full of holes. Rather than tell their own American story, they're leaving their vilest opponents free to link patriotism to stripping constitutional rights while casting the left as the true enemies of free speech.

Biden has left Democratic office-seekers from Tampa to Tucson without a leg to stand on as Republicans pound them with charges that their party's leaders are in thrall to a leftist fringe that regards racial oppression as the entirety of the American experience. He has left DeSantis and Ted ("the left hates America") Cruz in charge of the cultural colosseum, waving their book bans and crowing about their "values."[53] To Thomas Edsall's question—"How should Democrats deal with the 'weaponization' of critical race theory?"—Biden's answer has been to bear down harder on paving roads and controlling the prices of Valium and Viagra. Such avoidance is pure low-dominance politics.

Underlying this behavior is the assumption that culture is *the Republicans'* terrain; that's where they have the folks on *their* side. But all the data we've seen shows how erroneous that thinking is.

It doesn't hold in Virginia any more than it does nationally. A survey conducted shortly after Youngkin's election showed that Virginians overwhelmingly supported (63-33 percent) continuing to teach about how racism affects American society.[54]

How could Biden talk about culture, in this case race, in a way that captures his combination of guts, liberal passion, and distance from the excesses of the "Just America" story? Biden, after all, *does* have guts; he *is* a passionate progressive; and he *isn't* a woke extremist. The question is how he can convey those realities in his messaging. How could he tell his own national-democratic story in response to questions on race?

What could Biden say specifically in response to a question on CRT? How could he—and other leading Democrats—appeal to Americans' patriotism, longing for strong leadership, and progressive spirit? In Bidenesque language, it might sound something like this:

Critical race theory? Not sure what the hell it even is. I think the Republicans made it up to divide our great nation. But I can tell you this: If by "CRT" you mean America is a racist nation, I'll tell you it's a pile of crap. Our country has a horrific history of racial oppression, but overcoming it is a big part of what Americans are all about. From enslaving fellow Americans to electing my old boss—*twice, and by absolute majorities*—as head of the American tribe. From the idiocy of Jim Crow to the brilliance of Justice Ketanji Brown Jackson—*that's* America's destiny, folks, and it's where we're headed under us Democrats.

But if by "critical race theory" you mean teaching our kids the truth about slavery, how can a patriot be against that? Telling the truth about ourselves is the American way. If you don't face up to your mistakes, you can't up your game. Learning the whole truth about our past helped make our country great and makes it greater still today.

I wanna learn about great Americans like Cassius Clay. He was the old Kentucky planter from back in the 1800s. If his name rings a bell, it's because another great Kentuckian, Odessa Clay, named her son after him, and he would later rename himself Muhammad Ali, the greatest fighter of all time. The old Cassius Clay freed the slaves on his father's plantation and spent his life trying to end slavery. Defenders of slavery shot, beat, and stabbed him. He not only survived, he kicked their asses every time. Kentuckians elected him head of their Constitutional Convention when he was 80 years old. Not a bad age for a leader to be. He kept fighting the good fight until he died at 92.

He and Abraham Lincoln and Frederick Douglass and the 360,000 Black and white soldiers who died in the Civil War to free their fellow Americans from bondage—these are *my* political ancestors. If you're an American patriot, you'll consider them *yours*, too.

So if what you mean by "critical race theory" is telling the story of all the American heroes who fought to free our country from slavery and racism, then hell yeah, *put me down as a critical race theorist!*

Now, it's not hard to imagine what the typical low-dominance, risk-allergic liberal mind will think of such a statement. That mind is now scurrying to calculate—and no doubt overestimating—the number of voters on the left who will be offended if the president denies that America is a racist nation and fetes the country's progress. And then there's the panic over Biden calling himself a critical race theorist. Good Lord, the no-risk-please liberal mind can see it now: FOX News playing the last phrase (*put me down as a critical race theorist!*) over and over again.

But here you'd overlook that there are so many provocative lines that even Tucker Carlson would have a hard time fixing on just one or two. He'd be so frothed up over Biden hailing Justice Jackson (who

Tucker is sure is a groomer) while saluting whites (who Tucker is sure are *his*) for fighting slavery that he'd never be able to focus. And his whole research apparatus and his old team at FOX would be scrambling to figure out who that white Cassius Clay was, anyway.

In other words, Biden would be *owning them* for a change.

The liberal, risk-averse mind is also underestimating the confidence Biden would inspire among hardcore lefties for uttering *put me down as a critical race theorist!* The same could be said for phrases such as *a horrific history of racial oppression, the idiocy of Jim Crow*, and *enslaving fellow Americans*. This is harder, more evocative language than Biden or most other Democratic leaders typically use in their condemnations of racism. The skeptic is also underestimating the force that *the brilliance of Justice Ketanji Brown Jackson*—is there a more uniquely *American* name?—could have in the ears and hearts of African Americans.

These are phrases people *feel*, not just hear. This is the kind of language that earns *loyalty*, not just wan nods of approval before attention turns back to social media chatter about the state of play on *Succession* and *XO, Kitty*.

Perhaps our risk-averse critic is also underestimating the goodwill Biden would generate among the vast patriotic majority by celebrating the staggering scope of progress and dismissing the canard about America's racist essence. And that skeptic might be overlooking how appealing—even liberating—it would feel to many whites to be overtly included in the struggle for justice.

Finally, our fretting doubter isn't accounting for the benefits to Biden of finally saying something provocative that attracts attention.

Presidential messaging is especially important, but every day, in offices high and low throughout the land, liberals have the opportunity to up our nationalism game—and we are blowing it.

Consider the way the government of North Carolina justified its decision to stop—at long last—issuing specialty license plates bearing the Confederate flag. The plates were sponsored by the Sons of

Confederate Veterans, who protested the ruling, claiming it infringed on their speech rights. In response, the North Carolina Transportation Department sent the organization a letter stating that it would "no longer issue or renew specialty license plates bearing the Confederate battle flag or any variation of that flag" because the plates "have the potential to offend those who view them."[55]

How pathetic is that for a justification? This reasoning basically equates the Confederate flag—the American swastika—with racy words or profanity. Liberals have been tiptoeing around the delicate sensibilities of the Civil War cult since Robert E. Lee surrendered to General Ulysses S. Grant. Why not instead say that the state would "no longer issue or renew the plates bearing the Confederate flag because it symbolizes an act of treason against the United States of America that led to the deaths of 620 thousand American citizens and the ruination of many parts of our nation"?

Wouldn't that be a bolder, more patriotic response? Wouldn't it leave liberals looking less like overly sensitive suppressors of free expression and more like defenders of the country? Wouldn't fighting the right-wing speech police—and reducing their numbers in office—profit from wrapping the liberal case in a compelling national story that casts the far right's antics as threats to the oneness of the nation rather than just affronts to our delicate sensibilities?[56]

In the following pages, we'll turn from racial to socioeconomic equality. Again, we'll dig into the evidence to grasp how Democrats can craft a genuinely inclusive message that the majority, including working-class people, finds compelling.

20. Grappling with Class
in the Nation's Story

If you wander through rural areas and small towns where Trump polls highest, you'll see American flags all over the place. If you chat with the folks who fly them, you might run into some bigots. But you'll also find that many of the people who love Trump's Make America Great Again slogan don't just understand it as code for Make America White Again. You might even meet recent immigrants who are all in for Trump.

Farm bankruptcies soared during Trump's time in office, with little effect on support for him or his policies in rural areas. In a 2019 survey of Midwestern farmers, 76 percent agreed that farmers would bear the brunt of China's retaliation for Trump's tariffs, 62 percent said his trade policies would cost them markets, and just 14 percent thought their farm operations would be better a year hence.

And 56 percent supported Trump's tariffs.[57]

How can that possibly be? A week before the November 2020 election, in which three quarters of farmers would vote for Trump, Daryl Haack, an Iowa soybean and corn farmer, told Rebecca Beitsch, a reporter for *The Hill*: "I think most farmers realize [Trump' tariffs] needed to happen. China was taking and is still taking advantage of us." Tim Burrack, another Iowa farmer of soybeans and corn, said: "I've lost so much money under [Trump] it's really a crime, and COVID really took another chunk out of me, but I'm voting for Trump because I'm worried about the country." Jeff Samuelson, who raises pigs and grows corn in Iowa, estimated that he had lost $75–100k over the past year. He offered: "I hope that whoever is elected president understands agriculture has a vital role in the national economy and that there are a lot of jobs that are tied back to farming. But I'm not selfish enough to vote for someone who's just going to be 'good for the farmers'."

What these folks are saying, if any Democrat bothered to listen, is that they feel they're taking a hit for Team USA. It's rare for most liberals even to consider this possibility. Pam Johnson, Biden's surrogate at a Farm Foundation debate on the eve of the 2020 election, said she "cannot figure out why someone would vote against their own business livelihood." Reflecting on farmers who say they oppose "socialism" but still take government subsidies, she opined with more than a hint of sarcasm: "It's socialism if it's the other guy getting the money, but if it's me getting the money, that's OK?"[58]

Now there's a winning formula for appealing to American farmers: Don't make the case for free trade based on national interests or the free-market economics that most Americans, especially these folks, manifestly cherish. Tell 'em they're hypocritical, closet socialists instead—and none too bright, either.

These people know full well they often vote against their economic interests, just as I know I vote against mine. Like other overeducated, overpaid whites, I stand to benefit more from regressive tax cuts than from Medicaid expansion. Yet I believe the Democrats serve my country better than the Republicans do, so I vote Democratic. Why should I assume these farmers are any different?

Fighting economic inequality is a top priority for the Democratic Party, but it's not for most Americans. In a 2020 Pew survey, 61 percent agreed that "there's too much economic inequality in the country these days," yet just 42 percent said reducing it should be a "top priority" for the government. That's fewer than those who favored prioritizing "dealing with terrorism" (65 percent), "reducing gun violence" (58 percent), and "addressing climate change" (49 percent).[59]

To dig deeper, let's examine people's values by party and class. A survey item from the 2020 ANES states: "This country would be better off if we worried less about how equal people are."[60] The first column of numbers in Table 20.1 shows the percentage of people who disagree with the statement.

	"This country would be better off if we worried less about how equal people are" (percent who "disagree somewhat" or "strongly disagree")	"It is not really that big a problem if some people have more of a chance than others" (percent who "disagree somewhat" or "strongly disagree")
College-educated Democrats	84	84
Non-college Democrats	66	70
Non-college Republicans	26	38
Non-college Independents	44	45

Table 20.1. Valuation of Equality, by Class and Political Party, 2020

College-educated Democrats definitely care about inequality. A whopping 84 percent do *not* think the country would be better off if we worried less about it. Non-college Democrats are concerned about inequality, too, though at a lower level (66 percent). Among non-Democrats, however, the numbers are far lower. Just 26 percent of non-college Republicans and 44 percent of non-college Independents disagree with the statement.

The second column of numbers shows how people feel about inequality of *opportunity*, not just outcomes. Again, well-educated Democrats care, and how: 84 percent *are* bothered by some people having more of a chance than others. But we see much less concern among those who *have lesser* opportunities. Among non-college respondents, 70 percent of Democrats, 38 percent of Republicans, and 45 percent of Independents are concerned about some having more of a chance than others.

It's evident that privilege vexes privileged Democrats more than everyone else. We want others to have a better shake, and working toward that goal is a moral imperative for us. We also assume that those without the advantages we enjoy will reward us in elections for pursuing their interests. After all, if *our* privilege bothers *us*, surely it must grate on *them* even more.

But the data show nothing of the sort.

In her magisterial political ethnography of small-town Louisiana, Arlie Hochschild reports that libertarian beliefs and an idealized view of capitalism underlie white working-class thinking. She finds that the folks have little appetite for class-war rhetoric since they see big earners as worthy objects of emulation rather than greedy exploiters and ripe targets for tax hikes. Above all, people fear having to work for the government or rely on assistance programs. For that reason, they back just about any measure that will attract private investment into their communities, including tax breaks for big (and often polluting) energy companies that come at the expense of schools and public services. The folks do dislike their tax dollars flowing to supposedly indolent people. But deep attachment to self-reliance and a jagged sense of fairness appear to drive political opinion more obviously than racism per se.[61]

In *The Politics of Resentment*, political scientist Katherine Cramer explores the political views and values of small-town and rural people a thousand miles due north of where Hochschild conducted her research. A Wisconsin native and University of Wisconsin professor, Cramer relied on personal chats with folks at coffee klatches (Wisconsinese for get-togethers over cups of joe) in the Badger State. She wanted to better understand the rise of Scott Walker, the right-wing governor from 2011 to 2019. In her account, the objects of resentment were urbanites, particularly state-government employees in Milwaukee and Madison who rural and small-town dwellers see as pampered at taxpayer expense.

While African Americans in Milwaukee are potential targets of resentment, racism doesn't figure prominently in her account. Her research extended back to the time of Obama's rise, and at first, she encountered support for him. Many people believed that his being Black made him an outsider to power like they felt themselves to be. After some of Obama's statements seemed to show that he didn't understand folks like them very well, they cooled on him. While not ruling out racism as a possible motivator of political behavior, Cramer didn't report racial animus—or even serious discomfort with a Black man being president. Nor did she recount people feeling that the Democrats had abandoned their pocketbook concerns.

But Cramer did locate a deep sense of community, patriotism, and personal independence. She also found that some people were impressed with Walker's boldness and apparent commitment to principle. One woman told her: "I give Walker a lot of credit for standing up for what he believes and saying this is what I told you I was going to do and this is what I have done. Now he may not have gone about it in the real, ethical right way, but at least he made an effort . . . so many of these governors . . . are wishy-washy, is what they are."[62]

In *Broke and Patriotic*, sociologist Francesco Duina explores how poor people in Montana and Alabama view themselves and their country.[63] He aims to understand what some well-educated liberals regard as a paradox: How can people be poor and love their country, too? Those Duina interviewed all struggled with health or financial problems. Despite their circumstances, they're proud and patriotic and place a premium on hard work, freedom, and independence.

A 45-year-old white veteran commented on what values he wanted to pass on to his kids: "I think we really need to get back to teaching our young about taking pride in our country, taking pride in themselves, taking pride in accomplishments . . . taking pride in working hard."

In response to a question about how he viewed America, a middle-aged Black man said: "I think America is the last best hope of man on earth. . . . We try to uphold the principles of liberty and freedom to the best of our abilities. . . . It's an exceptional country because nobody does what we do. There's no country as diverse as America." An unemployed African American woman in her forties answered a question about the connection she felt to her country: "[F]or me to give up hope on the country in which I live in is almost to give up hope for self. So, I gotta keep the light burning for me and for my country, or I'm gonna be dark."

On inequality, a white man in his thirties said: "Well, there's always inequality. Show me a country that's equal in the world . . . We do pretty well in this country; like I'm not doing too bad and I'm living outside [laughs]!" When asked about whether it was unfair that the wealthy had so much while people like her had so little, a white woman in her 70s offered a response that echoed the answers Duina found among many others: "Those people with the money have earned it. So, what do we want them to do, give it away? And there are a lot of those people with money that are giving it away." In response to the author's query about whether the government bore responsibility for his problems, a young drug addict on disability said: "No. Get your ass up and go get a job and man up . . . that's your fault, not the government's fault. Everywhere is hiring every day. Anybody can get a job anywhere . . . I've been in pain . . . but it's my fault cause I chose that life."

In *The Forgotten*, former *Boston Globe* editor Ben Bradlee Jr. recounts conversations with residents of a county in Pennsylvania that voted heavily for Trump in 2016. A devout Christian woman who grew up as a Democrat in Detroit but became a strong Trump supporter explained Trump's appeal like this: "Trump was very aggressive when he dealt with his Republican opponents . . . He had balls . . . Trump was successful, and he wasn't afraid to speak his mind and tell people what he thought." She liked that he "brushed off any sort of incoming fire he encountered . . . and he always gave better than he got."[64]

These findings match what I find when chatting with working-class friends and acquaintances who voted for Trump. They're also consistent with what I hear when I'm mixing it up with old friends from back home in Kentucky, as well as new friends I meet during dive-bar crawls near home and in the small towns I drive through on red-state road trips.

I wouldn't necessarily expect everyone to have their beef with the Democrats on the tip of their tongues. But if the standard story were valid, I would expect *some* of these folks to complain about how liberals don't care about their wages or billionaire tax cheats anymore. I would expect *some* to say that the Democratic Party of their parents' or grandparents' day used to protect their labor unions and provide services, but now they don't.

But I never hear such complaints.

Now, I *do* hear people characterize the Democrats as wimps, socialists, and weak patriots. Some say that the liberals don't care about freedom—including freedom of speech, not just the right to bear arms—as much as they do. And I do encounter resentment over liberals thinking that people like them are bigots.

For insights into their mindsets, we can turn to two classics on the way Americans think about politics. One was penned by Louis Hartz in the 1950s. According to Hartz, from our origins as a nation, Americans have been wedded to the tenets expressed by the 17th-century English philosopher John Locke. In part because Americans never had feudalism and hereditary aristocracy, Locke's philosophy—which treated property rights, freedom of mobility, and individual choice as natural parts of the human condition and the key requisites of political liberty—became the basis of our political instincts and values.[65] It was a phenomenon also noted with singular genius by Alexis de Tocqueville, the sojourning French aristocrat whose 1840 book, *Democracy in America*, continues to read like a guide to Americans' political manners and mentalities today.[66]

Americans have a mile-wide libertarian streak rooted in the country's history and founding principles. It's more pronounced among Americans than people from other countries. One way it's expressed is in the importance people attach to freedom relative to other values.

In its most recent wave, the World Values Survey includes two relevant questions. The first asks: "Which is more important, freedom or equality?" The second asks: "Which is more important, freedom or security?" Table 20.2 provides the data for the first question; Table 20.3 shows those for the second.

"Most people consider both freedom and equality to be important, but if you had to choose between them, which one would you consider more important?" (percent of respondents)		
Country	Freedom	Equality
United States	**78**	**21**
Netherlands	69	19
UK	69	29
Germany	64	31
Canada	64	36
Japan	57	34
Brazil	46	50

Table 20.2. Valuation of Freedom versus Equality in Select Countries

"Most people consider both freedom and security to be important, but if you had to choose between them, which one would you consider more important?" (percent of respondents)		
Country	Freedom	Security
United States	**70**	**28**
UK	54	44
Canada	49	51
Germany	43	53
Netherlands	41	48
Brazil	24	72
Japan	14	82

Table 20.3. Valuation of Freedom versus Security in Select Countries

Americans' famed (or infamous, depending on your perspective) preference for liberty shows in the numbers. On freedom versus equality, the Dutch and British are in league with the United States, though not quite as strongly for freedom. On freedom versus security, no one comes close.[67]

The evidence might seem like a counsel of despair for those who support progressive reforms, but that need not be the case. During the Progressive Era (1890s-1920s) and the times of the New Deal (1930s) and the Great Society (1960s), a critical mass of Americans supported massive government spending programs. Americans aren't fundamentally different people than we used to be.

That directs us to the way liberals frame their economic policies. With only a bit of exaggeration, we could say that the party's central message to working-class Americans since the onset of Obama's presidency has been: *The American Dream is dying—especially for people like you. The only way you can revive it is by accepting government aid. And if you're not smart enough to realize how desperately you need it, just wait until you get old and sick and the Republicans won't cover your preexisting conditions!*

It's all about what the government gives you, not what you have earned with your tax dollars—and helping poor folks to boot. It's all about what your country—or, rather, your government—can do for you, not what you can do for your country.

The Democrats' messaging isn't just politically tone-deaf; it's also largely out of sync with reality. Ever since Franklin Roosevelt powered Social Security into existence in 1935, the Democrats have wisely framed it as something we get for our own contributions rather than as the tax-financed government support scheme that it actually is. That might have helped make it the most popular and politically durable component of the American welfare state.

But the Democrats have largely taken the opposite tack with Obamacare—even though the program is *not* government-financed healthcare. Rather, it was the product of a tough deal with private insurance companies to furnish coverage at a much fairer price. The program does include help for those who can't afford healthcare on their own, and there is an individual mandate. But that mandate was demanded by the insurance companies as part of the deal to keep prices affordable, *not* a government scheme to make people buy government insurance.

The Democrats have largely allowed the Republicans to get away with casting Obamacare as government health insurance with a government mandate. That's the scheme Bernie Sanders might have wanted, but he never got it (which is part of why Bernie keeps howling).

Social Security is, in fact, rather "socialist"; Obamacare decidedly isn't. Who knew?

Our messaging isn't just patronizing and mindless of Americans' libertarian instincts. It also fails to tap the immense potential inherent in people's better natures. The Democrats seem so convinced of Americans' pure egotism that even Bernie Sanders frames his pitch in terms of the welfare of the "middle class." He speaks less often of the poor, who are really and laudably the main objects of his concern. Nor do he or most other Democratic leaders typically cast aiding the poor as a heroic, patriotic endeavor, a way of showing the world what America is made of.

Another losing component of liberal messaging is the notion that poverty and prosperity are a function of structural privilege. Current-day progressives roll our knowing eyes at the "Horatio Alger myth." Alger's novels depicted poor kids making their way to the middle class through hard work and morally exemplary behavior. Rather than cheer Americans' affection for tales of American pluck and exceptionalism, we often treat them as the one-percenters' tools for brainwashing people into working harder for less—and blaming only themselves if they don't succeed.

Liberal elites' rhetorical contempt for a bootstrap mentality must look like a particularly rich pose to working-class voters who strive to get ahead. After all, it often comes from meritocrats who have been working 12-hour days since college to secure their tickets to the slopes at Vail and send their kids to Penn.

I'm acutely aware of the role that unearned privilege can play in getting ahead. I might be pumping fuel into farm equipment back in my native Kentucky rather than teaching at Berkeley if I weren't blessed with parents who worked hard to create every opportunity a kid could ever have. And I can hardly argue against affirmative action since Ivy League schools like to boast that they have students from all fifty states—and I was Kentucky 1980 in the entering class at Cornell. There, I spent part of my first year in a remedial writing program after failing the first essay assignment in world history. (At this point in the book I'll understand if you think the program didn't quite take).

But I also know how hard my unlettered, fatherless father worked as he rose from deep poverty to gas station attendant to builder of a retail shop, the revenue from which paid for my higher education. He also financed the college educations of the children of his warehouse workers, who rose to join the middle class without having college degrees themselves. My Mom went back to work as a nurse on a geriatric ward the month I started college to cover my tuition. Many of my maniacally hard-working students and their parents, some first-generation Americans, have similar stories.

Denial of the importance of individual effort isn't just disingenuous; it's out of step with how Americans think. According to the GSS survey for 2018, 73 percent of respondents, including 80 percent of non-college whites and 68 percent of non-college Blacks, said "hard work" rather than "lucky breaks or help from other people" was the key to "getting ahead."[68]

Americans stand out. In a 2019 Pew survey, respondents were asked whether they agreed that "success in life is pretty much determined by forces outside their control." Sixty-seven percent of Americans disagreed with that statement, compared to 55 percent of Brits, 41 percent of French people, and 39 percent of Germans.[69]

Hard work is a core American value. In a 2023 *Wall Street Journal*/NORC poll, 94 percent said that they regarded "hard work" as very or somewhat important—more than those who felt the same way about tolerance for others (90 percent), money (90 percent), community involvement (80 percent), or religion (60 percent).[70]

Opportunities for social mobility might be less favorable than many people think.[71] So what? Does marinating in that fact and trying to "educate" people to believe it really make them like and identify with the Democrats? Does it help us enlist their support for reforms that will propel greater social mobility?

Belief in the possibility of moving up by one's own efforts *is* the American worldview. If mindful of people's attachment to self-reliance—as well as their patriotism and capacity for transcending self-interest—might the Democrats not enhance the popularity of our programs? If our rhetoric relentlessly tethered the quest for equality to national greatness while appealing to people's charitable spirits and natural hunger for optimism, might we not stand a better chance come even-year Novembers?

Let's look at how the three most popular Democratic presidents of the 20th century made their pitches for justice. Alone among Democratic presidential candidates over the past century, two of them (Franklin Roosevelt and Bill Clinton) won the white working-class vote and the presidency twice, and the third (John Kennedy) came within a hair's breadth of winning the white working class the one time he ran. Each was also wildly popular with African Americans.

Roosevelt spoke of his economic reforms in a nationalist idiom less commonly heard from current-day Democratic leaders. In a 1936 speech given shortly before his landslide reelection, here is how the president touted his New Deal tax reforms:

First, we gave a credit to earned income—that is, income from personal work or service—thus substantially reducing taxes paid by the working citizen. Wasn't that the American thing to do?

Second, we decreased the tax rates on small corporations. Wasn't that the American thing to do?

Third, we increased the taxes paid by individuals in the higher brackets—those of $50,000 a year. Wasn't that the American thing to do?

Fourth, we increased still further, more steeply, the taxes paid by individuals in the highest brackets—those with incomes over one million dollars. Wasn't that the American thing to do?

Fifth, we increased the tax on very large estates. Wasn't that the American thing to do?

...Once more this year we must choose between democracy in taxation and special privilege in taxation. Are you willing to turn the control of the Nation's taxes back to special privilege?

I know the American answer to that question.[72]

This was stock rhetoric for Roosevelt, who justified his policies in terms of national traditions, interests, and values. It enabled him to enact the deep reforms needed to restore the economy and reduce inequality. It also helped him put down threats to democracy, which were legion in his time as they are in ours. The fact that he was authoring the story as he went—the United States in fact had little tradition of the radical economic measures he pursued—testified to his appreciation of the power of narrative and *Americanizing* his every reform.

Roosevelt's rhetoric also showcased his high-dominance approach. He didn't fret about whether his reforms were *really* the "American" thing to do. He *made* them the American thing to do.

He *led.*

His pitch for economic justice is often famed for its class-warfare rhetoric, but there was more to it than that. In addition to casting his quest for greater equality in terms of Americanism, he made everyone feel like a giver, a producer, and a promoter of the common good rather than just a recipient of government benefits. In the same speech, he asserted:

> I have spoken in Chicago and elsewhere of the simple fact that the overwhelming majority of business men are like the rest of us. Most of us whether we earn wages, run farms or businesses, are in one sense business men. All they seek and all we seek is fair play based on the greater good of the greater numbers—fair play on the part of the government in levying taxes on us and fair play on the part of government in protecting us against abuses.

Imagine that: calling wage earners *businessmen* instead of *struggling working families.*

Indeed, Roosevelt relentlessly tied the fate of all classes together while treating all Americans as makers of a single national destiny. The oneness of the nation, along with the indivisibility of democracy and freedom from want, were staples in his messaging.[73]

John Kennedy also tethered his progressive policies to national greatness and the heritage of self-reliance. As his administration drew up plans for what became the Great Society programs under Lyndon Johnson, Kennedy initiated a drive for much more extensive government involvement in healthcare. Republicans condemned his efforts as a quest to "socialize medicine" (sound familiar?). In a May 1962 rally at Madison Square Garden on behalf of the legislation that would lay the groundwork for Medicare, Kennedy defended the measure and pushed back against its detractors like this:

> And then I read [from the bill's opponents] that this bill will sap the individual self-reliance of Americans. I can't imagine anything worse, or anything better, to sap someone's self-reliance, than to be sick, alone, broke—or to have saved for a lifetime and put it out in a week, two weeks, a month, two months...We are concerned with the progress of this country, and those who say that what we are now talking about spoils our great pioneer heritage should remember that the West was settled with two great

actions by the National Government: one, in President Lincoln's administration, when he gave a homestead to everyone who went West, and in 1862 he set aside Government property to build our land grant colleges. This cooperation between an alert and progressive citizenry and a progressive Government is what has made this country great.[74]

About a year after Kennedy gave that speech and four months before his assassination, he greeted a delegation of American Legion Boys State and Boys Nation programs at the White House. It's the kind of thing presidents do routinely, and it's unlikely that the kids Kennedy met made any lasting impression on him. But it did leave one, a 16-year-old Arkansan who idolized the president, inspired beyond measure and dead set on pursuing a career in public service. Thirty years later, he would hang the photo of his handshake with Kennedy in the White House.[75]

Bill Clinton's first policy love—and he *really* loved policies—was healthcare, and immediately after arriving in office he launched his effort to universalize coverage. Strident, united Republican opposition blocked him. It took another 17 years of spade work and a different Democratic president to bring universal healthcare to the United States. After he failed to realize this ambition, Clinton turned to poverty reduction, where he had better luck. Child poverty fell from 28 to 18 percent during his tenure. The overall poverty rate fell from 15 to 11 percent, the steepest decline of any postwar presidency.[76]

Since Clinton, Democratic leaders have built on his policies and achieved stunning success. In 2021, due largely to Biden's child tax credit, the child poverty rate fell to five percent, the lowest ever recorded.

But the Democrats' anti-poverty programs are ever under attack by the Republicans and sustaining them has proven difficult. The 2021 child tax credit, which was part of the $1.9 trillion COVID relief package, lifted four million children above the poverty line and dramatically lowered the number of households that reported not having enough food. But the Republicans disrupted the program and the Democrats have struggled to renew it. Writes poverty specialist Natasha Pilkauskas of the child tax credit, "It's baffling to me that it wasn't more popular."[77] And, as we saw earlier, the consequences of Republican sabotage were tragic and immediate: In the fall of 2023, the Census Bureau reported child poverty had recently risen sharply, wiping out some earlier gains.[78]

We presented one explanation for that baffling problem earlier: the Democrats' abject failure to celebrate and claim credit for the fruits of their policies. That's an especially crippling aspect of their low-dominance messaging. The vast majority of Americans have no idea how precipitously child poverty fell, any more than they know that Biden's economy is crackling. The Democrats' messaging failure has left even their most effective policies vulnerable to Republican attacks. It's also left the Democrats looking like strivers who never succeed.

Bill Clinton didn't make that mistake. He knew that trumpeting the results of his policies was vital to sustaining support for them. His messaging team saw to it that the folks were kept abreast of their results.

Clinton also did something else that his Democratic successors usually fail to do: He always framed his programs as vehicles for getting ahead by one's own efforts. He worked to destigmatize the recipients of government aid by helping them into the workplace. He honored Americans' affection for capitalism rather than trying to reeducate them about its cruelties.

Personal responsibility was his rhetorical creed. In Berkeley, Bernie Sanders's *It's OK to Be Angry about Capitalism* has sold like vegan roasted kale tacos. But the breadth of its readership among working-class Americans likely matches the popularity of said tacos among this demographic. And while neither Obama nor Biden embrace Sanders's rhetoric, they haven't done as good a job as their

20th-century predecessors at presenting their programs as tools that make markets work better and contribute to national greatness.

Instead, along with most current-day Democratic leaders, they have tended to treat the Republicans' refusals to help the poor as acts of cruelty. While that critique is fully justified, it doesn't necessarily carry much bite with folks who have a rough notion of just deserts—which includes a very large proportion of Americans and not just MAGA Republicans.

Clinton himself recognized that fact, and it shone through his dazzling September 5, 2012, speech to the Democratic National Convention nominating Obama for a second term.[79] The address was 48 minutes and 21 seconds of jubilation, punctuated by piles of statistics demonstrating the economy's superior performance under the Democrats. Ever aware of what gave his policies political legs, he launched the substantive portion of his address by shooting down "a lot of talk" the Republicans had just offered in their nominating convention "about how the president and the Democrats don't believe in free enterprise and individual initiative, how we want everybody to be dependent on the government." Clinton bore down hard on falsifying the Republicans' claim that Obama had weakened the work requirements in the program Clinton had initiated when he ended "welfare as we know it."

Clinton's speech wasn't all verses; it had a clear refrain. After each raft of numbers on job creation, Clinton summed it up: "So what's the score? Republicans, 24 million; Democrats, 42 million." A few minutes later: "President Obama: plus 4 ½ million. Congressional Republicans: zero." A few minutes after that: "So here's another jobs score: Obama, 250,000; [Mitt] Romney, zero." By the third time, the crowd was roaring "zero!" along with Clinton like he was proclaiming the Second Coming.

And all the policy details were just flexes, anyway. Clinton wielded them the same way he had when he was in office: to burn into listeners' brains that *This man knows what he's talking about; personal responsibility is his dogma; he believes in America's boundless promise; he eats Republicans for lunch with a smile on his face; and his party is a mighty force that really delivers.*

The speech electrified the Democrats and gave Obama a big bounce. According to the Pew Research Center, "The perception that the Democratic convention—highlighted by a much-lauded speech from former President Bill Clinton—gave Obama's campaign a lift was reinforced by national surveys that showed the president expanding his narrow lead."[80]

While he was in the White House, Clinton won high marks for economic stewardship. In 1996, he enjoyed the approval of 60 percent of working-class whites for it. In 2000, during his last year in office, that number stood at 68 percent, unsurpassed by any president before or since. In the electorate as a whole, 71 percent approved of Clinton's economic management.[81] In March 2024, 37 percent of Americans give Biden such marks, though his economy is as good as Clinton's.[82]

Perhaps working-class folks sensed a more optimistic, less patronizing tone from Clinton and his messenger on the economy, Louisiana redneck populist James Carville, than they've gotten since. Clinton's high-dominance inclination to always advertise his and his party's accomplishments, his efforts to convince everyone of his policies' market-friendly nature, and his reassurance that "There is nothing wrong with America that cannot be cured by what is right with America" might have helped as well. They enabled him to weather Republican attacks over his tryst with Monica Lewinsky and left most Americans indifferent to where he was parking the presidential limousine.[83]

The Democratic National Committee website's homepage leads with: "We are the Democratic Party. We're fighting for a brighter, more equal future: rolling up our sleeves and organizing everywhere to build a better America for all."

That message contrasts with how the Republican National Committee presents itself on the party website: "Initially united in

1854 by the promise to abolish slavery, the Republican Party has always stood for freedom, prosperity, and opportunity."

It takes some gall for today's Republicans to claim to be the party of Lincoln. But setting that aside, how appealing are the parties' messages?

"A more equal future" is the worthiest of aims. But making it the *only* goal in the short mission statement (besides the hot air about "rolling up our sleeves and organizing everywhere to build a better America for all") can sound uninspiring to everyone who sees themselves as above the 50th percentile or aspires to be—which of course includes the vast majority. The Republicans' message is very likely more appealing to most Americans.

To be sure, what the parties say on their websites doesn't matter much. But these statements roughly encapsulate the parties' messaging—and the Republicans hold the advantage.

Little wonder that when respondents in a 2022 survey were given a list of terms and phrases and asked which applied to each political party, 58 percent said the Republican Party "values hard work" versus just 43 percent who said it describes the Democrats.[84] Why not punch up the Democrats' pitch by casting ourselves as champions of a more powerful, freer, and prosperous—rather than just "more equal"—America?

It's no mystery that people in rural areas and small towns are especially attached to the nation's founding stories, values, and traditions (what overeducated liberals often refer to as "myths"). We also know that these are the demographics where Democrats have been hemorrhaging support.

Americans' self-reliance is a big part of what makes the country wealthy and distinctive. Devotion to this value is also an essential element of what makes heartland folks invaluable contributors to American prosperity and greatness. We esteem these qualities in Emerson and Thoreau. Why not honor them in our fellow Americans today?

21. Pride, Respect, Trumputin

O ne of the most baffling things to liberals is why in the world people in red states turn down federal aid. It's easy to dismiss their claims that it's a matter of principle, all the more since accepting the help costs their taxpayers next to nothing. Surely racial resentment against the beneficiaries of the largesse must be driving the resistance. That, in fact, is the claim that a host of liberal analysts make.[85]

Let's have a closer look.

The Summer Electronic Benefits Transfer (EBT) program started during the COVID pandemic. It furnishes poor kids with $40 per month for free or reduced-price lunch from June to August at the schools they attend during the academic year. The federal government pays the benefits. The states pick up half the administrative costs—which amount to practically nothing.

Still, Nebraska's Republican governor, Jim Pillen, is having none of it. His reason: "I don't believe in welfare."[86]

Apparently, Kim Reynolds, Iowa's Republican governor, doesn't either. She's also refusing the money. According to her, "An EBT card does nothing to promote nutrition at a time when childhood obesity has become an epidemic."[87]

Child obesity a problem? No problem! Just starve 'em down to training weight—that'll do the trick.

Cruel? Unusual? Cruel, yes, but unusual, no: Nebraska and Iowa are among 15 states that are refusing the assistance. And most Cornhuskers, Hawkeyes, and folks in the other 13 states are neither cruel nor unusual. Still, their governors aren't backing down for fear of the political costs. Most of their constituents apparently "don't believe in welfare" either.

Even many who are, in one form or another, receiving it. Social Security is "welfare."

Nebraska and Iowa are among the 10 whitest states in the country, and just one in twenty people in each state is Black. The vast majority of the kids who would get the lunch money are white. This can't just be a matter of resisting government programs because folks don't want Blacks to get benefits.

Denying the kids basic nutrition—and this, of course, is just one small, if especially lurid, manifestation of the hostility to government assistance—is taking a gruesome toll. In fact, the partisan division on *government* welfare is now creating a geographic divide on *human* welfare.

As of 2023, all nine of the states that have life expectancies of 80 years or higher are blue and 12 of the 13 states where it is 77 or lower are red. Some of the difference is due to the fact that African American life expectancies run six years behind the national average and red deep-Southern states have large Black populations. New Mexico, the one blue state with a life expectancy of 77 or lower, has a large Native American population, and members of this group on average can expect to live just 65 years.[88]

But the color divide isn't just black-and-white; it's red-and-blue as well. Seven of the 13 states with life expectancies of 77 or lower—Indiana, Missouri, Ohio, Arkansas, Tennessee, Kentucky, and West Virginia—have populations that are whiter than the national average. Buckeyes and Missourians can now expect to live no longer than Peruvians and Iranians; in 1990, they lived a decade longer.[89]

Red-state resistance to "welfare," environmental regulations, gun control, tobacco control policies, COVID masking mandates, vaccine requirements, and everything else that seems to smack of "more government" is contributing to the disparity in life prospects.

The phenomenon, moreover, is relatively new; in 1990, the life-expectancy gap between red and blue states was nothing like it is now.[90]

Some analysts who embrace the standard story we examined earlier in this book hold that people are voting red *because* their circumstances have grown worse. But all the evidence we've seen suggests that despair born of rising economic frustration and declining life prospects doesn't provide a good explanation for why people support Trumpism. Working-class whites in particular aren't as despairing as we might have thought.

They aren't as prejudiced, either. We've seen copious data on this matter. Here's one more piece of evidence that goes right to the heart of the questions we are examining here: The GSS asks, "Are we spending too much, too little, or about the right amount on improving the conditions of Blacks?"[91] Respondents are given the choice of "too little," "about the right amount," and "too much." In 1973, 73 percent of non-college whites and 77 percent of all respondents favored boosting or sustaining current spending, rising to 89 and 92 percent, respectively, in 2018. That included 88 percent of Republican respondents.

So where does that leave us?

A more plausible causal story is that any correlation between declining living standards, such as they may be, and voting Republican is largely spurious. Instead, the evidence indicates that a gut-level aversion to government assistance drives *both* working-class Republican voting *and*, wherever it might be happening, declining life prospects. It's possible that there's a feedback loop, with the health consequences of hostility to government action making some people more wretched and therefore amenable to Trump's antics. But that isn't the heart of the story. Instead, deeply held—and to some extent distinctly American—resistance to state intervention is driving *both* the Republican vote *and* health crises in some red states.

So people's political choices *are*, in some cases, having detrimental effects on their own lives. To the extent that they *are* suffering, people may be bringing at least a bit of it on themselves.

But that only deepens the mystery of why they are making these choices. As we've discussed, American political culture has long included a bootstrap mentality and suspicion of government paternalism. But until the 21st century, Republican-led state governments didn't reflexively refuse federal funds to help their poor children. They didn't normally cut taxes to the point that their states were driven to the brink of bankruptcy—and then wear their fiscal irresponsibility as a badge of pride, as some red-state governments have done in recent years. What explains that turn?

It's possible that the growing prosperity of the vast majority has given the anti-government impulse freer rein. During the times of Franklin Roosevelt and Lyndon Johnson, people—including working-class whites—needed government programs just to get by more than they do today. So rising incomes and falling need for government aid may have given people greater latitude for rejecting help.

We might also point to the FOX News propaganda machine and other media that have helped turn hatred of government into a kind of uncivil religion. But blaming the media rarely gets us very far. They are as diverse as national opinion, and outlets thrive by feeding us what we want to hear and putting it in terms that make sense to us. The question of why such a large portion of the public has become so responsive to anti-government propaganda remains.

What's more, we might expect the increasingly glaring consequences of hostility to government to cool the libertarian abandon. And why would the majority that might not need government assistance grow stingier toward their neighbors in need than they once were?

Mississippi long led the country in vaccinations against infectious diseases, despite the state's low personal incomes. Its record was a source of pride for Mississippians and a model for the rest of the country. But recently the state has begun granting religious exemptions from the formerly strict requirement that children receive vaccines against measles, polio, hepatitis, tetanus and pertussis, mumps and rubella, diphtheria, and chickenpox before attending daycare or public or private school. Thousands of parents received exemptions in 2023, and the applications keep pouring in. All the nightmares you can imagine, of course, are sure to follow.

MaryJo Perry is the president of Mississippi Parents for Vaccine Rights, which calls itself a "health freedom" organization. Having worked to undermine the vaccine mandate, Perry and her group have now set their sights on ridding the state of its health officer. Perry states: "I'm not concerned about being wrong, because the scripture says, 'Where the Spirit of the Lord is, there is freedom'."[92]

Freedom from what? Why do anti-vaxxers nationwide now call themselves advocates of "health freedom"?

Maybe it's not freedom to do the Almighty's work that really motivates anti-vax activists. There isn't an iota of Scriptural basis for regarding vaccinations as a violation of God's will.

Instead, maybe it's freedom from liberal interlopers who tell these people what's good for them. Perhaps it's fierce—if in practice dysfunctional—resistance to do-gooder Democrats who insist that they must have government assistance to save them from their own uninformed selves.

Indeed, liberal attitudes, and the messaging they yield, may be partial drivers of the turn to MAGA. These factors, more than supposedly rising material desperation, bias, and ignorance, help explain growing red-state resistance to taking government funds that don't even require higher taxes. They can help us begin to make sense of the seemingly bizarre vehemence of opposition to measures such as government-mandated COVID masking. They can clue us in to how so many millions can regard Dr. Anthony Fauci, the mild-mannered face of COVID prevention, as an agent of government tyranny.

We have assumed that the folks are angry—and they are, but not at what we thought. According to the standard story that's guided our thinking and actions, they're enraged by the effects of globalization—growing job insecurity, stagnant or declining incomes, dead-end jobs, escalating inequality, and the rest. But as we've seen, jobs haven't grown scarcer or less rewarding and inequalities haven't been shooting up recently. In any event, the people who are most angered by inequality aren't voting Republican. And the champion of globalization who opened up trade with China and Mexico, Bill Clinton, won white working-class voters twice while racking up astronomical margins with working-class people of color.

Yes, Bill Clinton felt their pain—he famously claimed he did. But the manner in which he framed his progressive programs never failed to honor Americans' solemn attachments to work and personal initiative.

Long before he came along, Franklin Roosevelt felt their pain as well. But he called wage-earners "businessmen" and told them that his measures were just "the American thing to do." John Kennedy framed his progressive programs as a heroic national combat task that was designed to unfold America's glory and refute the communists' arguments that they had a better way.

These leaders summoned our better natures as well. They made their pitch for the poor at least in part on behalf of the poor—and invited us to join the crusade.

In place of such daring appeals, today we have organized a cheerless cult of empathy that largely omits heroic petitions to pull together and aid the poor among us. Instead, it's all about "restoring the middle class," "growing the middle class," "growing the economy from the middle out," and other such drivel.

Unqualified reverence for the flag, service to country, religious faith, hard work, individual responsibility, and the moral merit of aiding the less fortunate pervaded successful 20th-century Democrats' messaging. It figures less prominently today. It's also not typically what kids hear from their (overwhelmingly liberal) teachers and professors in the classroom these days. It's possible to see why many non-liberal Americans now regard liberals as unenthusiastic about these things—even as harboring contempt for those who cherish them without qualification. And a mountain of data shows that many—perhaps most—non-liberals now *do* question liberals' commitments to these values.

Some liberals love the language of "resistance" in our response to Republican machinations. Well, MAGA's minions have their own forms of resistance to us—and showing us what they think of our efforts to aid them figures prominently in their repertoire. At least here, on the territories they control as well as within their own persons, they can show those who they fear look down on them what they think of our rejection of their values and attempts to control them. At least here, they can make their own choices and let their freedom-flags fly.

Their "resistance" can now take the form of rejecting *everything* liberals treasure simply because liberals treasure them. That can include not just an activist state, but even vaccines, scientific evidence, the rule of law, civility, decency, and democracy. The irony, of course, is that these, too, like religious commitment and ardent patriotism, were once shared values.

The standard story we have believed has left us in a prison of our own making. It's got us scratching our heads and chasing our tails as we try to reach out. And as Trump consolidates his lock on white working-class people, and even expands his support among working-class people of color, we think we *still* must not be showing the folks that we feel their pain quite hard enough.

But they don't want our empathy. They don't want us to tell tales of their woe and offer to console them with our well-thought-out policies.

Given the choice between respect and material well-being, people will always choose the first. Putin's imperial war on Ukraine damages the Russian economy—and most Russians applaud his course anyway. All he has to do is tell Russians the West disrespects them and that invading a neighboring country allied with the West is the only way to strike back. Listen to his speech announcing the "annexation" of Ukrainian territories and justifying his invasion. It doesn't even focus on Ukraine. Instead, it's a litany of ways in which the West supposedly looks down on Russia. But now, he says, maybe they'll take us seriously and quit trying to tell us what to do. They might hate us even more, but now at least they'll respect us.

He's got hostages, too. Every time Putin wants to stick it to the West—and especially when his war seems to be faltering—he imprisons another crop of liberals. They are already scattered, isolated figures who pose no threat to him or his beloved war. He even trots out a few who have been languishing in prison, pressing new charges on them before adding to their sentences and sending them off to still harsher camps. He did that to Alexey Navalny. And when Navalny's spirit couldn't be crushed even in a torture-chamber of a prison located 40 miles above the Artic Circle, Putin finished him off.

You see, Western liberal humanitarians? Here in the territories I rule, I can do anything I wish to these objects of your concern. You might control world culture and be richer and better educated, but here we call the shots. We know you suffer for these dissidents, but your appeals for them will not move us. These are our lands, and on them you shall not tread. In fact, the more monstrous our deeds appear to you, the more we will keep on doing them.

And even if they could, most Russians—including many good and moral people—would refrain from protesting Putin's actions.

You see, coastal liberal humanitarians? Here in the states we control, we can do anything we wish to these objects of your concern. You might control national culture and be richer and better educated, but here we call the shots. We know you suffer for the poor in our states, but your appeals for them will not move us. These are our lands, and on them you shall not tread. In fact, the more repulsive our actions seem to you, the more we will keep on doing them.

And even though they enjoy full freedom of political action, Nebraskans, Iowans, and Alabamans—including many good and moral people—will keep turning down federal aid and electing Republicans.

Trump is Putin's revenge. Trump is *their* revenge.

There may be more than meets the eye in the Republicans' seemingly mystifying desertion of Ukraine and growing embrace of Putin.

Thirst for respect obviously doesn't always bring out the best in us. But there it is. Those of us who already get a great deal of the esteem we need from our solid incomes, self-driving cars, and professional status need to recognize that an ounce of R.E.S.P.E.C.T. is worth more than a pound of policy promises. And let's face it: We started rather enjoying the view from atop our high horses as we rode in with our programs of rescue and relief.

In any event, it couldn't be clearer that our condolences and condescension to the working-class is bringing us no closer to a solution on how to save our programs—and democracy—from these folks' political decisions.

It's time to acknowledge that they know what they want better than we do. Let's internalize that fact—now. The sooner we do, the sooner we can really confront Trumpism, in all its malevolent manifestations.

Now let's grasp this as well: The standard story about why they follow Trump further polarizes politics. It plays into Trump's hands by reinforcing *his* story. Trump and his party polarize people intentionally, but we might be contributing—if inadvertently and just around the edges—to polarization ourselves.

There's a vicious circle here that may be polarizing *feelings* as well as opinions. The more they resist our efforts to aid them, the surer we become that they must be infected with bias and false consciousness. The more vicious they seem to the poor among them, the more we regard them as—let's just say it—moral inferiors. And as long as we believe their resistance to us is rooted in resentment over their own rising material desperation and bigotry, the more our attempts to show we feel their pain will feel to them like disrespect for their freedom to make their own choices.

Even if we don't come out and say what we think. Even if we try to hide how we feel. They know. They aren't stupid.

The good news is that their political behavior isn't as puzzling as we have thought. We've been at least partially wrong about their motivations.

But the main reason it's good news isn't about them; it's about us. Now that we've seen that the standard explanation for their turn to Trump is mistaken, we can finally be rid of the notions that have yielded messaging so tone-deaf that it has helped drive almost half of our compatriots into the arms of a man who—even at the cost of democracy itself—promises to put us in our places on their behalf.

All we have to do is listen and act on what we hear. That means listening with a different ear to the folks who have turned against us, listening to the story told by the data in this book, and following the examples of our own liberal heroes who enacted every progressive program we are now fighting a rearguard action to save.

It's time to scrap our pathos-soaked appeals to "struggling working families" for whom the American Dream is fading in favor of a vision of self-reliance, shared sacrifice for the common good, and national greatness. Let's have a look at how it might be done.

22. Claiming the Flag for Freedom's Sake: Toward a National-Democratic Narrative

D emocratic Party leaders can't seem to let go of their belief that the key to earning voters' loyalty is offering them more material benefits than the Republicans do. But do you or anyone you know choose friends and forge allegiances according to who offers you more stuff? Would you even trust someone who thinks that's the best way to win you over?

We form bonds based on common affections and commitments. We trust people who love the same things we do and work for similar ends. The same is true in politics—all the more in an age where cultural values rather than economic interests form the basis of political loyalties. People join the party they feel people like them belong in.[93]

The most important common bond in our political lives is the nation to which we belong. It's also a part of our personal identity. Love of country can overcome practically all manner of political divisions—or at least foster mutual respect. Capture the flag, and you'll have the wind at your back.

So how do we do that?

Let's start with a roundup of the practices that define a skilled politician's approach to claiming the nation. As with our inventory of high-dominance practices, we'll take our list to 11:

1. Always embrace patriotism. Unfailingly express gratitude for, pride in, and optimism about the nation.

2. Tout and identify yourself with the nation's accomplishments, traditions, and heroes.

3. Integrate national symbols, frames, and language into all aspects of messaging.

4. Use the language of freedom. It's fine to include justice-talk, and it appeals to progressive audiences. But never forget that Americans as a whole care more about liberty than equality or fairness.

5. Cast justice for traditionally underprivileged groups as inseparable from the progress of the entire nation. Treat the fight for equality as a heroic task to be joined with relish by all Americans of goodwill. Convey a sense of national oneness and purpose that cuts everyone in on the project.

6. Treat traditionally underprivileged groups and immigrants as the nation's creators, not its casualties.

7. Use language that elevates rather than chastises, emphasizes individual agency rather than haplessness, and aims to improve rather than redress.

8. Confront opponents squarely in cultural conflicts across the board, not just on abortion. Stop trying to sit out the culture wars by turning the conversation to the "kitchen table."

9. Scrap any hint of talk that could suggest that you regard working-class people as driven by desperation, ignorance, or bigotry.

10. Quit telling working-class people that the American Dream is "dying" or "fading" for them, all the more when you're in power.

11. Embed the quest for economic justice in language that celebrates Americans' enterprising spirit, bootstrap mentality, and belief in personal responsibility.

Democrats should be mindful of these imperatives in messaging on any issue and in every campaign. Even more importantly, these principles should be integrated into an overarching national-democratic narrative. Thinking and speaking in grand narrative terms, much like many of our most effective 20th century predecessors did, would create a bigger, bolder framework for pursuing liberal aims. It would help restore popular faith in liberals' self-confidence as national leaders, as well as in our unconditional love of country, commitment to freedom, bravery in confronting injustice, and capacity for appreciating, including, and uniting all people of goodwill.

Thinking and speaking in terms of a national-democratic narrative would frame our fight against Trumpism as the heroic work of combat that it is rather than as scattered resistance to the outrage of the moment. It would also provide a framework for taking political advantage of the Republicans' anti-American treacheries.

The Democrats haven't even begun to tap the potential of Trump's loyalty to Putin and relentless sell-out of American honor and security to dictators. Nor have we managed—or even really tried—to cast the Republicans' nonstop attacks on democracy at home as the assaults on American *culture* that they are. We have too often remained mired in fact-checking and indignation when we should be driving home the story of Trump's annihilation of America's *sacred traditions*. As political psychologist Drew Westen argues: "Democrats can't hope to achieve anything but default victories— victories that occur when the Republicans are so incompetent, corrupt, or morally bankrupt that voters have no direction to turn but left—if they do not develop a master narrative, an ideology that stands *for* something, other than disparate liberal causes."[94]

With this in mind, let's define the four pillars of Americanism to lay the foundation for a national-democratic narrative. These are ideals; in practice, of course, history contains many instances when the country has failed to live up to them. But they remain the core of what America is, and what it can yet become. These four pillars are:

- o Democracy
- o Demographic dynamism
- o Economic freedom
- o Defense of democratic allies against their foreign enemies

Let's dig a little deeper into why these concepts define the essence of who we are.

We'll start with democracy. The United States was founded for the purpose of freedom and self-government, and the nation's central drama has always been the struggle to expand these blessings to all Americans. It took a century-and-a-half after the country's founding to enfranchise the female half of the population and another half-century for most African Americans to obtain the right to vote. Full democracy arrived on American shores only after nearly two hundred years of blood-and-sweat-drenched political labor. Along with universal voting rights and free elections, freedom of speech, assembly, and religion are etched in the Constitution. In practice, moreover, these liberties have typically been more jealously guarded in the United States than in most other democracies.

The second pillar of Americanism is the continuous expansion of the nation to include new members from all corners of the world. No people can boast that their country *is the world* to the extent that Americans can. And in no other country is this demographic dynamism so central to national identity, achievement, and prominence. The party that deepens the nation's demographic dynamism by facilitating lawful immigration can lay claim to being the truly *American* party.

The third pillar of Americanism is economic freedom. The right to invest, trade, and operate a business independent of government control are core American values. The spirit of free enterprise has helped drive America's spectacular economic development. Economic freedom, of course, doesn't preclude strong social protections. In the 2023 Index of Economic Freedom, the Netherlands, Germany, and the Scandinavian countries, all of which outpace

America in social protections, rank higher than the United States.[95] Americans' attachment to economic freedom can—and, liberals believe, should—go hand in hand with a more robust welfare state. But given Americans' cultural beliefs, reforms are likely to attract more support if pursued in the name of advancing economic freedom rather than constraining it.

The fourth pillar of Americanism is the defense of democratic allies from the predations of foreign dictatorships. Hitler and Stalin taught Americans that freedom cannot be sustained in a fortress. Putin and Xi refresh that lesson today. As America has become the guarantor of democracy around the world over the past century, its guardianship of global democracy has joined democracy at home, demographic dynamism, and economic freedom as a mainstay of national identity.

In each of these areas, the Democratic Party enjoys plentiful grounds for claiming preeminence. Even before the Democrats shed their segregationist wing, they led the way in democratizing America by expanding the franchise and civil rights. The Civil Rights Act of 1964 and the Voting Rights Act of 1965 were the handiwork of John Kennedy, Lyndon Johnson, and other Democratic Party leaders, alongside their allies such as the Freedom Riders and Martin Luther King. Democrats remain the defenders of the rights these laws protect today.

So too have Democrats led the way in opening America to the new citizens who ensure the country's enduring demographic dynamism. The Immigration Act of 1965, which banished color codes from the nation's immigration policy, secured American greatness. Like the Voting Rights Act, it was enacted under the Democrats.

The Democrats have also led the way in deepening economic freedom and ensuring prosperity. Franklin Roosevelt saved American—and global—capitalism from its communist (or state socialist) and fascist (or state corporatist) alternatives. Barack Obama saved the country and the world from a financial meltdown in 2009-2010. Had he dawdled as Herbert Hoover did during the Great Depression, the disaster could have reached 1930s proportions. In fact, the economic history of the past century prominently features Democratic administrations sweeping in and cleaning up the messes left by their Republican predecessors. The liberals have continuously striven to modernize capitalism and expand its beneficiaries.

The Democrats have also played an outsized role in defending America's democratic allies from autocratic imperialists. Franklin Roosevelt led the struggle against fascism. Under his successor, Harry Truman, NATO established the framework that stopped Stalin and his Soviet successors from expanding into Western Europe, the Middle East, and East Asia. Truman managed the brilliant airlift that overcame the Soviet blockade of West Berlin in 1948-1949. Kennedy stared down Nikita Khrushchev in the Cuban Missile Crisis of 1962. The liberal party has done more than its fair share on behalf of building and sustaining this pillar of Americanism.

While the Democrats have long led the way in fortifying the four pillars of Americanism, for much of the past century the Republicans joined them. Barry Goldwater, the Republican presidential nominee in 1964, opposed the expansion of civil rights, but a bipartisan congressional coalition worked to make the Voting Rights Act law in 1965. Measures to renew and extend voting rights were passed in 1975, 1982, 1992, and 2006 with overwhelming bipartisan congressional majorities and were signed into law by Republican presidents.

Immigration was also once embraced by Republican leaders. Ronald Reagan and George H. W. Bush championed liberal immigration policies. The Republicans' brand of capitalism, moreover, might not have been as focused on reducing abuses as the progressives' approach, but it generally defended economic freedom. Finally, Republican and Democratic administrations alike sustained America's commitments to democratic partners' security with equal vigor and verve. There was no partisan divide when it came to NATO and America's security commitments to its Asia-Pacific allies.

What a difference a Trump makes. The Republicans have abandoned all four mainstays of Americanism. In the gravest presidential assault on democracy in American history, Trump sought to prevent the peaceful transfer of power to his elected successor. Thereafter, he relentlessly claimed the election was rigged—and his party stood by him. Since 2013, when the Supreme Court gutted the Voting Rights Act in *Shelby County v. Holder*, Democratic efforts to renew the law have met with almost united Republican opposition. Even the John Lewis Voting Rights Act, a limited measure named for the congressman who began his political career as a leader of the Freedom Riders in 1961, has been scotched by Republican stonewalling. And the Republicans turned freedom of speech on its head, rushing to ban thousands of books from libraries and control what may be taught in schools.

In a frontal attack on the nation's demographic dynamism, the Republicans have resorted to color-inflected nativism. Rather than live up to the spirit of Reagan on immigration, they turned their backs on this essential driver of American economic and cultural excellence.

In the economic realm, the party of Reagan and John McCain has been replaced by one that revels in Putin-style crony capitalism. Trump and his party don't intend to liberate market forces; they seek to leverage office to make themselves rich. Trump sold out American interests in the Middle East for a ten-figure Saudi payout to his son-in-law. He abandoned Kurdish allies to protect his investments in Istanbul. MAGA Senator Ron Johnson reaped an eight-figure payday by dumping stocks in his family's business after being briefed on the severity of the COVID pandemic. Russian oligarchs have gifted millions to the G.O.P.[96] The graft-happiness on the right side of the aisle far outstrips anything on the left, and Republicans barely even try to hide or condemn it anymore. When a Democrat is caught with his hand in the kitty, as Senator Robert Menendez has been, the Democrats turn against him. When a Republican is found out, his party rallies behind him. The blatant corruption of today's G.O.P. contrasts with both its predecessor's bygone market fundamentalism and the Democrats' progressive capitalism.

Finally, Trump has thrown Republican devotion to America's democratic allies into reverse. Reflecting on his foreign relations in late 2021, he said: "The ones I did the best with were the tyrants...for whatever reason, I got along great with Putin. I got along great with President Xi of China, I got along great with Kim Jong-un of North Korea! And isn't that good?"[97]

Not for America, it's not. And while his predecessors didn't spurn, belittle, or sideline America's traditional democratic allies, Trump threatens to defund and even withdraw the United States from NATO. That move would destroy the alliance, fulfilling Putin's fondest dream. Trump had multiple one-on-ones with Putin that he went to great pains to keep secret. In contempt for all precedent, he sometimes barred even his secretaries of state or anyone else from attending his conversations. On at least one occasion when he met Putin alone, he confiscated his interpreter's notes and told her not to disclose what she had heard to his advisers.[98] Given the indictments Trump now faces for hoarding top-secret intelligence information after he left office, and in light of his determination to monetize everything he can, one wonders what else he might have passed on to Putin—and what Putin might have promised in return. Since departing office, Trump has shilled for Putin's invasion of Ukraine, blamed the United States for provoking it, and pledged to terminate support for Ukraine if reelected in 2024.[99] At the behest of their cult master—and in defiance of public sentiment—congressional Republicans are now abandoning Ukraine to Putin.

The Republicans' astounding assault on the four pillars of Americanism leaves the Democratic Party as the sole major defender of the nation's core traditions. How hard should it be for the Democrats to overcome the shocking fact that the Republicans hold the edge on public perceptions of patriotism?

The task should be all the easier since Trump, while armed with strong dominance skills and a national story of sorts, does a singularly abysmal job of glorifying the nation. It's not just that his portrait of America divides the country and doesn't appeal to liberals.

It's that it characterizes the United States as rather pathetic. Trump can't hold a candle to more skilled demagogues. While India's Modi and Turkey's Erdoğan portray their countries as global power-houses-in-the-making, Trump never quits moaning that America can't compete with its trade partners or afford to sustain its alliances. Modi and Erdoğan surround themselves with national cultural luminaries; the best Trump could manage were Ted Nugent and Kid Rock. Trump makes America look *weak*—and the Democrats have failed to capitalize.

Now let's turn to Westen's formula for telling a story that connects. He argued in 2020 that politics "is less a marketplace of ideas than a marketplace of emotions. To be successful, a candidate needs to reach voters in ways that penetrate the heart at least as much as the head. That makes political messaging critical—and perhaps about to determine the course of American history."

According to Westen, the Republicans seem to intuit the primacy of feelings, while "the Democrats, in contrast, talked about their policy prescriptions, bewitched by the dictum that 'a campaign is a debate on the issues.' . . . Armed with a vision of the mind in which good ideas, even when described to people in terms they might not understand or find emotionally compelling, would somehow sell themselves, Democrats consistently lost elections." Westen holds that the Democrats' approach ignores an abundance of data from social science confirming that voters' choices rest much less on how the parties position themselves on policy matters than on how party leaders make voters *feel* about their leadership and actions.

He also offers a second recommendation: "Tell a coherent, memorable story." What defines such a story? He writes:

> Issues are not narratives. Nor are 10-point plans. Narratives have protagonists and antagonists. At least in the West, narratives tend to have a particular story structure, or grammar, recognizable even to preschool children. It includes, among other elements, an initial situation, a problem, a battle to be

fought or hill to be climbed, and a resolution. Stories also tend to have a moral . . . Perhaps the most important lesson I have learned from testing hundreds of thousands of narratives on the most important issues of our time, from contraception and abortion to climate change and economics, is that virtually every successful political narrative has a structure derivative of this grammar. . . . [E]ffective messages begin with a statement of values that transcends political divides (to establish a connection between speaker and listener), then raise concerns in vivid ways that activate emotions, particularly moral emotions, such as fairness or indignation. Finally, after briefly describing a solution, but skipping details, they end with a sense of hope.[100]

Now, you would think that this would be a no-brainer for liberals. After all, most of the storytellers in popular culture—novelists, actors, musicians, filmmakers, and other creators—tend to be liberals. So why do we neglect this skill set in the political arena?

For answers, consider how each of these components of a strong political message might rub many current-day liberals the wrong way. In political messaging, we tend to dismiss anything that is, as Westen says, "recognizable even to preschool children." We distrust such simplicity, regarding it as the cheap province of demagogues. Liberal politicians typically detail their entire legislative agenda when hitting hard on a few highlights would pack more punch. For example, as Jonathan Allen and Amie Parnes describe Hillary Clinton's 2016 nomination acceptance speech: "Like most of her major speeches, though, Hillary tried to squeeze in too many ideas. It remained impossible to decipher her priorities or her theory for her candidacy."[101]

Second, a good narrative "includes protagonists and antagonists." True, but many 21st-century liberals are allergic to us-versus-them politics. Many also tend to think and speak in terms of "systemic" and "institutional" culprits for injustice, instead of relentlessly attacking real-life villains. We also have become reluctant to build up heroes. In part that's because we distrust the personalization of politics. But strong progressives may also fear that anyone we lionize might fail our ethical purity tests.

Third, as we've already discussed, we distrust "activat[ing] emotions." What good can come of people getting all frothed up with feelings, anyway?

Finally, while you might think that the essential coda of a good narrative—ending "with a sense of hope"—would be uncontroversial, for many current-day liberals it doesn't come easy. Franklin Roosevelt, John Kennedy, Lyndon Johnson—and, perhaps less dramatically, Bill Clinton and Barack Obama—laced their messages with redemption, but many of their successors have been reluctant to do so. We can fear trumpeting how good we've made things and how great they will become under our leadership, not least because we worry about offending those who might feel they're not keeping pace.

To sum up: A compelling narrative contains readily comprehensible storylines. It speaks in terms of battles waged and won and fights ongoing for still greater gains. It has heroes and villains, stirs powerful emotions, and includes the promise of redemption. In the story that liberals would tell, a justice-seeking people governed by tenacious progressive leaders would secure the nation and go to bat for our values against those who would betray us all.

So who's in and who's out of the story? A national-democratic narrative must set a high bar for excluding anyone from its concept of the loyal citizen. A national-*democratic* story is not specifically a national-*progressive* story. It conveys liberal values that will appeal to progressives but has just as much room for real conservatives.

But anyone who seeks to prevent the nation from governing itself is categorically excluded as a patriot; loyalty to democracy must be a prerequisite for status as a decent citizen. A national-democratic narrative would also have little room for those who treat others as second-class citizens due to how they look or love, their national origins, or the recentness of their citizenship. Thus, racial supremacists would be cast as disloyal Americans. So-called Christian nationalists, meaning people who treat non-Christians as lesser Americans, would be as well.

In May 2023, Alabama Senator Tommy Tuberville, who single-handedly blocked the appointment of hundreds of nominees for top positions in the armed forces to protest the Pentagon's position on abortion, was asked in a radio program what he thinks of white supremacists serving in the military. He answered: "I call them Americans."[102]

No, they're not. At least they're not decent ones. They betray their country, just like Tuberville does. They are the "them" in any national-democratic story.[103]

Those who leverage office to enrich themselves are, too. They and those who abide such profiteering—which most Republican leaders do in the case of Trump's corruption—strike at America's economic freedom, undermining elementary fairness and national prosperity.

Finally, by the lights of any national-democratic narrative, opposition to external powers who assault America's democratic allies is also required. There is plenty of room for loyal Americans to disagree over foreign policy. But siding with America's greatest sworn enemy against our democratic allies qualifies one as a traitor.

The passions liberals must rouse and leverage differ from those stoked by democracy's enemies, and that is a source of a national-*democratic* story's power. That story must appeal to people's better natures. Resentment and shame can be motivating, but ultimately they harm our hearts and degrade everything we touch. The emotions a national-democratic narrative elicits should make us feel powerful, grateful, and united with our fellows. And while authoritarian narratives invariably exalt a single savior, our story must hold up the whole justice-minded people, acting through its chosen representatives, as the vehicle of national redemption.

Like any emotionally compelling story about a large collective entity, a national-democratic narrative must satisfy people's thirst for recognition, distinction, and equal dignity. That is and has always been the central motivator of political action, heroic and barbaric alike. To tap strong emotions, a national-democratic narrative can't be based purely on a thin, "civic" nationalism that's just about enjoying rights and obeying laws under a democratic constitution. That kind of nationalism appeals to the head but not the heart. Nor can it be based primarily on economic matters, which do not—at least not under conditions in which the vast majority has adequate food and shelter—stir emotions as readily as cultural matters do. In practice, that means it must be rooted in and celebrate cultural—but not ethnic—specificities, uniqueness, authenticity, and greatness.

Every country is exceptional and excellent in some respects, and its people have grounds for regarding it as the best place in the world. An emotionally resonant notion of the nation therefore must embrace national exceptionalism and tell a tale of extraordinary national exploits. It need not claim national superiority, but in some realms it will.

Liberals sometimes look askance at the idea of national exceptionalism. Some fear it will lead people to impose their ways on other countries or dull their taste for reform. But as we have seen, gratitude for and pride in one's country need produce no such effects. Liberals must see to it that a spirit of exceptionalism doesn't turn into either messianism or complacency. But it is decidedly *not* our right to tamp down popular feelings of enthusiasm for the nation's exceptionalism—unless the aim is to leave the flag in the hands of the ethnonationalists. Strong leaders, of whatever political stripe, never hesitate to celebrate what makes their country extraordinary.

Americans, like people in other countries, find our nation to be exceptional in many ways. America is the world's oldest democracy and the guardian of liberty in the world. It's the world's preeminent experiment in a multiethnic people governing themselves in freedom. The United States by far tops all other dreamed-of destinations among people worldwide who wish to move abroad.[104]

As we saw above, moreover, Americans' attitudes toward human equality have evolved at an astonishing pace. Despite our sordid history on race and enduring inequalities, we have made enormous strides. America is also a pioneer in gender equality and LGBTQ rights. Liberals often fail to flag these truths, which are self-evident to others. They make America the scorn and scourge of Putin, Xi, Kim Jong-un, the Iranian mullahs, and other despots who strive to stamp out liberalism. To the extent that liberals shrink from trumpeting these truths, we limit our ability to cast our causes as integral to the American tradition.

The United States is by far the world's most prosperous major country and the home of a grossly disproportionate share of technological innovation. Its leadership in higher education is nothing short of hegemonic; most of the world's best universities are in the United States. Any compelling national-democratic story must express gratitude for such blessings.

Finally, a compelling national-democratic narrative must contain the promise of a glorious tomorrow. This facet of the story is core to its emotional appeal. It requires that the story include a mighty current of optimism based on past victories over evil. It's what breeds hope—and renders its teller as one who deserves to be followed.

Any liberal politician who aspires to capture the country's imagination is going to have to convey that she deeply believes in the nation, with a full grasp of realities but without reservations. Any liberal narrative that can overcome the MAGA story must make people feel better about being Americans than the Trumpian tale does. Effective messaging will refrain from blaming "America" for failures rather than identifiable culprits.

"America" isn't trying to whitewash slavery; the servants of the MAGA narrative are. "America" isn't trying to make it more difficult for people to vote; the Republicans are doing that. "America" isn't failing to attack poverty; the Republicans are blocking the Democrats' efforts. "America" isn't at fault for horrific gun violence; the

Republicans are scotching all gun control measures. "America" isn't sluggish in confronting climate change; the Republicans are sabotaging Democratic efforts to tackle the problem. "Americans" don't thirst for authoritarianism; America's traitors do.

These statements aren't partisan pieties. They are simple facts. Such an us-versus-them narrative isn't just smart politics. It's just being honest.

Fighting for economic justice lies at the heart of the Democrats' program, and that isn't going to—nor should it—change. But economic policies and rhetoric can't *substitute* for engaging on culture. And as long as the Democrats remain the "materialist party," we will struggle to appeal outside our class-justice-minded base.

And our struggle for economic and racial justice must embrace a mentality and rhetoric of *freedom* rather than *constraint.* Americans treasure their liberties—possibly more than anyone else in the world. Those perceived as curbing their exercise—in political communication, economic affairs, or any other realm—will always be at a disadvantage. By rights that should handicap the Republicans, with their book bans and lunge toward market-distorting crony capitalism. But the liberals can't take advantage of MAGA snowflakery if we're perceived as no less censorious than our opponents. Nor can we exploit the Trumpian flight from market fundamentalism to corrupt pseudo-capitalism if we aren't seen as more committed to free entrepreneurship than the Republicans.

None of this will win over the deplorable quarter; in fact, it will drive them to distraction. But it promises to reduce their numbers in high office. It's the best shot the Democrats have for exciting our own base and convincing a small but crucial slice of centrists and (real) conservatives that our party is the place to be—or at least the party to hold one's nose at and vote for in a pinch.

We've discussed the elements of a national-democratic narrative in broad strokes. Now let's summarize the specific components of a rich and meaningful story. What would an inspiring national narrative, offered by democracy's defenders at the current moment in history, look like? It would:

First, offer a simple storyline with a good-vs-evil—not merely better-or-worse or more-or-less advantageous—frame. The conflict is over our way of life and sacred values, not mere interests. It takes the form of an encompassing moral war.

Second, specify the central conflict. Democracy is under attack. We face determined enemies who threaten our right to govern ourselves in a context of nonviolence, fair play, and rights. Our adversaries are working to subvert elections and disenfranchise voters. They are applauding insurrections, threatening violence, and promising to dismantle the agencies that ensure the rule of law.

Third, spell out the stakes. Everything that freedom- and justice-loving people cherish hangs in the balance. That includes our ability to determine who governs us; equal treatment for all of us under the law; freedom from arbitrary state action; and recognition of every person's worth.

Fourth, contain a plot that specifies the initial condition, the turning point, the problem, the war to be waged, and the climactic moment. For all its imperfections, our democracy was long secure, and forward-thinking Americans endeavored to spread liberty to all. Both major parties honored our right to elect our representatives in free elections, after which the winners took office and the losers accepted defeat. But Trump marked a turn. He not only captured the presidency but—worse—took his party with him. As a result, democracy and all its attendant benefits are now under immediate threat, regardless of Trump's political fate. Our opponents are tearing down democratic institutions from within to perpetuate their power, leverage their offices for personal gain, and remake our nation in their own twisted image. They are armed with powerful new technologies, media mouthpieces, and national narratives that many find compelling. They cannot be shamed; they can be overcome only with overwhelming electoral force. The climax of the story will come when we defeat the authoritarian menace and establish stable electoral dominance.

Fifth, feature heroes and villains. The protagonists are all democracy-loving people who stand ready to defend their own and their compatriots' rights. Our heroes are those who have made outstanding contributions and sacrifices to defend democracy and spread its blessings to those who have lacked them or still lack them in full today. The antagonists are those who would deprive their compatriots of the right to govern themselves in freedom or limit the blessings of liberty to certain groups. The villains are the authoritarian leaders, their henchmen, and their enablers.

Sixth, end with a redemptive resolution and a call to action. Democracy's partisans, armed with moral superiority, greater elan, higher dominance orientation, a more inspiring national narrative, and majority support, *will prevail*. The central pillars of Americanism will be placed on a firmer foundation than ever before. Protecting democracy over the long haul, however, will require deepening our faith in the nation's democratic project. It will also call for continuous political action—the donation of time and money, an iron commitment to always vote, readiness to aid our compatriots in need, and willingness to tell our national-democratic story to those who are detached or unconvinced. Guided by devotion to our nation's highest purposes, we will never again allow democracy's enemies to control our halls of power.

Delivery of the story is also important. A compelling national narrative can be told only by a reasonably high-dominance actor. Here is a crucial place where dominating the authoritarians and reclaiming the nation come together as the cornerstone of a democratic comeback.

A stirring national narrative can't be told effectively by one who is allergic to simplified, good-versus-evil distinctions. Nor can it be purveyed by one who is concerned with avoiding "triumphalism," who regards skepticism as a high virtue, or who looks down his nose at exuberance. Telling an absorbing national story requires generating elation about the nation rather than fretting about the depth and complexities of its difficulties.

Risk-aversion and telling a potent national narrative don't go together, since a story that *reclaims the nation* requires an act of faith and entails offending many. The story can't be told effectively by one who is uncomfortable with us-versus-them framing, since a captivating narrative always features heroes and villains. Fixation on self-examination and reluctance to "other" the political enemy— still more to even think of him as an enemy—won't do. Nor can one who is disinclined to tell a tale that ends with a shining future, or who regards everyone as motivated strictly by calculations of their own interests, be very effective. Also consistent with the requirements of high-dominance politics, meeting the challenge means giving pique a rest and turning to spirited attack.

A convincing teller of the story must be deeply grateful for and proud of the nation. She must be unfailingly hopeful about its prospects, no matter how dark the hour. Only a nationalist—an inclusive, anti-ethnonational one—can convey a gripping *national-democratic* story that generates zeal for the Democrats and contempt for our detestable foes.

Look at it another way. Which boss inspires greater loyalty and devotion to the task at hand? One who is devoted to her job but fails to tout the company's accomplishments and seems uncertain about its prospects? Or one who is on fire with excitement about the firm's mission and future?

The president is the captain of Team America. That fact was never lost on Franklin Roosevelt, John Kennedy, or Barack Obama, but it's not so clear that most current-day Democratic leaders grasp this truth.

You might think that the authoritarians would have an easier time telling a riveting narrative than we do—perhaps all the more since we have failed to tell our story in recent years. But liberals—at least high-dominance ones—hold the advantage. Democracy's foes tend to be resentful, cynical pessimists who exclude whole parts of the nation from their national stories. While their emotional appeals might be motivating for a time, the feelings they stoke ultimately weaken their followers. Obama's constant refrain that hope beats fear encapsulates this truth.

When we think back over American history, who told the stories that ring through the ages? Jefferson Davis or Abraham Lincoln? Father Charles Coughlin, who proposed a fascist alternative during the Great Depression, or Franklin Roosevelt, who never lost faith in democracy? George Wallace or John Kennedy, who slapped Wallace down? Barry Goldwater or Martin Luther King, who slapped Goldwater down? Even many people who don't share liberal values remember the latter figures in each pair with reverence and respect, while the former are largely forgotten.

A national-democratic story can be told in a single sentence or a long speech (though the single-sentence version of course can't incorporate all the elements we presented).

Here is the Trumpian narrative, as David Brooks summarizes it: "Their central story is that the good, decent people of the heartland are being threatened by immigrants, foreigners and other outsiders while corrupt elites do nothing."[105]

What would a one-sentence encapsulation of a national-*democratic* narrative be? Here's one possibility:

A patriotic, justice-seeking people will secure our democracy and its sacred values against the bigots, liars, grifters, and thugs who would deny liberty and justice for all.

You can probably think of a better line than this. What's yours?

America's glorious story is all over the place. Democrats can and should be looking for examples of it and telling them all the time. Here's a story I came across recently: From a land America strafed with munitions made in Japan, our nation brought forth the Vietnam-born Viet Xuan Luong, who became Commanding General for the section of the U.S. Army that protects Japan from neighboring dictatorships.

Such is the tale of America's democratic and demographic destiny, and its redemptive power.

How about a slightly longer narrative? We'll examine fuller expositions of the American national-democratic story in the final part of this book. But first, let's listen to what a certain 18-year-old said after winning the gold in boxing for Team USA at the 1960 Rome Olympics:[106]

To make America the greatest is my goal,
So I beat the Russians, and I beat the Pole,
and for the USA won the medal of gold.

Italians said, "You're greater than Cassius of Old,
We like your name,
We like your game,
So make Rome your home if you will."

I said I appreciate kind hospitality,
but the USA is my country still,
'cause they're waiting to welcome me in Louisville.

Fourteen years later, facing the professional championship fight of his life in which his undefeated opponent was the 4-1 favorite, this man offered a lesson in the power of infectious, high-dominance buoyancy. It followed a pattern that ran through his whole public life. It's something that Democrats, whose jaws have been broken and who've been knocked down a couple of times and are now facing the fight of our lives, might take a page from today:[107]

I'm experienced now, professional!
Jaw's been broke
been lost
knocked down a couple times.

I'm *bad*!
Been choppin' trees, I done somethin' *new* for this fight!

I done wrestled with an alligator
That's right!
I have wrestled with an alligator
I done tussled with a whale.
I done handcuffed lightning,
Thro'ed thunder in jail!

That's *bad*!

Only last week
I murdered a rock,
Injured a stone,
Hospitalized a brick.
I'm so mean I make *medicine* sick.

There's no beating that, ever—and, boxing cool and smart, the utterer of those lines went on to knock out his bigger, stronger, younger opponent in the eighth round. And few have done more for racial equality and dignity in America and the broader world—not to mention for bringing Americans to our senses about the Vietnam War—than the exuberant progressive poet who uttered those verses. But while The Greatest he shall remain, let's have a look at how other champions of democracy also told a story that sang.

PART FOUR

DEMOCRACY'S CHAMPIONS SHOW HOW IT'S DONE

23. Time for a Democratic Comeback

"**T**he liberal idea has become obsolete. It has come into conflict with the interests of the overwhelming majority of the population." So said Vladimir Putin in a June 28, 2019, interview.[1] As the *New York Times's* Andrew Kramer noted, Putin's notion of "the liberal idea" was "the postwar dominance of democracy, human rights, multiculturalism, and tolerance."[2] It was a story Putin had rehearsed for years, and he had it down cold.

That same day, the presidents of the two leading nuclear powers met on the sidelines of the G-20 summit in Osaka, Japan. As always, Donald Trump showed deference he pays no one else in the world. "It's a great honor to be with President Putin," Trump gushed. "We have a very, very good relationship." When asked by a reporter if he had warned Putin not to reprise his 2016 intervention in the forthcoming 2020 election, Trump wagged a finger at Putin and said with mock seriousness: "Don't meddle in the election, please." Putin smirked, cameras snapped, and the Russian dictator's dominance of the president of the United States hit the airwaves.

Kramer captured the moment: "President Vladimir V. Putin, already well established as a geopolitical superstar, had a splashy day on the global stage at the Group of 20 meeting on Friday, even by his own standards." The self-styled sword of the global antidemocratic movement bestrode the world like an authoritarian colossus.

What a difference a few years can make. Putin remains in the limelight, but his fame has shrunk to infamy since his man in the White House lost reelection in 2020 and Ukraine mauled his marauders on the battlefield. Then, the International Criminal Court issued a warrant for Putin's arrest. The charge: kidnapping hundreds of thousands of Ukrainian children. Autocracy's Prince of Darkness couldn't leave home anymore for fear of being extradited to the Hague.

While democracy's enemies might seem to be prevailing, democrats are scoring some remarkable victories. Perhaps the brightest ray of hope emanates from the darkest place—the grisly battlefields of Ukraine. The Ukrainians' mighty resistance under Volodymyr Zelensky, the pro-Ukrainian solidarity of the democratic world under Biden's leadership, and the reduction of Putin to a desperate, child-molesting warlord have helped give global democracy a second wind.

Let's look at an example of a democratic comeback in a country whose political predicament closely resembles what we find in the United States. When Luiz Inácio "Lula" da Silva decided to take on Jair Bolsonaro in Brazil's 2022 presidential election, he framed the contest as exactly what it was: "Polarization in Brazil is different now. It is not between two sides, a right and a left. The polarization in Brazil is between fascism and democracy. I represent democracy because I am from a democratic party that has a history of very democratic governance. And Bolsonaro represents fascism. So that is what's at stake."[3] During the campaign, he mercilessly attacked and ridiculed his rival's COVID-denial policies. Often sporting wonderfully tacky green, yellow, and blue ties bearing the colors of the Brazilian flag, Lula told a story of a nation whose ineffable greatness had been temporarily eclipsed by Bolsonaro's authoritarianism and incompetence. Lula ran first and foremost on saving democracy, while Bolsonaro copied Trump in every way, including by threatening to ignore the election's results if he didn't win.

On October 30, 2022, Lula terminated one of the gravest threats to democracy Latin America had faced since the 1980s. He won even though the economy was recovering strongly after COVID under

Bolsonaro. The Trump wannabe fled to Florida, camping out a couple hours' drive from Mar-a-Lago.

In his first speech as the new president, Lula harkened to his compatriots' struggles of the 1980s to rid themselves of military despots, who Bolsonaro had lauded while in office: "Under the winds of redemocratization, we used to say: dictatorship never again! Today, after the terrible challenge we have overcome, we must say: democracy forever." He attributed Brazil's grim COVID toll to "the criminal attitude of a denialist government that was also insensitive to life. Responsibilities for this genocide must be ascertained and must not go unpunished." He inveighed against Bolsonaro's encouragement of private gun ownership and vowed to tighten restrictions. Lula would have no part of reconciliation with democracy's enemies: "The mandate we have received, in the face of opponents inspired by fascism, will be defended with the powers that the Constitution confers on democracy. To hatred, we will respond with love. To lies, with truth. To terror and violence, we will respond with the law and its harshest consequences."[4]

Just a week later, Lula faced the challenge of making good on his promise, and that he certainly did. In the copycat crime of the 21st century, on January 8, 2023, thousands of Bolsonaristas stormed the presidential, congressional, and Supreme Court buildings in Brasília. Having unsuccessfully tried to recruit the military to block a peaceful transition, they besieged the halls of government, wreaking vast damage.[5] Staring the crime in the face, Lula toured the wreckage the next day and declared that the "vandals, neo-fascists, and fanatics" would be swiftly brought to justice. He followed up by sacking heads of the army and military police who had failed to stop the assault and by prosecuting the insurrectionists. His fierce response might explain why every major parliamentary party—including Bolsonaro's—condemned the insurrection.[6]

He also launched a raft of progressive reforms. Confronting powerful agribusiness groups, he commenced an ambitious plan to halt illegal deforestation in the Amazon. Vowing that "Brazil will once again become a global reference in sustainability," he promised zero net deforestation by the end of his term in 2027.[7]

Lula's mind never strays far from economic justice, but he doesn't shrink from the culture wars, either. After four years of a president who treated indigenous people as foreigners and allowed agricultural interests to push them off their lands, Lula decreed a slew of protected indigenous reservations into existence. By the end of his first half-year in office, he had driven thousands of illegal gold miners out of the Amazon and reduced deforestation by a third. He also signed a sweeping order to tighten gun control, declaring: "Only the police and the army must be well-armed."[8]

Shortly after Bolsonaro returned to Brazil following his three-month hiatus in Florida, the superior electoral court informed him that his assault on democracy had earned a ban on running in the next two presidential elections.[9] Lula doesn't control the judiciary, but his uncompromising approach to democracy's antagonists created a zeitgeist that was also felt on the bench.

The difference between Lula and Biden is hard to miss. Lula, like Biden, is militantly committed to progressive social reforms, but Lula keeps the focus on what matters most: democracy. While Biden *once* dared to liken MAGA *philosophy* to "semi-fascism," Lula always frames his struggle as a showdown between democrats and fascists.

Lula's adversaries are every bit as numerous and well-organized as the Republicans, and he has to cut deals with the center and the center-right to govern. But his approach to depolarization focuses on quelling rather than soft-peddling the polarizers. He wraps himself in the flag every chance he gets. He shares no part of the nation with those who would tear down democracy, treating them as traitors who are unworthy to call themselves Brazilians. He dominates the airwaves and leaves his detractors sputtering.

Try Googling Biden's tweets from the night he was elected, and you won't find anything but *Trump*'s tweets; Biden said nothing memorable. Google Lula's tweets from the night he was elected, and this is what you'll find: A photo of Lula's hand, missing a finger he lost in an industrial accident when he was a metallurgical factory worker, pressed on a Brazilian flag. It was captioned with a single word: *Democracìa.*

Poland's recent democratic comeback is also instructive. The Law and Justice Party's disrespect for their country's proud democratic tradition handed liberals the chance to discredit their illiberal opponents' patriotism. Poland's democrats did eventually seize the flag and, under the leadership of the brazenly high-dominance truth-teller, Donald Tusk, ended the authoritarian party's eight-year reign of bigotry and lies.

Tusk had long been skeptical about nationalism. He instinctively identified it with ethnonationalism and opposition to the EU, and the last thing he wanted to do was sound like Law and Justice. His devotion to the EU (he headed its executive branch from 2014 to 2019), and his upbringing in Gdansk, a city that has been torn for centuries between Polish and German rule, led him to believe, as he stated in 2014, that it is "best to be immune to every kind of orthodoxy, of ideology and most importantly, nationalism."[10]

But that left Law and Justice's bigoted ethnonational story as the main one Poles heard, and the liberals looking like skeptics about Polish distinctiveness and greatness. Law and Justice took that to the bank in Poland's 2015 and 2019 elections. They won big enough to control government and impose a democracy-busting program that resembles what the Republicans are striving to enact in the United States.

But as the 2023 campaign wore on, the liberals' messaging shifted. At previous demonstrations staged by Law and Justice's liberal opponents, the dark blue banners of the EU often seemed to outnumber the Polish red-and-white.

No more.

Reporting on an immense demonstration by democracy's defenders in the campaign's closing days, *The Guardian's* Shaun Walker noted: "A large part of Tusk's campaign has been about reclaiming the language of patriotism for the opposition, leading to the red-

and-white hearts that have become a symbol of the campaign. On Sunday, thousands in attendance at the rally were waving red-and-white Polish flags." An exhilarated Tusk proclaimed to the crowd: "I see a sea of red and white banners . . . we all share the view that our red-and-white homeland can be home to free people again."[11]

What's more, Tusk didn't run on economic policy. He ran on saving democracy and always framed the fight as a showdown between liberal good and illiberal evil. In June 2023, he told the crowd at the largest demonstration in Poland since 1989—and perhaps the largest prodemocracy demonstration in the world in recent years: "We are going to these elections to win and to right human wrongs. I promise you victory, as settlement of evil, compensation for human wrongs and reconciliation among Poles."[12]

He wore his famed self-assurance on his sleeve, refusing even to consider the possibility of defeat. "A breakthrough is coming in the history of our homeland," Tusk intoned at a rally in Warsaw. "Let no one have any illusions. Change for the better is inevitable." Often a man of dour countenance who seems more comfortable meeting with Eurocrats in Brussels than rousing crowds at home, he showed an ebullient side during the demonstrations, exclaiming: "No one believed that such crowds and such emotions could happen again in our history. This is a sign of the great Polish revival."[13]

Indeed it was, and Tusk's tactics worked. The economy was doing fine under Law and Justice, but the party's vote share fell to 37 percent, down from 44 in 2019. Along with fellow illiberal parties, it won 212 seats to 248 for Tusk's Civic Platform and its prodemocratic coalition partners in the lower house of parliament. The prodemocratic parties did even better in the Senate. The election wasn't even close.

It bears note that Tusk didn't make it on personal popularity. His approval ratings in the year preceding the election ran at a Biden-level 30-40 percent, lower than those of the sitting president and the prime minister, both of whom hail from Law and Justice.[14] But now Tusk is prime minister, and he's restoring democratic protections and relations with the EU while running the table on democracy's ousted foes.

It happened in Poland. It happened in Brazil. It can happen in America, too.

Democracy is on a roll in parts of the world, even as it's under threat in others. Whether that roll continues depends vitally on the performance of the Democratic Party in the United States.

So now let's examine some of America's most promising liberal leaders. In Maryland, 44-year-old Wes Moore became the third Black elected governor in American history in January 2023. Calling himself "a very proud, progressive patriot," the former Army paratrooper and head of an antipoverty NGO tells his fellow progressives: "I want people to understand that we still have work to do, but at the same time...if we're not acknowledging what we've gotten done, if we're not taking a moment and taking a beat and giving thanks to those who put in the work before us, then we're not just being disrespectful, we're being disingenuous."[15] Maryland voters handed Moore a 65-32 percent margin over his Republican opponent.

Another rising Democratic star, Michigan Governor Gretchen Whitmer, beat her MAGA opponent by double digits in a state that swung to Trump in 2016 and that Biden won by just two points four years later. Whitmer's hard-edged commitment to liberal causes and non-patronizing approach to working-class Michiganders has helped establish a Democratic lock on government: Riding her coattails, the Democrats flipped both houses of the state legislature from red to blue in 2022.[16]

Kentucky Governor Andy Beshear shows how a liberal can govern in a deep-red state while retaining voter confidence. In 2019, at age 41, he edged out his MAGA opponent by winning several Appalachian counties that had earlier swung to the Republicans. You might think Beshear governs as a conservative Democrat, but he pushes progressive economic policies and never hesitates to take on the right in the culture wars. One of his first acts in office was to reopen the Planned Parenthood clinic in Louisville, and he followed that up by vetoing a bill imposing new abortion restrictions.[17]

The strapping Kentucky governor, whose dorky, earnest countenance recalls that of Ron Howard's Richie Cunningham in the 1970-80s *Happy Days* sitcom, marches in Pride Parades. When a Republican lawmaker displayed a photo of Beshear with a drag queen and accused him of corrupting kids, the governor shot back that he'd be happy to have more such photos taken. He then turned the tables on his detractor: "I don't think he's the fashion police for the Capitol. I believe he owes each and every one of [the participants in the Pride Parade] an apology. They are as much Kentuckians as anybody else." The Republican tucked his tail between his legs, whimpering: "My problem is not with the gay movement. I didn't say anything about the 'Pride Celebration'."[18]

When the state legislature voted to prohibit transgender minors from receiving what some people refer to as gender-affirming care in March 2023, Beshear vetoed it, stating: "Every child is a child of God. Every. Single. One.... These types of bills will lead to an increase in suicides for Kentucky's teens."[19] As COVID raged, and in defiance of public opinion, Beshear mandated masks for Kentucky students. He held nightly televised "COVID briefings," solemnly reading out the names of Kentuckians who had recently succumbed to the disease and chiding those who refused to get vaccinated.[20]

Many of his liberal policies aren't popular in Kentucky. But by all indications, Beshear couldn't care less.

Neither could most Kentuckians. In November 2023, he won reelection by beating a Mitch McConnell protégé by five points in a state that Trump won by 26 points in 2020.

The son of a Mexican mother and a Colombian father, Ruben Gallego grew up in poverty in Chicago's South Side. He worked as a janitor and meat packer before joining the Marines. First elected to Congress in 2014 at the age of 34, he's running to replace Senator Kyrsten Sinema, an erratic Democrat who left the party and has sided with the Republicans on crucial votes.

Gallego often speaks of the Republican threat to democracy, casting it as rank anti-Americanism. He brings a distinctive attitude to dealing with opponents. In a 2022 conversation with *Vox* reporter Christian Paz, Gallego remarked: "Too many young Democrats grew up watching West Wing thinking that's what politics is." On the contrary, he argued, "Politics is dark and hard. It's not a bunch of people trying to do their best. It's who can shank each other in a smarter way." As Paz noted in his article, "Ruben Gallego's Ready for a Fight—Even if the Democratic Party Isn't," Gallego thinks "politics should be treated like more of an existential fight."[21]

Gallego doesn't hesitate to jump into the culture wars—and always on his own terms. Following the 2020 election, when 10 percent of Hispanic voters shifted to Trump, a concerned liberal asked Gallego: "[H]ow do we as a party improve our work with the LatinX community? It's so frustrating to see so many republican LatinX voters." Gallego, a leader of the Congressional Hispanic Caucus, responded: "First start by not using the term LatinX." He explained: "For this name to be kind of imposed upon the community, what a lot of Latinos felt was [that it was] inappropriate, especially because we felt it was coming mostly from white progressives."

When Kari Lake, the 2022 MAGA G.O.P. nominee for Arizona governor who's now running against Gallego for the Senate, endorsed a bigot in an Oklahoma state primary race, Gallego tweeted: "Only reason @KariLake supports an antisemite or a homophobe for office is that she is both." He followed up: "Imagine losing your shit defending a bigot . . . just ditch the fucker. Why keep endorsing a bigot unless you are trying to keep the bigot vote." And he kept cranking up the heat: "hi Kari so the candidate you endorsed said 'Jews will go to hell' do you agree with that statement?" A few Gallego tweets later, Lake withdrew her endorsement of the Oklahoma extremist.

Other high-dominance liberal patriots include Adam Schiff, the California congressman who now appears to be headed to the Senate on the strength of his hardcore campaign against the Republicans' betrayal of democracy. Another is Eric Swalwell, the 42-year-old California congressman who chairs the Future Forum, a group of 50 young members of Congress. While most Democratic leaders have punted on taking political advantage of Trump's Russia ties, Swalwell has led the charge to unmask Trump's fealty to Putin.[22] The former prosecutor and the son and brother of police officers was a constant thorn in the side of short-lived Republican House Speaker Kevin McCarthy. As McCarthy shepherded through a surreal censure of Schiff for conducting the January 6 investigation, Swalwell stood next to the Speaker, staring at him and saying: "This is pathetic. You're weak. You're a weak man."

The next day, McCarthy confronted Swalwell outside the men's room, telling him: "If you ever say something like that to me again, I'm gonna kick the shit out of you." After some heated back and forth, McCarthy said: "Call me a pussy again, and I'll kick your ass." Swalwell leaned in: "You. Are. A. Pussy." McCarthy stepped back and Swalwell brushed past him to relieve himself.

Many liberals might feel uncomfortable adopting high-dominance tactics themselves, but we love seeing one of our own taking it to the other side. Noted the reporter who covered the Swalwell-McCarthy encounter: "While Democrats may not love the particular insult—a gendered slur denoting that someone lacks courage—they are absolutely delighting in the exchange. They believe it's indicative of McCarthy's empty threats and ultimate weakness."[23]

Democracy's defenders have plenty of would-be mentors, past and present, to inspire and guide us, as we'll see in the following chapters. As we make our way through their words, let's bear in mind that the challenges they faced were every bit as formidable as ours. Each leader, moreover, had flaws, large and small. You don't have to be a saint—and no one is—to be a democratic hero. And there's nothing they said and did that we and our leaders can't say and do today.

24. Frederick Douglass: The Greatness and Grandeur of the Future of the Republic

America knows no greater intellect, more committed patriot, or mightier builder of democracy than Frederick Douglass. Born into slavery, Douglass went on to become the most eloquent spokesperson for Americanism the nation has ever known. He had to teach himself to read in secret, away from the prying eyes of his owners, but he became one of the most masterful literary voices in American history. He dominated his detractors with his contempt for prevailing opinion, the force of his mind, and his capacity to appeal to the best in human nature. No horrors he or his fellow African Americans suffered quenched his nationalism, which stands as a largely untapped example for liberals today.

Here we will read portions of "Composite Nation," which Douglass delivered, in various iterations to audiences across the country, during the early years after the Civil War.[24] Like King's "Speech on the Civil Rights Movement in the United States and the Anti-Apartheid Movement in South Africa," which we discussed earlier, "Composite Nation" is poorly known but full of minable riches. No one had more bitterly condemned America's closed door to Blacks while slavery was in force, but after the Civil War, Douglass saw no end to the nation's potential for advancement. He regarded his mission as lifting Americans' eyes from their nation's near-death experience and pointing their gaze to everything they had already achieved and everything they could yet become.

This speech focuses specifically on the wave of new immigration from China that was picking up at the time. Douglass knew that most Americans despised Chinese immigrants and that the few who welcomed them were former slavers who sought a new influx of cheap labor. But that didn't keep Douglass from envisioning the Chinese as full members of the nation, long before most Americans imagined such a thing. He saw welcoming them as the next step in building on America's demographic dynamism, helping the nation prove the ineffable power of ethnic multiplicity. His iron faith in American democracy, his description of the nation's demographic destiny, and his belief in the nation's mission to lead the world by example perfectly articulates America's national-democratic story.

Douglass's vision is obviously aspirational, and it may never be fulfilled. As we read it now, however, might we not ask ourselves: Has it not in part already been realized, to a greater extent than many of us dare admit? And wouldn't its optimistic vision help arm democrats to defeat those who would define the nation as the possession of the native-born ethnic majority?

Douglass's opening pays eloquent tribute to the centrality of the nation in human life. The set-up he uses leaves little doubt as to the irresistible—and positive—power of nationalism:

> As nations are among the largest and the most complete divisions into which society is formed, the grandest aggregations of organized human power; as they raise to observation and distinction the world's greatest men, and call into requisition the highest order of talent and ability for their guidance, preservation and success, they are ever among the most attractive, instructive and useful subjects of thought, to those just entering upon the duties and activities of life.

The simple organization of a people into a National body, composite or otherwise, is of itself an impressive fact. As an original proceeding, it marks the point of departure of a people, from the darkness and chaos of unbridled barbarism, to the wholesome restraints of public law and society. It implies a willing surrender and subjection of individual aims and ends, often narrow and selfish, to the broader and better ones that arise out of society as a whole. It is both a sign and a result of civilization.

Douglass then expresses his vision of the American nation—strong, rising, ethnically plural, overflowing with promise:

I am especially to speak to you of the character and mission of the United States, with special reference to the question whether we are the better or the worse for being composed of different races of men. I propose to consider first, what we are, second, what we are likely to be, and, thirdly, what we ought to be.

Without undue vanity or unjust depreciation of others, we may claim to be, in many respects, the most fortunate of nations. We stand in relation to all others, as youth to age. Other nations have had their day of greatness and glory; we are yet to have our day, and that day is coming. The dawn is already upon us. It is bright and full of promise. Other nations have reached their culminating point. We are at the beginning of our ascent. They have apparently exhausted the conditions essential to their further growth and extension, while we are abundant in all the material essential to further national growth and greatness.

Large swaths of the country still lay in ashes, and former slaves labored under what could be regarded as re-enslavement in the form of debt peonage and a convict-leasing system. But in passages that should embarrass current-day liberal brooders and skeptics, Douglass ridicules those who regard the past as a golden age and the country as incapable of advancement. I admit to feeling shame at my own occasional bouts of bleakness in the face of my country's current challenges when I read these passages:

> It is thought by many, and said by some, that this Republic has already seen its best days; that the historian may now write the story of its decline and fall.
>
> Two classes of men are just now especially afflicted with such forebodings. The first are those who are croakers by nature—the men who have a taste for funerals, and especially National funerals. They never see the bright side of anything and probably never will ... They usually begin by telling us what we never shall see.
>
> ... During the late contest for the Union [the Civil War], the air was full of nevers, every one of which was contradicted and put to shame by the result, and I doubt not that most of those we now hear in our troubled air, will meet the same fate.

Douglass spells out what renders American democracy an affront to despots abroad as well as to bigots and pessimists at home:

> A Government founded upon justice, and recognizing the equal rights of all men; claiming no higher authority for existence, or sanction for its laws, than nature, reason, and the regularly ascertained will of the people; steadily refusing to put its sword and purse in the service of any religious creed or family is a standing offense to most of the Governments of the world, and to some narrow and bigoted people among ourselves.
>
> To those who doubt and deny the preponderance of good over evil in human nature; who think the few are made to rule, and many to serve; who put rank above brotherhood, and race above humanity; who attach more importance to ancient forms than to the living realities of the present; who worship power in whatever hands it may be lodged and by whatever means it may have been obtained; our Government is a mountain of sin, and, what is worse, it seems confirmed in its transgressions.

He again chides reformers who marinate in skepticism about the nation's promise and treats ignoring progress as an impediment to tackling the formidable tasks at hand:

> [Americans] have a right to be impatient and indignant at those among ourselves who turn the most hopeful portents into omens of disaster, and make themselves the ministers of despair when they should be those of hope, and help cheer on the country in the new and grand career of justice upon which it has now so nobly and bravely entered. Of errors and defects we certainly have not less than our full share, enough to keep the reformer awake, the statesman busy, and the country in a pretty lively state of agitation for some time to come. Perfection is an object to be aimed at by all, but it is not an attribute of any form of Government.

America's political problem, according to Douglass, isn't defects in its form of government or the principles on which it is based. They provide all the institutional and philosophical wherewithal needed to ensure continual progress. He also casts doubt on claims that changes in political institutions, public consciousness, or economic structures are prerequisites for preserving and improving democracy. Instead, group inequality and relations stand as the greatest obstacle to national advancement. His message is more relevant than ever today:

> Something different, something better, or something worse may come, but so far as respects our present system and form of Government, and the altitude we occupy, we need not shrink from comparison with any nation of our times. We are today the best fed, the best clothed, the best sheltered and the best instructed people in the world.
>
> . . . The real trouble with us was never our system or form of Government, or the principles underlying it; but the peculiar composition of our people, the relations existing between them

and the compromising spirit which controlled the ruling power of the country.

. . . Heretofore the policy of our government has been governed by race pride, rather than by wisdom. Until recently, neither the Indian nor the negro has been treated as a part of the body politic. No attempt has been made to inspire either with a sentiment of patriotism, but the hearts of both races have been diligently sown with the dangerous seeds of discontent and hatred.

But rather than be deterred by current injustices, Douglass unfolds his concept of a "composite nation" that is destined to augment the country's potential and atone for its past by welcoming a new wave of people from a land whose customs differ from America's:

Before the relations of these two races are satisfactorily settled, and in spite of all opposition, a new race is making its appearance within our borders, and claiming attention. It is estimated that not less than one hundred thousand Chinamen, are now within the limits of the United States. Several years ago every vessel, large or small, of steam or sail, bound to our Pacific coast and hailing from the Flowery kingdom, added to the number and strength of this new element of our population.

Douglass is under no illusions about the motives that drive many of those who welcome the new wave of immigrants:

Not only is there a Chinese motive behind this probable immigration, but there is also an American motive which will play its part, one which will be all the more active and energetic because there is in it an element of pride, of bitterness, and revenge.

Southern gentlemen who led in the late rebellion, have not parted with their convictions at this point, any more than at others. They want to be independent of the negro . . . Hence these gentlemen have turned their attention to the Celestial Empire. They would rather have laborers who will work for nothing; but as they cannot get the negroes on these terms, they want China-men who, they hope, will work for next to nothing.

Still, he regards mass immigration from across the Pacific as the next step in the advancement of America's mission, just as immi-gration from other regions had been and continued to be in his day:

> ... Assuming then that this immigration already has a foothold and will continue for many years to come, we have a new ele-ment in our national composition which is likely to exercise a large influence upon the thought and the action of the whole na-tion.
>
> ... I have said that the Chinese will come, and have given some reasons why we may expect them in very large numbers in no very distant future. Do you ask, if I favor such immigration, I answer I would...Would you have them naturalized, and have them invested with all the rights of American citizenship? I would. Would you allow them to vote? I would. Would you allow them to hold office? I would.
>
> ... I want a home here not only for the negro, the mulatto and the Latin races; but I want the Asiatic to find a home here in the United States, and feel at home here, both for his sake and for ours.

In Douglass's mind, America's manifest destiny lay not so much in settlers moving West but in accommodating a new wave of arri-vals from the East. Doing so would give rise to a historically unprec-edented national entity that would demonstrate to the wider world just how high humankind could reach:

> And here I hold that a liberal and brotherly welcome to all who are likely to come to the United States, is the only wise policy which this nation can adopt.

278

It has been thoughtfully observed, that every nation, owing to its peculiar character and composition, has a definite mission in the world.

. . . I need to stop here to name or describe the missions of other and more ancient nationalities. Ours seems plain and unmistakable. Our geographical position, our relation to the outside world, our fundamental principles of Government, world embracing in their scope and character, our vast resources, requiring all manner of labor to develop them, and our already existing composite population, all conspire to one grand end, and that is to make us the [most] perfect national illustration of the unit and dignity of the human family, that the world has ever seen...We are not only bound to this position by our organic structure and by our revolutionary antecedents, but by the genius of our people.

Americans had nothing to fear and everything to gain from absorbing new arrivals. The wave of immigration from a culturally distant land would expand Americans' hearts and minds, enabling the nation to reach heights yet unattained:

Contact with these yellow children of The Celestial Empire would convince us that the points of human difference, great as they, upon first sight, seem, are as nothing compared with the points of human agreement. Such contact would remove mountains of prejudice.

. . . If we would reach a degree of civilization higher and grander than any yet attained, we should welcome to our ample continent all nations, kindreds tongues and peoples; and as fast as they learn our language and comprehend the duties of citizenship, we should incorporate them into the American body politic. The outspread wings of the American eagle are broad enough to shelter all who are likely to come.

For Douglass, America had already begun to show the world the manifold advantages of unity in diversity. Douglass celebrates the contributions of every nationality:

> Our Republic is itself a strong argument in favor of composite nationality. It is no disparagement to Americans of English descent, to affirm that much of the wealth, leisure, culture, refinement and civilization of the country are due to the arm of the negro and the muscle of the Irishman. Without these and the wealth created by their sturdy toil, English civilization had still lingered this side of the Alleghenies, and the wolf still be howling on their summits.
>
> To no class of our population are we more indebted to valuable qualities of head, heart and hand than the German. Say what we will of their lager, their smoke and their metaphysics they have brought to us a fresh, vigorous and child-like nature; a boundless facility in the acquisition of knowledge; a subtle and far reaching intellect, and a fearless love of truth. Though remarkable for patient and laborious thought the true German is a joyous child of freedom, fond of manly sports, a lover of music, and a happy man generally. Though he never forgets that he is a German, he never fails to remember that he is an American.

By bringing in Chinese immigrants, the nation would transform its new members, and they would transform America, to the benefit of both. By realizing its demographic destiny, the American nation, already immeasurably blessed by its form of government, geography, and economic potential, would stand as an unrivaled beacon to the world:

> It is objected to the Chinaman that he is secretive and treacherous, and will not tell the truth when he thinks it for his interest to tell a lie. There may be truth in all this; it sounds very much like the account of man's heart given in the creeds. If he will not tell the truth except when it is for his interest to do so, let us

make it for his interest to tell the truth. We can do it by applying to him the same principle of justice that we apply to ourselves.

. . . Let the Chinaman come; he will help to augment the national wealth. He will help to develop our boundless resources; he will help to pay off our national debt. He will help to lighten the burden of national taxation. He will give us the benefit of his skill as a manufacturer and tiller of the soil, in which he is unsurpassed.

. . . I close these remarks as I began. If our action shall be in accordance with the principles of justice, liberty, and perfect human equality, no eloquence can adequately portray the greatness and grandeur of the future of the Republic.

We shall spread the network of our science and civilization over all who seek their shelter whether from Asia, Africa, or the Isles of the sea. We shall mold them all, each after his kind, into Americans; Indian and Celt; negro and Saxon; Latin and Teuton; Mongolian and Caucasian; Jew and Gentile; all shall here bow to the same law, speak the same language, support the same Government, enjoy the same liberty, vibrate with the same national enthusiasm, and seek the same national ends.

These words were uttered by a man who was born into slavery in he knew not what year. He was taken from his mother as an infant, and then at six years old was torn from his grandparents. In a daring dash to freedom as a young man, he escaped bondage and then endured a life of harsh discrimination despite his fame and genius. As he spoke these words, practically all African Americans lived in penury, and life expectancy among all Americans averaged 35 years. Are we so arrogant as to believe that the challenges we now face are worse than those Douglass—and the nation—faced back then? If he embraced the vision of America articulated here, who are we to doubt the majesty and promise of the nation's ideals, both aspirational and attained?

Remarkably, "Composite Nation" is poorly known and rarely, if ever used by liberals as a basis for defining Americanism. Nor does it appear in many school curricula. The bit of Douglass most students encounter comes from *Narrative of the Life of Frederick Douglass, an American Slave.* Published in 1845, this autobiography is a masterpiece, and it transformed Americans' consciousness about the lives of enslaved Americans. But Douglass penned it when he was just 27. Many also know "What, to the Slave, Is the Fourth of July?," Douglass's bitter 1852 evisceration of the then-half-free, half-slave nation. These are among the most formidable and heartfelt condemnations of slavery ever penned, but they can't possibly convey the full scope of Douglass's subsequent role as a towering creator of the American nation. Far fewer know "Composite Nation" or Douglass's "Eulogy for Abraham Lincoln," which were written decades later and number among the most evocative expressions of Americanism ever offered.

Shouldn't these works enjoy pride of place in our kids' American history education? What could more effectively foster fellow feeling among all the groups that coalesce in the American nation? And who more effectively links America's greatness and liberal immigration policy than Frederick Douglass? He honors the contributions of German, English, and Irish immigrants, even though some members of these groups enslaved him and his fellow African Americans. He worked to open Americans' hearts to immigrants from across the Pacific, who now make up a plurality of new arrivals to the United States. Might not "Composite Nation" spark enthusiasm for racial justice among *all* who call ourselves Americans?

25. John F. Kennedy: That Pledge Has Been Fulfilled

I t was the fall of 1963, time for John Kennedy to gear up for reelection. With the 1964 contest about a year away, he headed to Texas to get things rolling. Bringing Texas Senator Lyndon Johnson onto the ticket had helped put Kennedy over the top by a whisker in the Lone Star state in 1960. But it was still a conservative place, and the president wasn't taking it for granted.

In his 1960 campaign against Vice President Richard Nixon, Kennedy argued that the Eisenhower Administration's unimaginative, laissez-faire response to the mild economic recession was slowing down recovery. A staunch liberal, he pressed for more vigorous government intervention.

But above all, he campaigned on nationalism and leadership. He charged that the Republicans were failing to confront the global authoritarian threat with adequate vigor. He wrapped his every progressive aim in the flag. He held that Republicans' limp social welfare policies and tepid approach to civil rights failed to show the world what America—and democracy—were made of. He argued that it was time for the baton to pass to a leader who fully grasped the magnificence of what the nation could become. His speeches were laced with talk of national greatness.

Now that the time was drawing near to face the voters again, Kennedy knew that not everything was going his way—to put it mildly. The economy wasn't doing much better than when his presidency began. On the foreign policy front, he'd seen the country through the Cuban Missile Crisis with aplomb. But he'd also engineered a national humiliation with the Bay of Pigs invasion, a botched effort to overthrow Fidel Castro. Shortly thereafter, Soviet leader Nikita Khrushchev was widely seen as having owned him during their summit in Vienna.

Kennedy had stood up for African Americans, not least in his searing June 11, 1963, address to the nation on civil rights. He knew his bold stand could cost him Southern states that had carried him over the line in 1960—and Texas in particular. What's more, as the 1964 election approached, his ambitious agenda on the economy, social programs, and civil rights was largely stalled by Republican resistance.

In private, Kennedy judged himself harshly, and his mood was often anything but buoyant. When his speechwriter, Theodore Sorensen, told him that some historians were planning to write books on his first year in office, Kennedy responded: "Who would want to write a book on disasters?"[25]

His mood was often dimmed by his physical condition. He struggled with a debilitating autoimmune disease that had set in when he was 15 years old. The unremitting pain he felt thereafter only intensified following the watery trek he made after his PT boat was cut in half by a Japanese destroyer in the South Pacific during World War II. He was 25 years old at the time, and he led his crew of 11 on a three-mile swim to safety, dragging one of them through the waves on a strap he used to bind their bodies together.

Kennedy could have used his illness to escape military service. Instead, he leveraged his well-connected father's influence to get into the Navy despite his medical condition. While in the military, he always wore a corset-like brace and kept a plywood board underneath his mattress, much as he did for the rest of his life. During his subsequent political career, he suffered from extreme back, stomach, and colonic pain. He often got around on crutches when the cameras weren't rolling.[26]

But the public never caught wind of his political insecurities or physical agony. What people outside his family and inner circle saw were unremitting displays of confidence—in himself, in the nation he led, and in the policies he purveyed.

That was the source—the main source—of his power and popularity. Nobody, of course, grasped this fact more than Kennedy himself.

So as he launched his reelection bid in the fall of 1963, it was no surprise that he didn't shrink from spelling out his accomplishments or boldly predicting victory—for himself and the Democratic Party. If he had advisers who warned him against doing so until a booming economy sent the stars into perfect alignment, it never showed in his messaging.

His speech to Democratic Party officials in Austin began with these words:

> One hundred and eighteen years ago last March, President John Tyler signed the Joint Resolution of Congress providing statehood for Texas. And 118 years ago this month, President James Polk declared that Texas was a part of the Union. Both Tyler and Polk were Democratic Presidents. And from that day to this, Texas and the Democratic Party have been linked in an indestructible alliance—an alliance for the promotion of prosperity, growth, and greatness for Texas and for America.
>
> Next year that alliance will sweep this State and Nation.

Then straight to the economy, which was steaming ahead, courtesy of his own policies:

> In Grand Prairie, I pledged in 1960 that this country would no longer tolerate the lowest rate of economic growth of any major industrialized nation in the world. That pledge has been and is being fulfilled. In less than 3 years our national output will shortly have risen by a record $100 billion—industrial production is up 22 percent, personal income is up 16 percent . . . No

period of economic recovery in the peacetime history of this Nation has been characterized by both the length and strength of our present expansion—and we intend to keep it going.

That pledge has been and is being fulfilled—and he intended to keep delivering.

The development of natural resources, of human potential—it was all coming together on Kennedy's watch:

In Dallas, I pledged in 1960 to step up the development of both our natural and our human resources. That pledge has been fulfilled.... A new national park, a new wildlife preserve, and other navigation, reclamation, and natural resource projects are all under way in this State. At the same time we have sought to develop the human resources of Texas and all the Nation, granting loans to 17,500 Texas college students, making more than $17 million available to 249 school districts. . . . Civilization, it was once said, is a race between education and catastrophe—and we intend to win that race for education.

That pledge has been fulfilled—and civilization itself was winning.

Under the president's leadership, moreover, civil rights were advancing as never before. And Kennedy's policies didn't just yield gains for justice; they promoted domestic tranquility and honored the Constitution. Above all, Kennedy was just doing what was right:

In San Antonio, I pledged in 1960 that a new administration would strive to secure for every American his full constitutional rights. That pledge has been and is being fulfilled. We have not yet secured the objectives desired or the legislation required. But we have, in the last 3 years, by working through voluntary leadership as well as legal action, opened more new doors to members of minority groups—doors to transportation, voting, education, employment, and places of public accommodation—

than had been opened in any 3-year or 30-year period in this century. There is no noncontroversial way to fulfill our constitutional pledge to establish justice and promote domestic tranquility, but we intend to fulfill those obligations because they are right.

That pledge has been and is being fulfilled—and his anti-Constitutional opponents could suck it up and get used to it.

Remarking on a policy that he cherished, Kennedy weighed in on his race to space:

In Texarkana, I pledged in 1960 that our country would no longer engage in a lagging space effort. That pledge has been fulfilled. We are not yet first in every field of space endeavor, but we have regained worldwide respect for our scientists, our industry, our education, and our free initiative.

That pledge has been fulfilled—and the whole world was standing in awe of America's prowess.

Back on Earth, the nation's defenses were stronger than they had ever been—and unquestionably the world's most capable:

In Fort Worth, I pledged in 1960 to build a national defense which was second to none—a position I said, which is not "first, but," not "first, if," not "first, when," but first—period. That pledge has been fulfilled. In the past 3 years we have increased our defense budget by over 20 percent . . . We can truly say today, with pride in our voices and peace in our hearts, that the defensive forces of the United States are, without a doubt, the most powerful and resourceful forces anywhere in the world.

That pledge has been fulfilled—and Americans had every reason to exalt in their nation's preeminence.

Propelled by the president's and his party's direction, America—and its values—were on the march in every conceivable way. The world couldn't help but take notice:

> Finally, I said in Lubbock in 1960, as I said in every other speech in this State, that if Lyndon Johnson and I were elected, we would get this country moving again. That pledge has been fulfilled. In nearly every field of national activity, this country is moving again—and Texas is moving with it. From public works to public health, wherever Government programs operate, the past 3 years have seen a new burst of action and progress—in Texas and all over America. We have stepped up the fight against crime and slums and poverty in our cities, against the pollution of our streams, against unemployment in our industry, and against waste in the Federal Government. We have built hospitals and clinics and nursing homes. We have launched a broad new attack on mental illness and mental retardation. We have initiated the training of more physicians and dentists. We have provided 4 times as much housing for our elderly citizens, and we have increased benefits for those on social security.
>
> Almost everywhere we look, the story is the same. In Latin America, in Africa, in Asia, in the councils of the world and in the jungles of far-off nations, there is now renewed confidence in our country and our convictions.

That pledge has been fulfilled—in fact, the wins were getting practically impossible to tally, and the winning would not stop.

As long as he and the Democrats were in charge and the country remained steadfast in fulfilling its destiny, nothing could ever stop its ascent. The president's speech concluded:

> For this country is moving and it must not stop. It cannot stop. For this is a time for courage and a time for challenge. . . . So let us not be petty when our cause is so great. Let us not quarrel amongst ourselves when our Nation's future is at stake. Let us

stand together with renewed confidence in our cause—united in our heritage of the past and our hopes for the future—and determined that this land we love shall lead all mankind into new frontiers of peace and abundance.[27]

If you have never heard these words, it's because they were never uttered. Hours before he intended to deliver his address in Austin, Kennedy was cut down by an assassin's bullet in Dallas. But this speech—with its unapologetically credit-claiming, Republican-owning, combative, flag-waving, self-assured, optimistic thrust—embodied how Kennedy addressed his fellow Americans.

And as always in political communication, *attitude* is everything. It's easy to find credit-claiming in any politician's statements, but the way Kennedy does it differs from the ass-covering, I-sure-hope-I'm-not-offending-anyone-who-might-not-have-felt-the-benefits-yet vibe that pervades Democratic messaging today. And while Kennedy's speech is chock-full of policy details, its thrust isn't wonkish. Kennedy doesn't just list his accomplishments; he conveys *I am a powerful leader, and my leadership has worked and will work for you in the future.* He often says the job isn't done yet, but he leaves no doubt that the country is on a roll under his leadership and that he'll surely finish the job.

His message, moreover, isn't just a collection of verses (the specific promises and policies); it's got a clear refrain (*That pledge has been fulfilled*). He gets to the bottom line quickly, intoning it immediately after stating the pledge he made earlier. Then, and only then, does he delve into specifics. The listener could forget every promise and policy detail and still come away feeling that this man is kicking ass, taking names, and getting the job done for them, day in and day out.

Maybe that's why we've never really stopped mourning his loss. Who has ever made us feel better about being Americans—and liberals—than President Kennedy? Today, in surveys on the popularity of ex-presidents, only Abraham Lincoln scores higher; Kennedy ties for second place with George Washington. Among Millennials, he and Lincoln tie for first; Washington and Obama come in second.[28]

26. Lyndon Johnson and Ronald Reagan: Opening America's Golden Door

R iding a wave of grief-stricken nostalgia for his predecessor, Lyndon Johnson overcame the Senate filibuster of Kennedy's proposed legislation to ban racial segregation in public accommodations and to prohibit discrimination in employment and voter registration. The Civil Rights Act of 1964 was the product of Kennedy's vision, King's moral pressure, and Johnson's matchless powers of persuasion, arm-twisting, and political manipulation. Johnson had perfected his high-dominance—perhaps a better term would be hyper-dominance—style during his years as what Robert Caro aptly called the "Master of the Senate" in his magisterial biography of the man who was born in a farmhouse near Stonewall, Texas, and raised in a land without electricity.[29]

Johnson went on to enact what was arguably the greatest crush of progressive legislation in American history. It was greater, perhaps, than Franklin Roosevelt's New Deal, since Johnson's Great Society programs and flurry of civil rights legislation explicitly cut everyone in, while Blacks were selectively excluded from some New Deal benefits. After swatting away a primary challenge from George Wallace and squashing Barry Goldwater in the general election, Johnson signed the Voting Rights Act of 1965. With his pen stroke, he ensured that descendants of those who had begun arriving in chains over a third of a millennium before would enjoy the franchise along with everyone else, thereby completing the democratization of America.

Less well-known than his civil rights and Great Society legislation, but of a vital piece with them, was Johnson's momentous immigration reform. America from its origins had been a land of immigration, but the path to Frederick Douglass's magnificent vision had proved to be long and strewn with obstacles. Shortly after Douglass urged his fellow Americans to open their borders and hearts to arrivals from East Asia in his Composite Nation address, the Chinese Exclusion Act of 1882 banned the immigration of Chinese laborers, making it the only law in American history that targeted a specific national group. Still, waves of immigration from other parts of the world grew, and some Chinese continued to gain admission. Between 1860 and 1910, the share of the foreign-born population rose from 10 to 15 percent.

The Immigration Act of 1924, however, radically cut the inflow and limited large-scale immigration to people from Western Europe. Consequently, the proportion of Americans born abroad fell to just five percent in 1965, and the country's foreign-born racial complexion lightened.

Without the wily hand of our second-greatest civil rights president, the nation might have continued its march away from Douglass's awesome ideal. But with the Immigration Act of 1965, America reopened its doors to people of color. Among its other effects, by 2020, the bill had enabled a ten-fold increase in Americans of Chinese origin.

Speaking in the shadow of the Statue of Liberty upon signing the law, this is how President Lyndon Johnson rekindled Frederick Douglass's dream and ensured America's enduring greatness:[30]

> [The Immigration Act] repair[s] a very deep and painful flaw in
> the fabric of American justice. It corrects a cruel and enduring
> wrong in the conduct of the American Nation...[T]he fact is that

for over four decades the immigration policy of the United States has been twisted and has been distorted by the harsh injustice of the national origins quota system. Under that system the ability of new immigrants to come to America depended upon the country of their birth. Only 3 countries were allowed to supply 70 percent of all the immigrants.

Families were kept apart because a husband or a wife or a child had been born in the wrong place.

Men of needed skill and talent were denied entrance because they came from southern or eastern Europe or from one of the developing continents.

This system violated the basic principle of American democracy—the principle that values and rewards each man on the basis of his merit as a man. It has been un-American in the highest sense, because it has been untrue to the faith that brought thousands to these shores even before we were a country.

Today, with my signature, this system is abolished.

We can now believe that it will never again shadow the gate to the American Nation with the twin barriers of prejudice and privilege.

Our beautiful America was built by a nation of strangers . . . The land flourished because it was fed from so many sources— because it was nourished by so many cultures and traditions and peoples.

And from this experience, almost unique in the history of nations, has come America's attitude toward the rest of the world. We, because of what we are, feel safer and stronger in a world as varied as the people who make it up—a world where no country rules another and all countries can deal with the basic problems of human dignity and deal with those problems in their own way.

Now, under the monument which has welcomed so many to our shores, the American Nation returns to the finest of its traditions today. . . .

Over my shoulders here you can see Ellis Island, whose vacant corridors echo today the joyous sound of long-ago voices.

And today we can all believe that the lamp of this grand old lady is brighter today—and the golden door that she guards gleams more brilliantly in the light of an increased liberty for the people from all the countries of the globe.

Does that sound anything like the hedged, morally muddled, defensive message you hear from Democrats in response to Trumpian nativism today? Or does it sound more like a leader who is *owning* the enemies of the second pillar of Americanism—demographic dynamism born of immigration?

Fast-forward a quarter-century, and we find the words of another president whose belief in America's promise, secured through immigration, inspired countless Americans—especially new ones. As an intellect and a builder of democracy, Ronald Reagan was no Frederick Douglass—nor, for that matter, Lyndon Johnson. But his far-less-than-stellar record on some fronts, combined with his conservative credentials, make his last public statement in office even more remarkable.[31] Current-day liberals' failure to echo his rhetoric, while perhaps understandable given his stance on many other issues, is a missed opportunity to confront MAGA's nativist assaults. His address was as brief as it was bravura, and it merits quotation in its entirety.

Reagan opened with his intention to reveal what he cherishes most about America:

> Since this is the last speech that I will give as President, I think it's fitting to leave one final thought, an observation about a country which I love.

He then universalized the nation. America is magnificent because *it is the world*. Ethnicity and national origin have nothing to do with it; *anyone* can be an *American*:

> It was stated best in a letter I received not long ago. A man wrote me and said: "You can go to live in France, but you cannot

become a Frenchman. You can go to live in Germany or Turkey or Japan, but you cannot become a German, a Turk, or Japanese. But anyone, from any corner of the Earth, can come to live in America and become an American."

America is special, so much so that people from everywhere are irresistibly drawn to its promise. Who wouldn't want to be part of such a sublime project?

> Yes, the torch of Lady Liberty symbolizes our freedom and represents our heritage, the compact with our parents, our grandparents, and our ancestors. It is that lady who gives us our great and special place in the world. For it's the great life force of each generation of new Americans that guarantees that America shall continue unsurpassed into the next century and beyond. Other countries may seek to compete with us; but in one vital area, as a beacon of freedom and opportunity that draws the people of the world, no country on earth comes close.
>
> This, I believe, is one of the most important sources of America's greatness. We lead the world because, unique among nations, we draw our people—our strength—from every country and every corner of the world. And by doing so we continuously renew and enrich our nation.

Reagan then issued a warning to any who would undermine American vitality by interfering with the nation's demographic dynamism. He cast the nation as youthful and rising, in contrast with other countries whose best days were behind them. While the comparison with other countries might rub some liberals the wrong way, this is exactly how Frederick Douglass portrayed America in Composite Nation:

> While other countries cling to the stale past, here in America we breathe life into dreams. We create the future, and the world follows us into tomorrow. Thanks to each wave of new arrivals to

this land of opportunity, we're a nation forever young, forever bursting with energy and new ideas, and always on the cutting edge, always leading the world to the next frontier. This quality is vital to our future as a nation. If we ever closed the door to new Americans, our leadership in the world would soon be lost.

Reagan spoke of his country's goodness, drawing on the story of a man from the part of Germany that labored under Soviet control between the end of World War II and 1989:

> A number of years ago, an American student traveling in Europe took an East German ship across the Baltic Sea. One of the ship's crew members from East Germany, a man in his sixties, struck up a conversation with the American student. After a while the student asked the man how he had learned such good English. And the man explained that he had once lived in America.
>
> He said that for over a year he had worked as a farmer in Oklahoma and California, that he had planted tomatoes and picked ripe melons. It was, the man said, the happiest time of his life.
>
> Well, the student, who had seen the awful conditions behind the Iron Curtain, blurted out the question, "Well, why did you ever leave?" "I had to," he said, "the war ended." The man had been in America as a German prisoner of war.
>
> Now, I don't tell this story to make the case for former POWs. Instead, I tell this story just to remind you of the magical, intoxicating power of America. We may sometimes forget it, but others do not. Even a man from a country at war with the United States, while held here as a prisoner, could fall in love with us. Those who become American citizens love this country even more. And that's why the Statue of Liberty lifts her lamp to welcome them to the golden door.

By bravely embarking on their American journey, immigrants bring themselves untold bounty:

It is bold men and women, yearning for freedom and opportunity, who leave their homelands and come to a new country to
start their lives over. They believe in the American dream. And
over and over, they make it come true for themselves, for their
children, and for others.

Even more important than what immigrants do for themselves
is what they do for America. They are vital to the American project,
fueling innovation and building national might. But this isn't their
only contribution, or even the greatest one. Still more critically, they
remind the native-born of the majesty of their country:

They give more than they receive. They labor and succeed. And
often they are entrepreneurs. But their greatest contribution is
more than economic, because they understand in a special way
how glorious it is to be an American. They renew our pride and
gratitude in the United States of America, the greatest, freest
nation in the world—the last, best hope of man on Earth.

Reagan, like Douglass and Johnson, wrapped his rhetoric on immigration in a vision of a great nation made still more excellent by
welcoming new arrivals. He didn't speak of immigration's merit primarily in terms of humanitarian obligation. While he hailed the
gains immigrants have made, he credited their own efforts and the
courage they showed by coming to America. He portrayed immigrants as makers of the American nation, not its hard-pressed casualties.

Reagan's rhetoric, with its emphasis on national competitive-
ness and greatness, armed him to achieve remarkable reforms. In
1986, he pushed through the most sweeping progressive immigration measure in recent American history: He amnestied everyone
who had entered the country unlawfully before 1982. He sold it as a
means of enhancing border security and seeing to it that new arrivals
would not be breaking the law as they strengthened the American

economy. With his signature, three million people, mostly Hispanics, gained legal status and protection from deportation.[32]

Reagan's approach and the results he achieved could hardly differ more starkly from the Democrats' messaging on immigration today—and what their efforts yield. Our approach is a contradictory mish-mash of arguments for immigration on humanitarian grounds, insinuations that calls for border controls are coded racism, and on-again, off-again crackdowns that amount to disingenuous appeasement of nativists. As *Washington Post* columnist Perry Bacon argued in July 2023: "The problem is that Biden and the broader Democratic Party's approach to immigration is largely defensive. The Democrats are (in theory at least) against Trump-style immigration policies and rhetoric. At the same time, they are against being portrayed by Republicans and FOX News as too immigrant-friendly." Bacon rightly claimed that "neither senior Democratic officials nor those on the broader left are articulating a clear vision of immigration policy to contrast with the right."[33]

There's little sign of Johnson's and Reagan's nationalistic, unapologetic case for liberal immigration policy in current-day Democrats' low-dominance, low-nationalism messaging. In the absence of such leadership, to cite Bacon, "The United States' current immigration posture is one of fear. We seem to be saying that our native-born workers can't compete with immigrants; our communities can't integrate new people; and our citizens, a huge percentage of whom are the descendants of European immigrants, won't welcome darker-skinned people." We might add that immigration has joined the basket of other hot-button cultural issues that the Democrats spend more time eluding than confronting and taking to the bank in elections.

The results are plain to see. Since the beginning of the century, the Democrats have been trying to pass the DREAM Act, which would afford temporary residency, along with a path to citizenship, for undocumented immigrants who entered the country as children. The DREAM Act is far less ambitious than Reagan's 1986 amnesty, but even though a large majority of Americans support the measure, the Democrats have been unable to enact it.[34]

Were Americans just more friendly to immigration in the late 20th century? Was it for that reason easier for Reagan to enact his far-reaching reform than it would be for liberal leaders today?

Exactly the opposite is true. When Reagan issued his blanket amnesty in 1986, 49 percent of Americans wanted immigration reduced, compared to 38 percent today. Seven percent wanted to increase immigration, compared to 31 percent today. Roughly one third wanted to keep it at present levels (35 percent then and 31 percent today). Public opinion is much more favorable to liberal immigration policy now than in the 1980s.[35]

Whatever his shortcomings as a civil libertarian, Reagan treated the ceaseless creation of new Americans from everywhere in the world as key to American greatness. The revival of Reagan's memory by anti-Trump Republicans might up their chances of de-throning Trump. In 2021, even as Trump retained his grip on the G.O.P. and 32 years after Reagan left office, a plurality of Republicans said that Reagan, not Trump, had been the best president of the past 40 years.[36] G.O.P. leaders who recognize Trump's drag on the party would be wise to resurrect Reagan, all the more given his impeccable tax-slashing and culturally conservative credentials. Their failure to do so leaves the Democrats a precious opening—if we can only overcome our qualms about speaking of American glory and exceptionalism with no ifs, ands, or buts.

Under Trump, the Republicans have retreated to rank nativism, betraying a core pillar of Americanism even in the face of a pro-immigrant public. Douglass's, Johnson's, and Reagan's muscular liberal nationalism sits on a shelf, awaiting Democratic leaders who will seize it and wield it to advance our causes and electoral prospects.

27. Jasmine Crockett: Republicans in the Shitter

L et's fast-forward to the present day, where Jasmine Crockett is emerging as one of the Democrats' highest-dominance assets. While the glamorous 42-year-old congresswoman from Dallas was an undergraduate at Rhodes College in Memphis, she planned to become an accountant, but after being the victim of a hate crime she decided to pursue law and became a civil rights attorney. She won election to Congress in 2020 and was reelected in 2022. It's a safe bet she'll be a fixture in the House for the foreseeable future.

Every element of the high-dominance archetype we laid out earlier shines through in Crockett's style and messaging. Her takedowns of Marjorie Taylor Greene, Lauren Boebert, and other MAGA miscreants on the House floor are becoming the stuff of legend.[37] On the Republicans' defense of the January 6 insurrectionists, whose assault led to the deaths of three police officers, Crockett said: "The party of law and order is now saying defund law enforcement. Right? The party that backs the blue is also the party that was bashing the blue on January 6."

She draws a contrast between MAGA and real conservatives: "[I]f you are a real Republican, like old-school Republican, you should be offended and saying hey, I want nothing to do with this. Because this isn't the Republican Party, this is something completely different...We know that they do not believe in law and order."[38]

Here Crockett is reaching out to Republicans, but not by going easy on the out-of-reach deplorables. Instead, she reminds potentially persuadable conservatives that they're no longer casting their ballots for a Reagan or a McCain. Her style also reminds these people that if they want to play on the team with the bigger cojones, she can show them a pair that no small-handed ex-president can match.

Is Biden paying attention?

Crockett has a passion for gun control but in a Texas-kind-of way. Shortly after the May 10, 2023, mass shooting in Allen, Texas, which lies just outside her congressional district, she spoke with *Guardian* Washington correspondent David Smith.[39]

First, some background: Clad in tactical gear, a gunman plastered with Nazi tattoos and an RWDS [Right Wing Death Squad] patch pulled up to a crowded shopping mall. Within four minutes, he used his AR-15 military assault rifle to murder eight people and wound seven others. After the massacre, the police found five more guns in his car. All of them, including the AR-15, had been purchased legally.

During his 2000 and 2004 presidential campaigns, George W. Bush had vowed to work with Congress to renew Bill Clinton's Assault Weapons Ban. But just as it was set to expire in 2004, congressional Republicans refused to take up the matter, and Bush let it go. Instead, the Republicans enacted federal legislation to protect gun manufacturers against lawsuits. Democrats have tried to renew the assault-weapons ban ever since, but united Republican opposition has blocked it.

Which brings us back to Crockett's *Guardian* interview, where she called the Republicans "cowards" on guns. She asserted: "No one wants to accept that part of the chaos and carnage is actually being stoked by the rhetoric that is being spewed by the Republican Party."

Crockett registered support for an AR-15 ban, but she did so with a twist: "I myself am a Texan. I own a gun—or a couple. I am licensed to carry." But, she continued, "There are definitely guns that we want to take away because it's the equivalent of some of these people having [a] cannon; I'm sorry, but it's not OK for my next-door neighbor to have a cannon."

Yes, she went there.

Other Democrats seldom do. They almost never say they intend to *take away* anyone's guns, even AR-15s. Nothing incites anxiety and hatred among the compensating men with gun racks in their Ford F-450 Super Duty pickup trucks like threats to *take away* their guns. So Democratic politicians take pains not to go anywhere near that kind of language—perhaps because they fear physical as well as political attack. But Crockett can talk with gun goons, gun-owner to gun-owner, and they certainly don't intimidate her.

She'll have no part of pessimism about her party's prospects anywhere. Smith asked her whether it was lonely to be a Democrat in the Lone Star state. He recounts: "Counterintuitively, however, Crockett contends that Texas is already a blue state." She told him: "I believe my state is blue because we're probably the only majority-minority state that is 'red'; most majority-minority states are blue. So demographically it's there." And in her estimation, MAGA madness just provides more opportunities for Democrats. Speaking of their post-Roe abortions bans, she said: "As a criminal defence attorney, I have had to deal with cases where fathers were raping their little girls . . . Honestly, the Republicans have thrown us a bone, and it is going to be moms and young people" who will ensure the Democrats' future gains.

When she's not owning illiberals in the press, she's taking it to them on the House floor. During a Republican hearing on crime in D.C., one of the G.O.P.'s favorite subjects, MAGA loon Anna Paulina Luna launched into a breathless and dubious claim of a rise in sexual assaults in the capital. Crockett responded: "I am so excited that my colleagues across the aisle care about sexual abuse considering that their front runner for the presidency has just been found liable of sexual abuse, so I'm excited! Because this may mean that, finally, some folk will back off from supporting him."

Predictably, videos of Crockett's pugnacity go viral and prompt comments such as these following the *YouTube* post of her exchange with Luna: "If I was a Dem on Jasmine's committee, I would just yield my time to her and let her continue to go off on MAGA Republicans"; "Rep. Crockett is a force to be reckoned with and I can't wait to see what else she does! She is intelligent, articulate & knows how to shove the Repubs face in their own crap so eloquently"; "I am a registered republican and i stand with Ms. Crockett on everything she just said"; "Ms. Crockett is genius at shutting up those clowns" [five clown-face icons]; "I love when a MAGA says something really stupid and they think is gonna really own a lib and the libs come back with the truth, aka facts!"; and "Jasmine Crockett is amazing. She is exactly the kind of person America needs in positions of power."[40]

Crockett is all that and more. And being new to Washington, she apparently hasn't gotten the memo from hapless party operatives telling her to dial it back and keep her eye on the ball—which would be the next supplemental bill on infrastructure or prescription drug prices. That, together with heartfelt expressions of sympathy for "struggling working families," would of course be the key to defeating Trumpism.

Crockett is having too much fun skewering MAGA opponents and defending democracy to be bothered with patronizing naysaying. She's doing her own thing, mixing lawyerly analytic mastery and gleeful gut punches wrapped in down-home—and often transgressive—language.

Her womanhandling of Republicans as they try to impeach Biden is a portrait of high-dominance prowess. House Oversight Chairman Rep. James Comer is presiding over the impeachment hearings. A MAGAman of manifestly modest mental means, Comer claims G.O.P. investigators have "uncovered a mountain of evidence revealing how Joe Biden abused his public office for his family's financial gain."[41] His evidence is—don't you just know it—crusty, debunked attacks on Hunter Biden's dealings in Ukraine, topped off with Trump's bizarre claims about Biden's supposed China ties.

Trump, who says Xi Jinping is "smart, brilliant, everything perfect," claims Biden is in hoc to the Chinese government. Trump's word, of course, is good enough for Comer's "investigators."[42]

Crockett's statement at the first hearing, which *Daily Kos* called "5 minutes of mic-drop moments," displays how she works.[43] The panel was hearing from a grab bag of Republican witnesses whose testimony kept falling flat, much to Comer's chagrin.

So Crockett got right to the point:

> Thank you so much, Mr. Chair. Before I begin my questioning, I want to remind everyone that the information recorded in the FBI Form 1023 that my Republican colleagues keep citing is not evidence of anything. This form reflects the years-old secondhand unverified information from a Ukrainian oligarch as relayed to the FBI by a confidential human source. These un-verified second-hand allegations have been repeatedly de-bunked and undermined, including by the confidential human source who relayed this information to the FBI.
>
> The tip, recorded in the Form 1023, was thoroughly explored by the U.S. attorney handpicked by Donald Trump, which was Attorney General William Barr and the assessment was closed. Finally, Devin Archer, Hunter Biden's former business partner who worked with the Ukrainian oligarch in question, told this committee in a transcribed interview in July that he had no knowledge of any such payments allegedly described in this form.

Unable to resist tying the deceitful basis of the impeachment ef-fort to the Republicans' favorite invention, Crockett offered words that Biden should be roaring three times a week:

> Repeating the same lies will not somehow turn them into truths. Kind of like the election that Trump lost: Say it with me. He lost it. Repeating the same lie that he won wasn't going to turn the

election around. The "lost" in this chamber keep pushing lies and lunacy on behalf of a multi-time loser.

Crockett then turned to the fabrications about Biden's corrupt China ties:

So if we gon' talk about China, let's go ahead and talk about China. And let's talk about the dealings. And let me point out the fact that right now each of you has admitted that none of you are fact witnesses. We walked in without facts. And unfortunately, because what we say isn't necessarily evidence, we have wasted the American people's time and we are going to walk out of this chamber, and we still have no facts that are leading to anything.

But let me give y'all a little bit of tea while we're here. So: I have a document that I will ask for unanimous consent to enter into the record. It's a fact sheet on President Trump's shady business dealings with the Chinese government.

Comer: What are you entering in? A record from who?

Crockett: This is from the Congressional Integrity.

Comer: Congressional Integrity Project, the dark-money PAC. I object. Object to that too.

Crockett: Of course y'all are going to object, but we gon' talk about it. So it says Trump has extensive financial ties to the Chinese government. President Trump collected millions from Chinese government-owned entities while in office: "I have the best tenants in the world." President Trump was well aware of the multiple million-dollar lease to Chinese interests. President Trump promised to donate foreign government profits while in office, but he donated less than a third of his proceeds from the Chinese government.

President Trump maintained three foreign bank accounts while in office, including one in China. President Trump's business with China raises legal and ethical concerns. President Trump: "President Xi loves the people of China. He loves his country, and he's doing a very good job."

Turning to Michael Gerhardt, a law professor from the University of North Carolina who served as the Democrats' witness, Crockett posed a question:

Let me tell you something: I don't want to talk about what y'all want to act like is some big mystery because we keep sitting here. And Professor Gerhardt, just to be clear: As my colleagues have even tried to provide evidence, which they're not the ones to provide evidence. Have you ever heard them say "if" since we've been sitting here for I don't know how long?

Gerhardt: Yes, I've been taking a tally.

Crockett: Oh, okay. Can you show us what the tally is?

Gerhardt: More than 35 times the Republican witnesses and Republican members of the committee have used the word "if."

Crockett: Thank you so much for that. Because honestly, if they would continue to say "if" or "Hunter," and we were playing a drinking game, I would be drunk by now.

But while the Republican witnesses' arguments seemed to indicate that they'd already reached that state, Crockett was far from it. Now she turned to taking apart their charges and the "evidence":

Because I promise you, they have not talked about the subject of this [hearing], which would be the president. But let me tell you something that was so disturbing as I walked into this chamber today. As I prepared, I said, *"What is the crime?"*

Because when you're talking about impeachment, you're talking about high crimes or misdemeanors. And I can't seem to find the crime. And honestly, no one has testified of what crime they believe the president of the United States has committed.

But there was plenty of criminal evidence against a certain former president to discuss. Crockett started with Trump's indictments for keeping top-secret documents related to national security in a bathroom at his private residence. Waving publicly available photocopies of papers Trump stored next to the toilet, Crockett proclaimed:

But when we start talking about things that look like evidence, they want to act like they blind. They don't know what this is. These are our national secrets. Looks like in the shitter to me. This looks like more evidence of our national secrets—say on a stage at Mar-a-Lago. When we're talking about somebody that's committed high crimes, it's at least indictments. Let's say 32 counts related to unauthorized retention of national security secrets. Seven counts related to obstructing the investigation. Three false statements. One count of conspiracy to defraud the United States. Falsifying business records. Conspiracy to defraud the United States. Two counts related to efforts to obstruct the vote certification proceedings. One count of conspiracy to violate civil rights. Twenty-three counts related to forgery or false document statements. Eight counts related to soliciting. And I could go on because he's got 91 counts pending right now.

Crockett had reached her crescendo. All that was left to do was defend Biden. In her virtuoso denouement, she reminded listeners that the sum total of charges amounted only to attacks on Hunter Biden, and that the only "crime" the president had committed was standing by his son:

But I will tell you what the president has been guilty of: He has, unfortunately, been guilty of loving his child unconditionally. And that is the only evidence that they have brought forward. And honestly, I hope and pray that my parents love me half as much as he loves his child. Until they find some evidence, we need to get back to the people's work, which means keeping this government open so that people don't go hungry in the streets of the United States.

She finished with:

And I will yield.

Well, not really. She never really does *that.*

As for her "in the shitter" comment about where Trump hid the classified documents: This time it was the Republicans who were consumed with umbrage, offended by her barnyard language. And they're apparently helpless to prevent the inclusion of the indeco-rous term in the Congressional Record. It would seem that such language is unprecedented—unprecedented!—in the august, age-old annals of congressional proceedings.

Now we're talking.

28. Franklin Roosevelt: The Forces of Selfishness and Lust for Power Meet Their Match

N ow let's again cast our eyes back to an earlier time that in some ways resembled the world we inhabit today, though economic circumstances were far more dire then than anything we can now imagine. Like today, authoritarian pressures were building, and they combined to imperil peace and democracy at home and abroad.

The address we will examine was delivered by President Franklin Roosevelt on October 31, 1936, six days before his first reelection. The audio is available on *YouTube*, and I hope you'll listen to it after reading the excerpts here. There's no way to capture it fully in print.[44]

Hitler, Mussolini, and Stalin were turning the lights of democracy off across Europe. In the United States, fascists found a mouthpiece in Father Charles Coughlin. His radio program prefigured Rush Limbaugh and Tucker Carlson, spreading a mix of evangelical fervor, "America First" isolationism, and ethnonational bigotry to tens of millions.

Coughlin had originally supported Roosevelt, but the president held him at arm's length. The demagogic priest then turned against him and became an apologist for foreign enemies of democracy, much like Trump-allied media have done on behalf of Putin and Hungary's Viktor Orbán. The Republican Party of Roosevelt's time did not openly side with America's enemies the way Trump and his party now line up with Putin. But the United States was mired in the Great Depression, and there was reason to fear that some Americans could prove susceptible to the wiles of demagogues as had happened in Europe.

Roosevelt's most urgent task was to convince the people that they had nothing to fear but pessimism and hopelessness—and, of course, fear itself. His iron self-confidence, optimism, commitment to democracy, and high-dominance style were the mightiest weapons in his arsenal.

The president began by spelling out the stakes and assuring his supporters that they were the champions. The showdown was indeed between the two major parties, and the American people—led by the Democrats—were in the mood to win:

> Senator Wagner, Governor Lehman, my friends:
>
> On the eve of a national election, it is well for us to stop for a moment and analyze calmly and without prejudice the effect on our Nation of a victory by either of the major political parties.
>
> The problem of the electorate is far deeper, far more vital than the continuance in the Presidency of any individual. For the greater issue goes beyond units of humanity—it goes to humanity itself.
>
> In 1932 the issue was the restoration of American democracy; and the American people were in a mood to win. They did win. In 1936 the issue is the preservation of their victory. Again they are in a mood to win. And again they will win.
>
> More than four years ago in accepting the Democratic nomination in Chicago, I said: "Give me your help not to win votes alone, but to win in this crusade to restore America to its own people."
>
> And we know tonight that the banners of that crusade still fly in the forefront of a Nation that is still on the march.

Who were the foot soldiers—the winners—in this noble quest? They included the tired, the poor, the masses who yearned to breathe free from the oppression of want. So too did they encompass employers and property owners who yearned for a better life:

> Tonight I call the roll—the roll of honor of those who stood with us in 1932 and still stand with us today. Written on that roll of honor are the names of millions who never had a chance— men at starvation wages, women in sweatshops, children at looms. Written on it are the names of those who despaired, young men and young women for whom opportunity had become a will-o'-the-wisp. Written on it are the names of farmers whose acres yielded only bitterness, business men whose books were portents of disaster, home owners who were faced with eviction, frugal citizens whose savings were insecure.

But those who struggled weren't the only winners and heroes. Americans who had less to fear from want but whose consciences dictated their actions figured prominently as well. Indeed, their names were written on the honor roll "in large letters":

> Written there in large letters are the names of countless other Americans of all parties and all faiths, Americans who had eyes to see and hearts to understand, whose consciences were burdened because too many of their fellow beings were burdened, who looked on these things four years ago and said, "This can be changed. We will change it."

All these soldiers of righteousness stood together with their president, and their ranks were only swelling:

> We still lead that army in 1936. They stood with us then, in 1932, because they believed. They stand with us today in 1936 because they know. And with them, with them stand millions. Yes, with

them stand millions of new recruits who have *come* to know. Their hopes have become our record.

We have not come thus far without a struggle, and I assure you we cannot go further without a struggle.

Roosevelt then reminded his listeners of the travails of the recent past. Here he was referring to the Republican administrations that had preceded his own and the catastrophes they had abided. But they were in charge no longer; they had been replaced by the partisans of justice and practitioners of effective government:

For twelve years our Nation was afflicted with hear-nothing, see-nothing, do-nothing Government. The Nation looked to that Government but that Government looked away. Nine mocking years with the golden calf and three long years of the scourge! Nine crazy years at the ticker and three long years in the breadlines! Nine mad years of mirage and three long years of despair! And my friends, powerful influences strive today to restore that kind of government with its doctrine that that Government is best which is most indifferent to mankind.

For nearly four years now you have had an Administration which instead of twirling its thumbs has rolled up its sleeves. And I can assure you that we will keep our sleeves rolled up.

Roosevelt extended no olive branch to those who refused to join him. Instead, having flashed a sublime portrait of his own arrayed armies, he painted a picture of the wicked forces they had begun to subdue. Give him four more years and he'd surely show you—they'd be wriggling under his heel. There is no hint of the fear of rousing enemies—or of calling them what they are. Instead, we witness one who never shrank from the high-dominance tactic of distinguishing between a virtuous, effective "us" and a treacherous, inept "them." Here we find a bold commander; let his words resound:

We had to struggle with the old enemies of peace—business and financial monopoly, speculation, reckless banking, class antagonism, sectionalism, war profiteering.

They had begun to consider the Government of the United States as a mere appendage to their own affairs. And we know now that Government by organized money is just as dangerous as Government by organized mob. Never before in all our history have these forces been so united against one candidate as they stand today. They are unanimous in their hate for me—and I welcome their hatred.

I should like to have it said of my first Administration that in it the forces of selfishness and of lust for power met their match. I should like to have it said of my second Administration that in it these forces met their master.

Roosevelt then turned the tables on those who claimed he was fomenting class war. In his national-democratic narrative, their path ran from injustice to class division; his own, from justice to class peace. They claimed they couldn't keep supplying the jobs if the Democrats kept having their way (sound familiar?). They wailed that the Democrats would wreck American capitalism. But the American people would never fall for the age-old tactic of despots who sought to delude them:

Here is an amazing paradox! The very employers and politicians and newspapers who talk most loudly of class antagonism and the destruction of the American system now undermine that system by this attempt to coerce the votes of the wage earners of the country. It is the 1936 version of the old threat to close down the factory or the office if a particular candidate does not win. It is the old strategy of tyrants to delude their victims into fighting their battles for them.

The people themselves powered the march to justice, but their vehicle was the government. Today's Democrats hardly confront the poisonous anti-government rhetoric of a Republican Party that seeks to defund the IRS and eviscerate the "deep state." They opt instead for wan, occasional commendations of "hardworking civil servants." Such defensive drivel was foreign to Roosevelt's high-dominance, opinion-making messaging. He stood up for the government's honor instead. He even tarred those who didn't like their government as foes of democracy and aliens to the American nation. And if they didn't like the new, more just America—well, they were free to leave:

> But they are guilty of more than deceit. When they imply that the reserves thus created [by higher taxes on employers to finance insurance for workers] . . . will be stolen by some future Congress, diverted to some wholly foreign purpose, they attack the integrity and the honor of American Government itself. Those who suggest that are already aliens to the spirit of American democracy. Let them, let them emigrate and try their lot under some foreign flag in which they have more confidence.

But, of course, most businessmen were honest, loyal Americans. They, too, grasped that they were ill-served by the propagandists of fear and division:

> I am sure that the vast majority of law-abiding businessmen who are not parties to this propaganda fully appreciate the extent of the threat to honest business contained in this coercion. I have expressed indignation at this form of campaigning and I am confident that the overwhelming majority of employers, and workers, and the general public share that indignation and will show it at the polls on Tuesday next.

Who did the president speak for? For the United States of America, that's who:

But aside from this phase of it, I prefer to remember this campaign not as bitter but only as hard-fought. There should be no bitterness or hate where the sole thought is the welfare of the United States of America. No man can occupy the office of President without realizing that he is President of all the people.

Roosevelt then turned to his program. He enumerated no legislation but instead presented the aims and highest purposes of his policies. If you listen to the speech, you will hear him lean hard on the words *of course* that precede his every statement. They create the impression that his programs—all of which were unprecedented and radical by the standards of his time—were nothing more than common sense, the mere pursuit of moral objectives that any American of goodwill was reflexively bound to embrace. And, as in the speeches of John Kennedy and Bill Clinton that we examined earlier, his song had a battle cry that served as its refrain. Roosevelt's refrain was: *We have only just begun to fight:*

Of course, of course we will continue to seek to improve working conditions for the workers of America—to reduce hours that are over-long, to increase wages that spell starvation, to end the labor of children, and to wipe out sweatshops.

Of course we will continue every effort to end monopoly in business, to support collective bargaining, to stop unfair competition and to abolish dishonorable trade practices. And for all these we have only just begun to fight.

Of course we will continue to work for cheaper electricity in the homes and on the farms of America, for better and cheaper transportation, for low interest rates, for sounder home financing, for better banking, for the regulation of security issues, for reciprocal trade among nations, and for the wiping out of slums. And my friends, for all these we have only just begun to fight.

Of course we will continue our efforts in behalf of the farmers of America. With their continued cooperation we will do all in our power to end the piling up of huge surpluses which spelled ruinous prices for their crops. We will persist in successful action for better land use, for reforestation, for the conservation of water all the way from its source to the sea, for drought control and flood control, for better marketing facilities for farm commodities, for a reduction of farm tenancy, for encouragement of farm cooperatives, for crop insurance and for a stable food supply for the nation. And for all these, too, we have only just begun to fight.

Why would the nation help its citizens in need? First, because employment beats idleness; second, because it's *right*. And of those who fail to honor the less fortunate? Well, they stood against the Scriptures:

Of course we will provide useful work for the needy unemployed because we prefer useful work to the pauperism of a dole.

And here and now I want to make myself clear about those who disparage their fellow citizens on the relief rolls. They say that those on relief are not merely jobless—they say they are worthless. Their solution for the relief problem is to end relief—to purge the rolls by starvation. To use the language of the stock broker, our needy unemployed would be cared for when, as, and if some fairy godmother should happen to come on the scene.

But you and I will continue to refuse to accept that estimate of our unemployed fellow Americans. Your Government is still on the same side of the street with the Good Samaritan and not with those who pass by on the other side.

But Roosevelt's battleplan wasn't yet exhausted:

To go on—what of our objectives?

Of course we will continue our efforts for young men and women so that they may obtain an education and an opportunity to put it to use.

Of course we will continue our help for the crippled, for the blind, for the mothers, our insurance for the unemployed, our security for the aged.

Of course we will continue to protect the consumer against unnecessary price spreads, against the costs that are added by monopoly and speculation. We will continue our successful efforts to increase his purchasing power and keep it constant.

And for these things, too, and for a multitude of things like them, we have only just begun to fight.

For all his thunder about living standards, Roosevelt wraps up by intoning an eternal truth: Democracy is neither centrally about nor mainly upheld by material interests. Far above politics or the economy, only devotion to high moral purpose could elicit what is best in us as individuals and as a nation; only that could sustain our democracy. He again draws on Scripture—here, the words of the evangelist Luke (2:14) and the Hebrew Prophet Micah (6:8)—to sacralize his cause:

"Peace on earth, good will toward men"—democracy must cling to that message. For it is my very deep conviction that democracy cannot live without that true religion which gives a nation a sense of justice and of moral purpose. Above our political forums, above our market places stand the altars of our faith, altars on which burn the fires of devotion that maintain all that is best in us and all that is best in our Nation.

We have need of that devotion today. It is that which makes it possible for government to persuade those who are mentally prepared to fight each other to go on instead, to work for and to sacrifice for each other. And that is why we need to say with the old Prophet: "What doth the Lord require of thee—but to do justly, to love mercy and to walk humbly with thy God." That is why the recovery we seek, the recovery we are winning, is more than economic. In it are included justice and love and humility,

317

not for ourselves as individuals alone, but for our Nation. And that—that—is the road to peace.

That following Tuesday, Roosevelt defeated his Republican opponent, Alf Landon, 61–37 in the popular vote and 538–8 in the Electoral College. Roosevelt's happy tirade proved prescient: The American people had been in the mood to win again—and so they won again.

Nor was Roosevelt's other promise an idle boast. By the time he rolled on to whip still another Republican to secure a third term in 1940, "the forces of selfishness and of lust for power" had met their master.

29. Mary McLeod Bethune: What American Democracy Means to Me

M ary McLeod Bethune was the daughter of slaves, and she and her 16 siblings grew up picking cotton in Sumpter County, South Carolina. As she advanced in years, Bethune became a renowned organizer. In 1935, at the age of 60, she founded the National Council of Negro Women. At that time, she and Eleanor Roosevelt became close friends.

Eleanor's husband was a proponent of civil rights, but he had to make compromises that limited African Americans' access to some New Deal programs to maintain the Southern portion of his coalition. The First Lady was a constant source of pushback against these concessions, and she urged her husband to make Bethune the Director of the Office of Minority Affairs in the National Youth Administration. She knew the quality of Bethune's mind, and the power of her faith and ideas.

Aside from her official post, Bethune emerged as an important figure in the civil rights movement. Every Friday evening, she convened an intimate gathering of the nation's Black leaders. One was A. Philip Randolph, who brought trade unionism to Black Americans during the New Deal Era. He also led the movement to abolish segregation of the armed forces, which Harry Truman did by executive order in 1948. Another was Walter White, the writer who led the NAACP between 1929 and 1955.

On November 23, 1939, about a year before Franklin won a third term in the White House, she joined "America's Town Meeting of the Air," a weekly radio broadcast on NBC. America was still in the grips of the Depression, and African Americans in the South were still a quarter-century away from gaining the right to vote.

The question posed to Bethune that evening was: "What does American democracy mean to me?" The structure, cadence, and spirit of her response resemble what Americans would later hear in the speeches of Martin Luther King.

Now that you've survived this book to the end, I have one last request of you: Listen to her words, don't just read them here. They're available on *YouTube*. Her majestic voice will dispel your darkest doubts about our ability to conquer the emergency we face today.[45]

Here is the story Mary McLeod Bethune told of what democracy meant to her:

> Democracy is for me, and for 12 million black Americans, a goal towards which our nation is marching. It is a dream and an ideal in whose ultimate realization we have a deep and abiding faith. For me, it is based on Christianity, in which we confidently entrust our destiny as a people. Under God's guidance in this great democracy, we are rising out of the darkness of slavery into the light of freedom. Here my race has been afforded opportunity to advance from a people 80 percent illiterate to a people 80 percent literate; from abject poverty to the ownership and operation of a million farms and 750,000 homes; from total disfranchisement to participation in government; from the status of chattels to recognized contributors to the American culture.
>
> As we have been extended a measure of democracy, we have brought to the nation rich gifts. We have helped to build America with our labor, strengthened it with our faith and enriched it with our song. We have given you Paul Lawrence Dunbar, Booker T. Washington, Marian Anderson and George Washington

Carver. But even these are only the first fruits of a rich harvest, which will be reaped when new and wider fields are opened to us.

The democratic doors of equal opportunity have not been opened wide to Negroes. In the Deep South, Negro youth is offered only one-fifteenth of the educational opportunity of the average American child. The great masses of Negro workers are depressed and unprotected in the lowest levels of agriculture and domestic service, while the black workers in industry are barred from certain unions and generally assigned to the more laborious and poorly paid work. Their housing and living conditions are sordid and unhealthy. They live too often in terror of the lynch mob; are deprived too often of the Constitutional right of suffrage; and are humiliated too often by the denial of civil liberties. We do not believe that justice and common decency will allow these conditions to continue.

Our faith envisions a fundamental change as mutual respect and understanding between our races come in the path of spiritual awakening. Certainly there have been times when we may have delayed this mutual understanding by being slow to assume a fuller share of our national responsibility because of the denial of full equality. And yet, we have always been loyal when the ideals of American democracy have been attacked. We have given our blood in its defense—from Crispus Attucks on Boston Commons to the battlefields of France. We have fought for the democratic principles of equality under the law, equality of opportunity, equality at the ballot box, for the guarantees of life, liberty and the pursuit of happiness. We have fought to preserve one nation, conceived in liberty and dedicated to the proposition that all men are created equal. Yes, we have fought for America with all her imperfections, not so much for what she is, but for what we know she can be.

Perhaps the greatest battle is before us, the fight for a new America: fearless, free, united, morally re-armed, in which 12 million Negroes, shoulder to shoulder with their fellow Americans, will strive that this nation under God will have a new birth of freedom, and that government of the people, for the people and by the people shall not perish from the earth. This dream, this idea, this aspiration, this is what American democracy means to me.

I bet it means something like that to you, too.

Source Notes

Introduction and Part One

[1] Kathleen Hall Jamieson, *Cyberwar: How Russian Hackers and Trolls Helped Elect a President* (New York: Oxford University Press, 2018).

[2] Marc Levy, "Lawmakers Ask Trump's Postmaster to Return Sorting Machines," *Associated Press*, September 1, 2020.

[3] "60 Percent of Americans Will Have an Election Denier on the Ballot This Fall," *FiveThirtyEight*, November 8, 2022; and Reid J. Epstein, "Echoing Trump, These Republicans Won't Promise to Accept 2022 Results," *New York Times*, September 18, 2022.

[4] Michael Gold, "After Calling Foes 'Vermin,' Trump Campaign Warns Its Critics Will Be 'Crushed'," *New York Times*, November 13, 2023.

[5] Donald P. Moynihan, "Trump Has a Master Plan for Destroying the 'Deep State'," *New York Times*, November 27, 2023.

[6] Quoted in Thomas B. Edsall, "What the Republicans Are Doing Is 'One of the Odd and Scary Things about Politics'," *New York Times*, April 19, 2023.

[7] David Brooks, "Republican or Conservative, You Have to Choose," *New York Times*, June 25, 2018.

[8] Katie Reilly, "Read Hillary Clinton's 'Basket of Deplorables' Remarks about Donald Trump Supporters," *Time*, September 10, 2016.

[9] Katie Reilly, "Hillary Clinton Says She Regrets Part of Her 'Deplorables' Comment," *Time*, September 10, 2016.

[10] Seema Mehta, "Clinton Apologizes for Calling Half of Trump's Supporters 'Deplorables'," *Los Angeles Times*, September 10, 2016.

[11] Roxanne Roberts, "Hillary Clinton's 'Deplorables' Speech Shocked Voters Five Years Ago—But Some Thought It Was Prescient," *Washington Post*, August 31, 2021.

[12] Philip Bump, "Trump's One-Day Dictatorship Becomes an Applause Line," *Washington Post*, December 11, 2023.

[13] Michael Gold, "Trump, Attacked for Echoing Hitler, Says He Never Read 'Mein Kampf'," *New York Times*, December 19, 2023.

[14] Riley Beggin, "Donald Trump Said He'd Be a Dictator for One Day. His Supporters Say They're Not Worried," *USA Today*, December 18, 2023.

[15] David Brooks, "Trump Came for Their Party but Took over Their Souls," *New York Times*, February 8, 2024.

[16] Derek Thompson, "Donald Trump and 'Economic Anxiety'," *The Atlantic*, August 18, 2016.

[17] Unless otherwise noted, data in this chapter are from the Federal Reserve Bank of St. Louis, Economic Data.

[18] "Decoupling of Wages from Productivity: What Implications for Public Policies?," *OECD Outlook* 1, 2 (2018) pp. 51-65.

[19] Nicolas Vega, "After Inflation, People Making U.S. Minimum Wage Are Earning Less Now Than 60 Years Ago," *CNBC*, July 20, 2022.

[20] "Share of Wage and Salary Workers in the United States Paid Hourly Wages at or below the Prevailing Federal Minimum Wage from 1979 to 2021," *Statista*.

[21] U.S. Department of Labor, "State Minimum Wage Laws," 2024.

[22] Ernie Tedeschi, "Americans Are Seeing the Highest Minimum Wage in History (without Federal Help)," *New York Times*, April 24, 2019; and Ernie Tedeschi, "Pay Is Rising Fastest for Low Earners. One Reason? Minimum Wages," *New York Times*, January 3, 2020.

[23] The General Social Survey, https://gss.norc.org/.

[24] Anne Case and Angus Deaton, "The Great Divide: Education, Despair, and Death," *Annual Review of Economics* 14, 2022, pp. 1-21 (quoted p. 3).

[25] Ryan Farrell and William Lawhorn, "Fast-Growing Occupations That Pay Well and Don't Require a College Degree," U.S. Bureau of Labor Statistics, June 2022; and "Made in America: The Past, Present, and Future of the American Steel Industry," Boyd Metals Blog.

[26] Jim Tankersley, Alan Rappeport, and Ana Swanson, "Factory Jobs are Booming Like It's the 1970s," *New York Times*, September 26, 2022.

[27] Jonathan Rothwell, "Does Loss of Manufacturing Jobs Lead to Lower Life Ratings?," *Gallup News*, September 5, 2017.

[28] Craig Copeland, "Trends in Employee Tenure, 1983-2022," Employee Benefits Research Institute, January 19, 2023.

[29] Robert Griffin and John Sides, "In the Red: Americans' Economic Woes Are Hurting Trump," Democracy Fund Voter Study Group, September 2018.

[30] Noam Gidron and Peter A. Hall, "The Politics of Social Status: Economic and Cultural Roots of the Populist Right," *British Journal of Sociology* 68, S1 (November 2017), pp. S57-S84; Noam Gidron and Peter A. Hall, "Populism as a Problem of Social Integration," *Comparative Political Studies* 53, 7 (2019), pp. 1027-1059; Justin Gest, Tyler Reny, and Jeremy Mayer, "Roots of the Radical Right: Nostalgic Deprivation in the United States and Britain," *Comparative Political Studies* 51, 13 (2018), pp. 1694-1719; Hans-Georg Betz, "The Emotional Underpinnings of Radical Right Populist Mobilization: Explaining the Protracted Success of Radical Right-Wing Populist Parties," Centre for the Analysis of the Radical Right Research Paper, June 2020; and

Zhen Jie Im, Nonna Mayer, and Jan Rovny, "The 'Losers of Automation': A Reservoir of Votes for the Radical Right?," *Research and Politics* 6, 1 (2019), pp. 1-7.

[31] Daniel Oesch and Nathalie Vigna, "A Decline in the Social Status of the Working Class? Conflicting Evidence for Eight Western Countries, 1987-2017," *Comparative Political Studies* 55, 7 (2022), pp. 1130-1157 (quoted pp. 1130, 1141-1143, 1145-1152).

[32] Anne Case and Angus Deaton, *Deaths of Despair and the Future of Capitalism* (Princeton, NJ: Princeton University Press, 2020).

[33] U.S. Congress Joint Economic Committee, "Long-Term Trends in Deaths of Despair," September 5, 2019; "Deaths from Excess Alcohol Use in the United States," Centers for Disease Control and Prevention; and "Drug Overdose Death Rates," National Institute on Drug Abuse, February 9, 2023. The data are age-adjusted, per 100k per year.

[34] All quoted passages from Case and Deaton, "The Great Divide."

[35] Matthew F. Garnett and Sally Curtin, "Suicide Mortality in the United States, 2001-2021," National Center for Health Statistics, NCHS Data Brief No. 494, April 2023.

[36] National Library of Medicine, "Death Rates for Suicide by Sex, Race, Hispanic Origin, and Age: United States, Selected Years, 1950-2018."

[37] Andrea M. Tilstra, Daniel H. Simon, and Ryan K. Masters, "Trends in 'Deaths of Despair' among Working-Aged White and Black Americans, 1990-2017," *American Journal of Epidemiology* 190, 9 (2021), pp. 1751-1759.

[38] David G. Blanchflower and Andrew Oswald, "Trends in Extreme Stress in the United States, 1993-2019," *American Journal of Public Health* 110, 10 (2020), pp. 1538-1544 (quoted p. 1539).

[39] Christopher J. Ruhm, "Deaths of Despair or Drug Problems?," Working Paper 24188.

[40] Lisa Marshall, "Opioids, Obesity—Not 'Despair Deaths'—Raising Mortality Rates for Whites," *CU Boulder Today*, July 19, 2017.

[41] Neil K. Mehta, Leah R. Abrams, and Mikko Myrskylä, "US Life Expectancy Stalls Due to Cardiovascular Disease, Not Drug Deaths," *PNAS* 117, 13 (2020).

[42] Bernice A. Pescosolido, Andrew Halpern-Manners, and Liyang Luo, "Trends in Public Stigma of Mental Illness in the US, 1996-2018," *JAMA Network*, December 21, 2021.

[43] "Drug Overdose Death Rates," figure 2.

[44] "DEA Laboratory Testing Reveals that 6 out of 10 Fentanyl-Laced Fake Prescription Pills Now Contain a Potentially Lethal Dose of Fentanyl," U.S. Drug Enforcement Administration, 2023; and Jan Hoffman, "Fentanyl Tainted Pills Bought on Social Media Cause Youth Drug Deaths to Soar," *New York Times*, May 19, 2022.

[45] "Drug Overdose Death Rates," figures 4 and 8.

[46] "The Tragic Rise of Fentanyl, Mapped," *Wall Street Journal*, December 14, 2022.

[47] Yuki Noguchi, "American Life Expectancy Is Now at Its Lowest Rate in Nearly Two Decades," *NPR*, December 22, 2022.

48 Hannah Ritchie, Max Roser, and Esteban Ortiz-Ospina, "Suicide," Our World in Data; and Hannah Ritchie and Max Roser, "Death Rate from Alcohol Use Disorders," Our World in Data. The numbers on suicide for the United States are not identical to those used above, since the WHO draws on a variety of sources from national governments to compile their global statistics. The WHO also calculates data on alcohol-related causes differently than the source used for the American data above.

49 Daniel Cox, Rachel Lienesch, and Robert P. Jones, "Beyond Economics: Fears of Cultural Displacement Pushing the White Working Class to Support Trump," PPRI/The Atlantic Report, May 9, 2017.

50 "U.S. Immigrants Are Seen More as a Strength Than a Burden to the Country," Pew Research Center, August 2020. See also Robert Wuthnow, *The Left Behind: Decline and Rage in Rural America* (Princeton, NJ: Princeton University Press, 2018).

51 "How the Political Typology Groups Compare: America's Openness," Pew Research Center, November 9, 2021.

52 Diana C. Mutz, "Status Threat, Not Economic Hardship, Explains the 2016 Presidential Vote," *Proceedings of the National Academy of Sciences* 115, 19 (2018), pp. E4330–E4439.

53 Lydia Saad, "Four in Ten Americans Still Highly Concerned about Illegal Immigration," *Gallup News*, April 19, 2022.

54 "Most Americans Are Critical of Government's Handling of Situation at the U.S.-Mexican Border," Pew Research Center, May 3, 2021; Andrew Daniller, "Americans' Immigration Policy Priorities: Divisions between—and within—the Two Parties," Pew Research Center, November 12, 2019; and "Immigration," *Gallup News*, July 28, 2022.

55 GSS.

56 Justin McCarthy, "Same-Sex Marriage Support Inches up to New High of 71%," *Gallup News*, June 1, 2022.

57 Harris-APNORC Report, "No Public Consensus on How Schools Should Discuss Sexuality and Racism," April 14, 2022.

58 Kim Parker, Juliana Menasce Horowitz, and Anna Brown, "Americans' Complex Views on Gender Identity and Transgender Issues," Pew Research Center, June 28, 2022.

59 Pippa Norris and Ronald Inglehart, *Cultural Backlash: Trump, Brexit, and Authoritarian Populism* (New York: Cambridge University Press, 2019). Quoted pp. 16, 90–91.

60 Erica Frankenberg and Rebecca Jacobsen, "The Polls—Trends: School Integration Polls," *Public Opinion Quarterly* 75, 4 (Winter 2011), pp. 788–811.

61 Frank Newport, "In U.S., 87% Approve of Black-White Marriage, vs. 4 Percent in 1958," *Gallup News*, July 25, 2013.

62 Thomas B. Edsall, "The Unsettling Truth about Trump's First Great Victory," *New York Times*, March 22, 2023. The paper is Justin Grimmer, William Marble, and Cole Tanigawa-Lau, "Measuring the Contribution of Voting Blocs to Election Outcomes," *SocArXiv Papers*, February 28, 2023.

[63] Ruy Teixeira, "Republicans Really Are the Party of the Working Class," *The Liberal Patriot*, March 30, 2023.

[64] Thomas Frank, *What's the Matter with Kansas? How Conservatives Won the Heart of America* (New York: Holt, 2005); and Thomas Frank, *Listen, Liberal: What Ever Happened to the Party of the People?* (New York: Picador, 2017). See also Sheri Berman and Maria Snegovaya, "Populism and the Decline of Social Democracy," *Journal of Democracy* 30, 3 (July 2019), pp. 5-19; Gary Gerstle, *The Rise and Fall of the Neoliberal Order: America and the World in the Free Market Era* (New York: Oxford University Press, 2022); Anna Grzymala-Busse, "Introduction to the Symposium on Global Populisms and the European Experience," *Polity* 51, 4 (October 2019), pp. 631-640; Matt Stoller, *Goliath: The 100-Year War Between Monopoly Power and Democracy* (New York: Simon and Schuster, 2020); David Leonhardt, *Ours Was the Shining Future: The Story of the American Dream* (New York: Random House, 2023); and Robert Kuttner, "Free Markets, Besieged Citizens," *New York Review of Books*, July 21, 2022.

[65] "Democrats Once Represented the Working Class. Not Any More," *The Guardian*, November 10, 2016.

[66] George Packer, "How America Fractured into Four Parts," *The Atlantic*, July-August 2021.

[67] Chang-Tai Hsieh, Erik Hurst, Charles L. Jones, and Peter Klenow, "The Allocation of Talent and U.S. Economic Growth," *Econometrica* 87, 5 (September 2019), pp. 1439-1474; "Doctor Demographics and Statistics in the U.S.," *Zippia*, 2023 Report; and U.S. Census Bureau, Jessica Semega and Melissa Kollar, *Income in the United States: 2021*, September 2022, p. 10.

[68] "Educational Attainment Distribution in the United States from 1960 to 2022," *Statista*.

[69] USDA Foreign Agricultural Service, "Record U.S. FY 2022 Agricultural Exports to China"; and U.S. Department of Commerce Office of Technology Evaluation, "U.S. Trade with China (2022)."

[70] "The Lessons from America's Astonishing Economic Record: The World's Biggest Economy Is Leaving Its Peers Even Further in the Dust," *The Economist*, April 13, 2023.

[71] Erica York, "Tracking the Economic Impact of U.S. Tariffs and Retaliatory Actions," Tax Foundation Report, April 1, 2022.

[72] Jonathan Rothwell, "The Miniscule Importance of Manufacturing in Far-Right Parties," *New York Times*, September 15, 2017.

[73] Art Swift, "Few U.S. Workers Worry about Tech Making Their Job Obsolete," *Gallup News*, August 14, 2017.

[74] Rothwell, "The Miniscule Importance of Manufacturing in Far-Right Parties."

[75] Congressional Budget Office, "The Distribution of Household Income, 2019," November 2022.

76 "Historical Tables," Office of Management and Budget, undated; "The Distribution of Household Income, 2018," Congressional Budget Office, August 4, 2021; Danielle Kurtzleben, "Understanding the Clintons' Popularity with Black Voters," *NPR*, March 1, 2016; and Robert J. Shapiro, "The Case for Bill Clinton's Economic Record," *Washington Monthly*, July 21, 2022.

77 Eric Van Nostrand and Laura Feiveson, "The Inflation Reduction Act and U.S. Business Investment," U.S. Department of the Treasury, August 16, 2023.

78 Jeffrey Sonnenfeld, "Yale Professor: Biden's Economy Most Successful since FDR's New Deal," *Yahoo News*, July 25, 2023; Ben Noon, "Biden Needs to Broaden Semiconductor Sanctions on China," *Foreign Policy*, April 3, 2023; Ana Swanson and Jim Tankersley, "Biden is Betting on Government Aid to Change Corporate Behavior," *New York Times*, February 28, 2023; Annie Lowrey, "Low-Wage Jobs Are Becoming Middle-Class Jobs," *The Atlantic*, March 4, 2023; and U.S. Department of Commerce, "By the Numbers: U.S. Economy Adds over 350,000 Jobs in January Exceeding Expectations," February 5, 2024.

79 "The State of American Jobs," Pew Research Center, October 6, 2016.

80 Lawrence Mishel and Josh Bivens, "Identifying the Policy Levers Generating Wage Suppression and Wage Inequality," Economic Policy Institute, May 13, 2021; and Jacob S. Hacker and Paul Pierson, *American Amnesia: How the War on Government Led Us to Forget What Made America Prosper* (New York: Simon and Schuster, 2016).

81 James Feigenbaum, Alexander Hertel-Fernandez, and Vanessa Williamson, "Right-to-Work Laws Have Devastated Unions—and Democrats," *New York Times*, March 8, 2018.

82 Eric Levitz, "Democrats Paid a Huge Price for Letting Unions Die," *Intelligencer*, November 18, 2018.

83 Harold Meyerson, "Why Can't Labor Get a Little More Help from Its Friends?," *The American Prospect*, March 28, 2010.

84 Eleanor Mueller, "Congress Thwarted Biden on Unions. Or Did It?," *Politico*, April 21, 2022.

85 Jesse Rhodes and Kaylee T. Johnson, "Welcoming Their Hatred: Class Populism in Democratic Rhetoric in American Presidential Campaigns, 1932–2012," *Presidential Studies Quarterly* 47, 1 (March 2017), pp. 92–121 (quoted p. 92).

86 Steven Levitsky and Daniel Ziblatt, *Tyranny of the Minority: How American Democracy Reached the Breaking Point* (New York: Random House, 2023).

87 "What Are the Current Swing States, and How Have They Changed over Time?," *USA Facts*, June 16, 2023; and Jocelyn Kiley, "Majority of Americans Continue to Favor Moving away from Electoral College," Pew Research Center, September 25, 2023.

88 J. Miles Coleman and Kyle Kondik, "A Brief History of the Electoral College," *Sabato's Crystal Ball*, UVA Center for Politics, July 6, 2023.

89 Nate Cohn, "Trump's Electoral College Edge Seems to be Fading," *New York Times*, September 11, 2023. See also Hunter Brown, "The Electoral College: It Doesn't

Always Lean Toward Republicans," *Sabato's Crystal Ball*, UVA Center for Politics, October 10, 2019.

90 Coleman and Kondik, "A Brief History of the Electoral College."

91 Morning Consult/POLITICO National Tracking Poll, October 2–4, 2021; and Sam Stein, "Dems Thought Giving Voters Cash Was the Key to Success: So What Happened?," *Politico*, October 11, 2021.

92 Noah Sheidlower, "The US Economy Is Doing Way Better Than the Rest of the Rich World," *Business Insider*, July 7, 2023; Bryan Mena, "The US Economy Grew at a Blistering Rate Despite High Interest Rates," *CNN.com*, October 26, 2023; Emily Peck, "Charted: Workers Win as Wage Growth Outpaces Inflation," *Axios*, February 5, 2024; Nicole Goodkind, "Dow Closes Just Points away from 40,000 as US Markets Rally to New Records," *CNN.com*, March 21, 2024; and Jeffrey Sonnenfeld and Steven Tian, "Bidenomics' Critics Are Being Proven Wrong. Happy Days Are Here Again," *Fortune*, July 23, 2023.

93 "State of the US Economy," *YouGov*, March 18, 2024.

94 "NBC News Poll: January 2024." See also David Brooks, "The Political Failure of Bidenomics," *New York Times*, February 22, 2024.

95 Timothy Noah, "No, the Republicans Aren't Better at Managing the Economy Than the Democrats," *The New Republic*, May 3, 2022.

96 "Cross-Tabs: October 2023 Times/Siena Poll of the 2024 Battlegrounds," *New York Times*, November 5, 2023.

Part Two

1 Steven J. Stanton et al., "Dominance, Politics, and Physiology," *PLOS ONE*, October 21, 2009.

2 Gulnaz Sharafutdinova, *Red Mirror: Putin's Leadership and Russia's Insecure Identity* (New York: Oxford University Press, 2020), p. 60.

3 "Owning the Libs," *Wikipedia*.

4 Dan P. McAdams, "The Appeal of the Primal Leader: Human Evolution and Donald J. Trump," *Evolutionary Studies in Imaginative Culture* 1, 2 (Fall 2017), pp. 1-13 (quoted pp. 2, 5).

5 Jeffrey E. Cohen, *Presidential Leadership in Public Opinion* (New York: Cambridge University Press, 2015), pp. 14, 15, 33.

6 Scott O. Lilienfeld et al., "Fearless Dominance and the U.S. Presidency: Implications of Psychopathic Personality Traits for Successful and Unsuccessful Political Leadership," *Journal of Personality and Social Psychology* 103, 3 (2012), pp. 489–505.

7 Cameron Anderson and Gavin J. Kilduff, "Why Do Dominant Personalities Attain Influence in Face-to-Face Groups? The Competence-Signaling Effects of Trait Dominance," *Journal of Personality and Social Psychology* 96, 2 (2009), pp. 491-503; and Hanna Aileen Genau and Gerhard Blickle, "Fearless Dominance: The Upside of

Psychopathy?," in Derek Lusk and Theodore L. Hayes, eds., *Overcoming Bad Leader-ship in Organizations* (New York: Oxford University Press, 2022), pp. 423-441.

[8] All surveys from the ANES. The question has been asked since 1980, but the response categories were altered between the earlier surveys and those conducted since 2008, so the analysts recoded responses on a zero-to-one scale, which is what is used here.

[9] Seth Masket, "Republicans Paid a Price for Overturning Roe. It May Have Been Worth It," *Politico*, November 19, 2022.

[10] Steven Shepard, "Early Exit Polls: Voters Say They Want a 'Strong Leader'," *Politico*, November 8, 2016.

[11] "What Traits Do Voters Prefer in a President," Sachs Media Group, July 7, 2016.

[12] Reena Flores, "Poll: Hillary Clinton, Donald Trump Neck-and-Neck in Na-tional Race," *CBS News*, June 29, 2016.

[13] "National Exit Polls: How Different Groups Voted," *New York Times*, undated 2020.

[14] McAdams, "The Appeal of the Primal Leader," p. 8.

[15] Douglas Schrock, Benjamin Dowd-Arrow, Kristen Erichsen, Haley Gentile, and Pierce Dignam, "The Emotional Politics of Making America Great Again: Trump's Working Class Appeals," *Journal of Working-Class Studies* 2, 1 (June 2017), pp. 5-22.

[16] "Vice President Harris Says She's 'Scared as Heck' That Trump Could Win," *PBS Newshour*, January 17, 2024.

[17] Jonathan Allen and Amie Parnes, *Shattered: Inside Hillary Clinton's Doomed Campaign* (New York: Crown, 2017), p. 353.

[18] George Lakoff, "'Whose Freedom'?," *New York Times*, July 23, 2006.

[19] Ritchel Mendiola, "Ressa Delivers Lecture at Harvard University," *Asian Jour-nal*, November 20, 2021.

[20] Mark Murray, "Poll: 61 Percent of Republicans Still Believe Biden Didn't Win Fair and Square in 2020," *NBC News*, September 27, 2022.

[21] Mark Danner, "The Real Trump," *New York Review of Books*, December 22, 2016.

[22] Jacob Bogage, "Whom Are You Voting for? This Guy Can Read Your Mind," *Washington Post*, June 23, 2016.

[23] Tamara Keith, "Evolution or Expediency? Clinton's Changing Positions over a Long Career," *NPR*, May 23, 2016; and Dan Merica, "Hillary Clinton Has a New Posi-tion on Same-Sex Marriage," *Equality California*, April 23, 2015.

[24] "Obama Hits Back at Clinton amid 'Bitter' Flap," *NBC News*, April 12, 2008.

[25] "Donald Trump 'Insulting Our Friends'—Hillary Clinton," *BBC News*, August 31, 2016; and "Hillary Clinton: Donald Trump Insults Women, and Has Also Targeted Immigrants, African Americans," October 9, 2016, *YouTube*.

[26] "Donald Trump Is Terrifying and I Hate What He Stands for: Hillary Clinton," *NDTV*, March 4, 2016.

[27] Carmen Sesin, "Why Latinos Turned out in Favor of Republicans," *NBC News*, November 15, 2022; and Adriana Gomez Licon and Steve Peoples, "GOP Rides Latino Support as Miami-Dade Turns Red," *Associated Press*, November 9, 2022.

[28] Margie Menzel, "Democrats Examine Their Mistakes in 2022—with a Focus on Black Voters," *WUSF Public Media,* November 21, 2022.

[29] Carmen Sesin, "Buoyed by Latinos, DeSantis Could Become the First Republican Candidate for Governor to Win Miami-Dade in 20 Years," *NBC News*, October 21, 2022.

[30] Glenn C. Altschuler, "Trump and DeSantis Race to the Bottom," *The Hill*, June 11, 2023.

[31] Tal Axelrod, Jay O'Brien, and Hannah Demissie, "DeSantis' Brand as a 'Fighter' on the Line as Trump Throws Haymakers," *ABC News*, May 16, 2023.

[32] Michelle Goldberg, "The Sickening Déjà Vu of Watching Trump Manhandle DeSantis," *New York Times*, April 21, 2023.

[33] Josh Marshall, "The Trumph of the Will," *Talking Points Memo*, January 28, 2016.

[34] Anthony Salvanto, Jennifer de Pinto, Fred Backus, and Kabir Khanna, "More Americans Label Republican Party Extreme and Democratic Party as Weak—CBS News Poll," *CBS News*, May 22, 2022.

[35] David Smith, "'This Is about Saving Lives': The Texas Democrat Fighting for Gun Control and Abortion Rights," *The Guardian*, May 17, 2023.

[36] Drew Westen, *The Political Brain: The Role of Emotion in Deciding the Fate of the Nation* (New York: PublicAffairs, 2007), pp. 160, 339.

[37] John T. Jost and Orsolya Hunyady, "Mass Psychology in the Age of Trump," *Democracy* 48 (Spring 2018), pp. 1–18 (quoted pp. 9–11).

[38] "Vital Statistics on Congress," *Brookings*, November 21, 2022. Members can choose more than one option.

[39] Madeline Albright, *Fascism: A Warning* (New York: Harper Collins, 2018), p. 209.

[40] Kelly Lawler, "Chris Rock Rips Trump, Police Violence, and (Mostly) Himself in Emotional Netflix Special," *USA Today*, February 14, 2018.

[41] Bill Eddy, "Negotiating with Bullies," *Psychology Today*, December 28, 2018.

[42] Shawn T. Smith, "The Most Important Thing to Know about Bullies and Predators," *IronShrink,* October 30, 2014.

[43] Kristen Harper et al., "Lessons from a Historic Decline in Child Poverty," *Child Trends,* 2022; Jason DeParle, "Expanded Safety Net Drives Sharp Drop in Child Poverty," *New York Times*, September 11, 2022; Isaac Shapiro and Danilo Trisi, "Child Poverty Falls to Record Low, Comprehensive Measure Shows Stronger Government Policies Account for Long-Term Improvement," *Center on Budget and Policy Priorities*, October 5, 2017; and John Creamer, Emily A. Shrider, Kalee Burns, and Frances Chen, "Poverty in the United States: 2021," U.S. Census Bureau, September 13, 2022.

[44] David Leonhardt, "Poverty, Plunging," *New York Times*, September 14, 2022.

45 Creamer, Shrider, Burns, and Chen, "Poverty in the United States: 2021."

46 Paul Krugman, "America Betrays Its Children Again," *New York Times*, September 14, 2023. See also "The 2022 Income, Poverty, and Health Insurance Reports," Council of Economic Advisers, September 12, 2023.

47 David Brooks, "The Terrifying Future of the American Right," *The Atlantic*, November 18, 2021.

48 David E. Broockman and Christopher Skovron, "Bias in Perceptions of Public Opinion Among Elites," *American Political Science Review* 112, 3 (August 2018), pp. 542–563 (quoted p. 542).

49 Danny Hayes and Jennifer L. Lawless, "There's Much Less Gender Bias in Politics Than You Think," *Washington Post*, May 24, 2016. See also Danny Hayes and Jennifer L. Lawless, *Women on the Run: Gender, Media, and Political Campaigns in a Polarized Era* (New York: Cambridge University Press, 2016).

50 Yascha Mounk and Roberto Stefan Foa, "This is How Democracy Dies," *The Atlantic*, January 19, 2020.

51 Milan W. Svolik, *The Politics of Authoritarian Rule* (New York: Cambridge University Press, 2012).

52 Daron Acemoglu, Suresh Naidu, Pascual Restrepo, and James A. Robinson, "Democracy Does Cause Growth," *Journal of Political Economy* 127, 1 (February 2019), pp. 47–100.

53 Thomas D. Zweifel and Patricio Navia, "Democracy, Dictatorship, and Infant Mortality," *Journal of Democracy* 11, 2 (April 2000), pp. 99–114.

54 Quan-Jing Wang, Gen-Fu Feng, Hai-Jie Wang, and Chun-Ping Chang, "The Impacts of Democracy on Innovation: Revisited Evidence," *Technovation* 108 (December 2021), 102333.

55 Ivar Kolstad and Arne Wiig, "Does Democracy Reduce Corruption?," CMI Working Paper 10057 (2011:4).

56 Stephen E. Hanson and Jeffrey S. Kopstein, *The Assault on the State: How the Global Attack on Modern Government Endangers Our Future* (New York: Polity, 2024).

57 Evie Papada and Staffan I. Lindberg, "Does Democracy Promote Gender Equality?," V-Dem Policy Brief #37, December 2022.

58 Omar G. Encarnación, "Gay Rights: Why Democracy Matters," *Journal of Democracy* 25, 3 (July 2014), pp. 90–104.

59 Timothy Snyder, *On Tyranny: Twenty Lessons from the Twentieth Century* (New York: Crown, 2017).

60 Kristian Vrede Skaaning Frederisksen, "Young People Punish Undemocratic Behavior Less Than Older People," *British Journal of Political Science*, December 15, 2023, pp. 1–9 (quoted p. 1). See also Roberto Stefan Foa and Yascha Mounk, "The Democratic Disconnect," *Journal of Democracy* 27, 3 (July 2016), pp. 5–17.

61 Paul Krugman, "Beware the New American Triumphalism," *New York Times*, July 20, 2023.

62 Nicholas Kristof, "This Was a Terrible Year, and Also Maybe the Best One Yet for Humanity," *New York Times*, December 30, 2023.

63 Sam Levine, "Investigation Debunks Bogus 'Audit' Claiming 300 Dead People Voted in Arizona in 2020," *The Guardian*, August 2, 2022.

64 "Most Say Fundamental Rights under Threat," Monmouth University Poll, June 20, 2023.

65 "Remarks by President Biden on Standing up for Democracy," Columbus Club, Union Station, Washington, D.C., November 2, 2022.

66 Stephanie Lai, Luke Broadwater, and Carl Hulse, "Lawmakers Confront Rise in Threats and Intimidation, and Fear Worse," *New York Times*, October 1, 2022.

67 Catie Edmondson, "Pelosi Attack Highlights Rising Fears of Political Violence," *New York Times*, October 29, 2022; Amy Gardner, "A Majority of GOP Nominees Deny or Question the 2020 Election Results," *Washington Post*, October 12, 2022; and Reid J. Epstein, "Echoing Trump, These Republicans Won't Promise to Accept 2022 Results," *New York Times*, September 18, 2022.

68 U.S. Department of the Interior, National Park Service, "1957 Crisis at Central High," January 29, 2021.

69 Jeffrey M. Jones, "U.S. Political Party Preferences Shifted Greatly During 2021," *Gallup News*, January 17, 2021; and "More Than 1 Million Voters Switch to GOP, Raising Alarm for Democrats," *PBS Newshour*, June 27, 2022.

70 John Della Volpe, "Ring the Alarm," *JDV on Gen Z+*, June 15, 2023. See also Myah Ward, "Young Voters Are Getting Less Likely to Identify as Dems. It Spells Trouble for Biden," *Politico*, July 13, 2023.

71 Jim Tankersley, "The Democrats Spent $2 Trillion to Save the Economy. They Don't Want to Talk about It," *New York Times*, October 16, 2022.

72 "Full Vance/Ryan Debate, FOX 8 News Cleveland," October 10, 2022, *YouTube*.

73 "Exit Polls for Ohio Results," *CBS News America Decides Campaign 2022*; "Exit Polls for Midterm Election Results 2022," *CNN.com* (undated); and Ximena Bustillo, "Trump-backed J. D. Vance Wins Senate Seat in Ohio over Democrat Tim Ryan," *NPR*, November 8, 2022.

74 Raphael Warnock, *The Divided Mind of the Black Church: Theology, Piety, and Public Witness* (New York: New York University Press, 2014); and Raphael Warnock, *A Way out of No Way: A Memoir of Truth, Transformation, and the New American Story* (New York: Penguin, 2022).

75 Jill Nolin and Riley Bunch, "New Poll Finds That Nearly Two-Thirds of Georgia Voters Object to State's New Abortion Restrictions," *Georgia Recorder*, October 12, 2022.

76 Tankersley, "The Democrats Spent $2 Trillion to Save the Economy."

77 Maya King, "Warnock Hammers Walker in a Senate Debate, Gesturing to an Empty Lectern," *New York Times*, October 16, 2022.

78 I received these and the other ads cited in this section as text messages and/or in my Facebook feed during the two months prior to the election.

79 Esther Tsvayg, "Do a Majority of Nevadans Support Legal Abortion?," *The Nevada Independent*, October 28, 2022; and Tabitha Mueller, "Laxalt Calls 1973 Roe v.

Wade Decision a 'Joke', Bemoans Nevada's Abortion Protections," *The Nevada Independent*, June 30, 2022.

[80] Ryan Brooks, "This Is B-A-D: Some Democrats Are Sick of a DIRE Email Strategy," *BuzzFeed News*, March 16, 2018.

[81] David L. Ulin, "Op-Ed: We Have Nothing to Fear but Email Fundraising Pleas," *Los Angeles Times*, September 28, 2022.

[82] Lara Putnam and Micah L. Sifry, "Fed Up with Democratic Emails? You're Not the Only One," *New York Times*, August 1, 2022.

[83] Ashley Kirzinger et al., "How the Supreme Court's Dobbs Decision Played in the 2022 Midterm Election," *KFF*, November 11, 2022; and Nate Cohn, "Trump's Drag on Republicans Quantified: A Five Point Penalty," *New York Times*, November 16, 2022.

[84] Edward-Isaac Dovere, "Democrats Won't Get as Much Obama as They Want in the Midterms. But He Has Other Plans," *CNN.com*, October 18, 2022.

[85] Craig Howe, "Obama to Stump in Three Key Races," *Politico*, October 15, 2022.

[86] Dovere, "Democrats Won't Get as Much Obama as They Want in the Midterms."

[87] "Final Presidential Job Approval Ratings," The American Presidency Project; and "The Most Popular Politicians," *YouGovAmerica*, March 28, 2024.

[88] Della Volpe, "Ring the Alarm"; Russell J. Dalton, *The Participation Gap: Social Status and Political Inequality* (New York: Oxford University Press, 2017); and "Voter Turnout, 2018-2022," Pew Research Center, July 12, 2023.

[89] "Former President Barack Obama Campaigns with Sen. Raphael Warnock at Pullman Yards in Atlanta," December 1, 2022, *YouTube*; and Natalie Allison, "Obama Closes for Warnock in Georgia Senate Race," *Politico*, December 1, 2022.

[90] John Nichols, "Barack Obama's Politics 101: Ridiculing Republicans Works," *The Nation*, December 6, 2022.

[91] "Arnold Schwarzenegger Has a Powerful Message for Those Who Have Gone Down the Path of Hate," *YouTube*, March 6, 2023.

[92] Michael Grunwald, "The Selling of Obama," *Politico*, May/June 2016.

[93] "President Obama Delivers Remarks at Northwestern University," October 2, 2014, *YouTube*.

[94] "Meet the Press Transcript—October 5, 2014," *NBC News*, October 5, 2014.

[95] "Gallup Economic Confidence Index, 1996-2023," *Gallup News*, July 2, 2023.

[96] "Full Transcript of Biden's State of the Union Speech," *New York Times*, March 8, 2024; and Jennifer Agiesta, Ariel Edwards-Levy, and Nicholas Anastacio, "CNN Poll: More Than 6 in 10 SOTU Viewers Had a Positive Reaction to Biden's Speech," *CNN.com*, March 8, 2024.

[97] Lora Kelly, "Is Biden Relying on the Wrong Slogan?," *The Atlantic*, October 3, 2023.

[98] Adam Cancryn and Holly Otterbein, "Dems Pressure White House to Change Economic Message," *Politico*, September 29, 2023.

99 Stef W. Kight and Alex Thompson, "House Democrats Ditch 'Bidenomics' Messaging," *Axios*, December 3, 2023.

100 Cancryn and Otterbein, "Dems Pressure White House to Change Economic Message."

101 *Ibid.*

102 Sonnenfeld and Tian, "Bidenomics' Critics Are Being Proven Wrong"; and Rich Miller and Enda Curran, "US Extends Lead over China in Race for World's Biggest Economy," *Bloomberg*, January 25, 2024.

103 Daniel Bush, "Joe Biden's Age Problem Tears Democrats Apart," *Newsweek*, February 26, 2024.

104 Rich Jaroslovsky, "The Other Time America Panicked over a President's Age," *The Atlantic*, February 15, 2024; David Weigel, "When Ronald Reagan Blew a Debate and Dropped Seven Points in the Polls," *Slate*, October 10, 2012; Lou Cannon, David S. Broder, and Cristine Russell, "Age Emerges as New Issue in Campaign," *Washington Post*, October 9, 1984; and Andrew Glass, "Reagan Recovers in Second Debate, October 21, 1984," *Politico*, October 10, 2021.

105 "President Ronald Reagan Addresses a Historic 100th Congress to Deliver the State of the Union," January 27, 1987, *YouTube*; and Lou Cannon, "Actor, Governor, President, Icon," *Washington Post*, June 6, 2004.

106 Jim Tankersley, "'Morning in America' Eludes Biden, Despite Economic Gains," *New York Times*, November 7, 2023.

107 Cancryn and Otterbein, "Dems Pressure White House to Change Economic Message."

108 Maureen Dowd, "James Carville, the Cajun Who Can't Stop Ragin'," *New York Times*, March 23, 2024.

109 McAdams, "The Appeal of the Primal Leader."

110 Raymond Arsenault, *Freedom Riders: 1961 and the Struggle for Racial Justice* (New York: Oxford University Press, 2006).

111 Frank Newport, "Martin Luther King Jr.: Revered More after Death Than before," *Gallup News*, January 16, 2006; and James C. Cobb, "When Martin Luther King Jr. Was Killed, He Was Less Popular Than Donald Trump Is Today," *USA Today*, April 4, 2018.

112 "MLK Day Special: Rediscovered 1964 King Speech on Civil Rights, Segregation & Apartheid South Africa," *Democracy Now!*, January 21, 2019.

113 "Goldwater Calls Opposition to Gays in the Military 'Dumb'," *Deseret News*, August 21, 1993.

114 Wendell Rawls Jr., "Wallace Captures 4th Term as Governor of Alabama," *New York Times*, November 3, 1982; and "Remembering George Wallace," *NPR*, September 14, 1998.

115 "Public Figures: Martin Luther King," *YouGov*.

116 David Pietrusza, *1920: The Year of the Six Presidents* (New York: Carroll & Graf, 2007), p. 269-270.

117 "Jesus and Eugene Debs," *Spending Time with Jim McGuiggan* (2004), Way Back Machine Internet Archive, 2011.

118 "'Fuck you Putin', vzkazuje Černochová ruskému prezidentovi," *Echo24*, October 7, 2022.

119 Nick Nordowanec, "Video of Finnish PM Explaining Putin's 'Way Out' of Ukraine Viewed 4M Times," *Newsweek*, October 7, 2022.

120 Nancy L. Cohen, "Sexism Did Not Cost Hillary Clinton the Election," *Washington Post*, November 16, 2016. See also Nancy L. Cohen, *Breakthrough: The Making of America's First Woman President* (Berkeley, CA: Counterpoint, 2016).

122 Deborah Jordan Brooks, *He Runs, She Runs: Why Gender Stereotypes Do Not Harm Women Candidates* (Princeton, NJ: Princeton University Press, 2013), p. 111.

122 "Nancy Pelosi Rips Up Copy of Donald Trump's State of the Union Address," February 4, 2020, *YouTube*.

123 Eric Ting, "Gavin Newsom Goes Scorched Earth on Ron DeSantis, Joe Manchin, Democratic Party, More over Roe v. Wade News," *SFGate*, May 4, 2022; and Maanvi Singh, "Will Gavin Newsom Run for President—and Could He Win over the Democratic Base," *The Guardian*, October 2, 2022.

124 Jonathan Lemire, Lauren Egan, Myah Ward, and Ben Johnson, "What Biden *Really* Says about Trump behind Closed Doors," *Politico*, February 1, 2024.

125 Victor Nava, "Trump Tells Supporters 'Biden Just Called Me a Sick-F Word!' in Fundraising Email," *New York Post*, February 3, 2024.

126 Kristine Parks, "CNN Finds Biden Relatable after Reportedly Cursing at Trump in Private 'Connects' with Voters," *FOX News*, February 2, 2024.

127 Eric Lipton and Alan Rappeport, "Bolton Book Puts New Focus on Trump's Actions in Turkey and China," *New York Times*, January 28, 2020.

128 Victor Madeira, "Trump's Betrayal of the Kurds Gifted Military Intelligence to Russia," *Insider*, November 21, 2019; and Robert Burns, Lolita C. Baldor, and Matthew Lee, "Trump Defends Decision to Abandon Kurdish Allies in Syria," *Associated Press*, October 8, 2019.

129 Donald Trump tweet, October 16, 2019. See also Anna North, "Trump's 'Nervous Nancy' Tweet Shows His Problem with Powerful Women," *Vox*, October 17, 2019.

130 Christine Pelosi tweet, October 16, 2019.

131 Mike Lillis, "Pelosi Explains What She Was Saying in Viral Photo: 'All Roads Lead to Putin'," *The Hill*, October 17, 2019.

132 Martin Pengelly, "Nancy Pelosi Calls Indictments against Trump 'Beautiful and Intricate'," *The Guardian*, August 7, 2023.

133 Richard Wike, Jacob Poushter, Laura Silver, Janell Fetterolf, and Mara Mordecai, "America's Image Abroad Rebounds Strongly from Trump to Biden," Pew Research Center, June 10, 2021.

134 "International Public Opinion of the U.S. Remains Positive," Pew Research Center, June 22, 2022; and Anne Applebaum, "The Brutal Alternate World in Which the U.S. Abandoned Ukraine," *The Atlantic*, December 22, 2022.

135 Ariel Edwards-Levy and Jennifer Agiesta, "CNN Flash Poll: Here's What Viewers Thought of Biden's Address," *CNN.com*, February 8, 2023; "CNN SOTU Reaction Poll," February 7, 2023; and Kerry Eleveld, "Surveys Show Biden Hit the State of the Union out of the Park," *Daily Kos*, February 8, 2023.

136 "The State of the Union Dial Test," *Navigator Research*, February 8, 2023.

137 "Full Transcript of Biden's State of the Union Address," *New York Times*, February 8, 2023.

138 "President Joe Biden Delivers 2023 State of the Union Address to Congress, 2/7/2023," *YouTube*.

139 Amanda Macias, "Insight into What U.S. Intelligence Knew about Hitler in 1943," *Business Insider*, July 27, 2016.

140 Anne Applebaum and Nataliya Gumenyuk, "'They Didn't Understand Anything, but Just Spoiled People's Lives'," *The Atlantic*, February 14, 2023.

141 "In Full: Vladimir Putin Officially Annexing Four Ukrainian Regions at Moscow Ceremony," September 30, 2022, *YouTube*.

142 "Former President Trump Announces 2024 Presidential Bid Transcript," *Rev*, November 16, 2022.

143 Mychael Schnell, "McConnell Asked if He Has Reaction to Trump's Attack on Wife Elaine Chao: 'No'," *The Hill*, August 23, 2022.

144 Matthew Chapman, "'Donald Trump Is a Coward': Conservative Lists All the Times the Ex-President Has Run Away," *Raw Story*, December 14, 2023.

145 See Jonathan Haidt, Jesse Graham, and Craig Joseph, "Above and Below Left-Right: Ideological Narratives and Moral Foundations," *Psychological Inquiry* 20 (2009), pp. 110-119.

Part Three

1 Aram Hur, *Narratives of Civic Duty: How National Narratives Shape Democracy in Asia* (Ithaca, NY: Cornell University Press, 2022), p. 134.

2 "Barack Obama: 'In No Other Country on Earth is My Story Even Possible'," *Greeley Tribune*, November 5, 2008.

3 George Packer, "Witnessing the Obama Presidency, From Start to Finish," *The New Yorker*, June 5, 2018.

4 Eric Bradner, "Democrats Seek New Identity after Autopsy of 2014 Midterm Losses," *CNN.com*, February 21, 2015.

5 Jefferson Cowie, "Reclaiming Patriotism for the Left," *New York Times*, August 21, 2018.

6 David Brooks, "Do Democrats Know What Unites Us?," *New York Times*, November 5, 2018.

7 David Brooks, "The Materialist Party," *New York Times*, October 22, 2018.

[8] Jill Lepore, "A New Americanism: Why a Nation Needs a National Story," *Foreign Affairs* March/April 2019, pp. 10-19 (quoted p. 19). For other accounts that have called on American liberals to put forward their own vision of the nation, see Tom Nichols, "Reclaiming American Patriotism," *The Atlantic*, July 4, 2023; Steven B. Smith, *Reclaiming Patriotism in an Age of Extremes* (New Haven, CT: Yale University Press, 2021); Amitai Etzioni, *Reclaiming Patriotism* (Charlottesville, VA: University of Virginia Press, 2019); Yael Tamir, *Why Nationalism* (Princeton, NJ: Princeton University Press, 2019); Yascha Mounk, *The People vs. Democracy* (Cambridge, MA: Harvard University Press, 2019); Francis Fukuyama, "A Country of Their Own: Liberalism Needs a Nation," *Foreign Affairs*, May/June 2022; Paul Gross, "The Case for Liberal Nationalism," *The American Interest*, February 27, 2020; Robert Kagan, "The Strongmen Strike Back," *Washington Post*, March 14, 2019; Colin Woodard, "How Joe Biden Can Help Forge a New National Narrative," *Washington Monthly,* January 10, 2021; and John Haplin, "America Needs a New Public Philosophy," *The Liberal Patriot*, February 1, 2022.

[9] George Packer, "How America Fractured into Four Parts," *The Atlantic*, July-August 2021. For a fuller elaboration, see George Packer, *Last Best Hope: America in Crisis and Renewal* (New York: Farrar, Straus and Giroux, 2021).

[10] Aliza Astrow and Lanae Erickson, "Overcoming the Democratic Party Brand," *Third Way*, November 7, 2022.

[11] Aliza Astrow and Rachel Reh, "Democrats: Don't Let the GOP Own Patriotism," *The Hill,* January 23, 2023.

[12] Gina Gustavsson and David Miller, "Introduction: Why Liberal Nationalism Today?," in Gina Gustavsson and David Miller, eds., *Liberal Nationalism and Its Critics* (New York: Oxford University Press, 2020), pp. 1-20 (quoted p. 5).

[13] GSS. See also Scott Clement, "Americans Love Their Country, but It's a Surprisingly Tough Love," *Washington Post*, June 3, 2015.

[14] Aaron Blake, "That Jarring New Poll on 'Patriotism'," March 27, 2023; and Megan Brenan, "Record-Low 38 Percent Extremely Proud to Be American," *Gallup News*, June 29, 2022.

[15] Jack Citrin, Morris Levy, and Matthew Wright, *Immigration in the Court of Public Opinion* (New York: Polity, 2023), p. 82.

[16] *Wall Street Journal*/NORC Poll, March 2023; and "Patriotism in the United States: Statistics and Facts," *Statista*, November 9, 2022.

[17] Gregory A. Petrow, John Transue, and Manuel Gutierrez, "How Do You Persuade Trump Supporters to Oppose the 'Big Lie'?," *Washington Post*, June 14, 2022.

[18] Jan G. Voelkel, Joseph S. Mernyk, and Robb Willer, "Moral Reframing Increases Support for Economically Progressive Candidates," *PNAS Nexus* 2, 2023, pp. 1-14 (quoted p. 1). See also Robb Willer and Jan Voelkel, "Why Progressive Candidates Should Invoke Conservative Values," *New York Times*, November 30, 2019.

[19] Jan Voelkel and Matthew Feinberg, "Morally Reframed Arguments Can Affect Support for Political Candidates," *Social Psychology and Personality Science*, September 28, 2017.

[20] Gina Gustavsson and Ludvig Stendahl, "National Identity, a Blessing or a Curse? The Divergent Links from National Attachment, Pride, and Chauvinism and Political Trust," *European Political Science Review* 12 (May 2020), pp. 449-469 (quoted p. 465; in-text citations of other work omitted here).

[21] Volha Charnysh, Christopher Lucas, and Prerna Singh, "The Ties That Bind: National Identity Salience and Pro-Social Behavior Toward the Ethnic Other," *Comparative Political Studies* 48, 3 (2015), pp. 267-300.

[22] Prerna Singh, "In India, Protestors Are Singing the National Anthem and Waving the Flag. Here's Why That Matters," *Washington Post*, January 20, 2020.

[23] Gustavsson and Miller, "Introduction: Why Liberal Nationalism Today?," p. 13.

[24] Martin Luther King, Jr., "Beyond Vietnam: A Time to Break Silence," *Black-Past*, January 28, 2007.

[25] Quoted in Michael Kazin, "The Best Dissent Has Never Been Anti-American," *Washington Post*, February 9, 2003.

[26] Clement, "Americans Love Their Country, but It's a Surprisingly Tough Love."

[27] Katherine Schaeffer, "On the Fourth of July, How Americans See Their Country and Their Democracy," Pew Research Center, June 30, 2022. See also Jonathan Haidt, "When and Why Nationalism Beats Globalism," *The American Interest*, July 10, 2016.

[28] Chelsea Bailey and Brandon Drenon, "Florida's Battle over How Race Is Taught in Schools," *BBC News*, March 11, 2023.

[29] Sarah Mervosh, "DeSantis Faces Swell of Criticism over Florida's New Standards for Black History," *New York Times*, July 21, 2023.

[30] Stephen Hawkins et al., *Defusing the Culture Wars: Finding Common Ground in Teaching America's National Story* (Common Ground, 2022).

[31] Daniel Yudkin, Stephen Hawkins, and Tim Dixon, *The Perception Gap: How False Impressions Are Pulling Americans Apart* (More in Common, 2019).

[32] Lydia Saad, "U.S. Political Ideology Steady; Conservatives, Moderates Tie," *Gallup News*, January 17, 2022.

[33] Charles M. Blow, "Is America a Racist Country?," *New York Times*, May 2, 2021. See also Charles M. Blow, "White Racial Anxiety Strikes Again," *New York Times*, November 3, 2021.

[34] Frederick Douglass, "Eulogy for Abraham Lincoln," Address at Cooper Union, New York, June 1, 1865, The Library of America.

[35] Charles M. Blow, "Tyre Nichols's Death Is America's Shame," *New York Times*, January 27, 2023.

[36] "Bipartisan Negotiations on Capitol Hill Failed to Produce a Police Overhaul Bill," *NPR*, September 24, 2021.

[37] "Deep Divisions in Americans' Views of Nation's Racial History—and How to Address It," Pew Research Center, August 12, 2021; Harris-APNORC Report, "No Public Consensus on How Schools Should Discuss Sexuality and Racism"; and Jonathan

Collins, "Poll Shows Support for Teaching of U.S. Racism—with or without Parental Consent," *The 74*, October 13, 2020.

[38] Jeffrey M. Jones and Camille Lloyd, "Larger Majority Says Racism against Black People Widespread," *Gallup News*, July 23, 2021.

[39] Maureen A. Craig, Julian M. Rucker, and Jennifer A. Richeson, "Racial and Political Dynamics of an Approaching 'Majority-Minority' United States," *Annals of the American Academy of Political and Social Science* 677, 1, pp. 204-214; Ashley Jardina, *White Identity Politics* (New York: Cambridge University Press, 2019); and Sabrina Taverise, "Why the Announcement of a Looming White Minority Makes Demographers Nervous," *New York Times*, November 22, 2018.

[40] Morris Levy and Dowell Myers, "Racial Projections in Perspective: Public Reactions to Narratives about Rising Diversity," *Perspectives on Politics* 19, 4 (December 2021), pp. 1147-1164 (quoted pp. 1147-1148). See also Richard Alba, "The Likely Persistence of a White Majority: How Census Bureau Statistics Have Misled Thinking about the American Future," *American Prospect*, January 11, 2016.

[41] Rachel Lienesch, "Testing the Limits of White Democrats' Support for Progressive Racial Messaging," unpublished paper, September 12, 2022, p. 1.

[42] Nyla R. Branscombe, Michael T. Schmitt, and Kristin Schiffhauer, "Racial Attitudes in Response to Thoughts of White Privilege," *European Journal of Social Psychology* 37, 2 (March-April 2007), pp. 203-215 (quoted p. 212).

[43] Martin Luther King, "Address Delivered at Albany Movement Mass Meeting at Shiloh Baptist Church," Albany, Georgia, August 15, 1962, The Martin Luther King, Jr. Research and Education Institute, Stanford University.

[44] Ruy Teixeira, "The Democrats' Nonwhite Working Class Problem Reemerges," *The Liberal Patriot*, August 7, 2023.

[45] Jennifer Agiesta, "CNN Poll: Trump Narrowly Leads Biden in Hypothetical Rematch," *CNN.com*, November 7, 2023.

[46] David L. Smiley, *Lion of White Hall: The Life of Cassius M. Clay* (Madison, WI: University of Wisconsin Press, 1962); Edward H. Richardson, *Cassius Marcellus Clay: Firebrand of Freedom* (Lexington, KY: University Press of Kentucky, 1976); and John Lockwood, *The Siege of Washington* (New York: Oxford University Press, 2011).

[47] Howell Raines, *Silent Cavalry: How Union Soldiers from Atlanta Helped Sherman Burn Atlanta and Then Got Written Out of History* (New York: Crown, 2023). These facts were flagged by Garry Trudeau in *Doonsbury*, February 18, 2024.

[48] Betsy Klein, "Biden and Harris Respond to Tim Scott's Claim That the US Is Not Racist, Stressing That Racism Must Not Be Ignored," *CNN.com*, April 29, 2021.

[49] Thomas B. Edsall, "Republicans Are Once Again Heating Up the Culture Wars," *New York Times*, November 10, 2021.

[50] Echelon Insights, "2021 Virginia State Elections," October 27-29, 2021; "Oct. 20-26, 2021, Washington Post-Schar School Virginia Poll," *Washington Post*, October 29, 2021; and Yascha Mounk, "You Can't Win Elections by Telling Voters Their Concerns Are Imaginary," *The Atlantic*, November 3, 2021.

51 "How a Loss in Virginia, Close Race in New Jersey Could Affect Dem Midterm Plan," *PBS Newshour*, November 3, 2021.

52 Remarks by President Biden on the Authorization of the COVID-19 Vaccine for Children Ages 5 to 11, November 3, 2021.

53 Paul Waldman, "The Roots of the Republican War on Democracy," *Washington Post*, November 19, 2021.

54 "Survey: State of the Commonwealth," The Watson Center, February 21, 2022.

55 "Supreme Court Won't Review North Carolina's Decision to Nix License Plates with the Confederate Flag," *Associated Press*, posted on *Daily Kos*, June 12, 2023.

56 For the idea of national "oneness," and its superiority to "unity" as a term liberals should use in messaging, I am indebted to my student Sarah Kadous, who developed the concept in a course essay.

57 Shuyang Qu et al., "Midwest Crop Farmers' Perceptions of the U.S.-China Trade War," CARD Policy Briefs, Iowa State University, October 2019.

58 Rebecca Beitsch, "Trump Winning Farm Vote Despite Pinch of Trade Policies, Pandemic," *The Hill*, November 1, 2020.

59 Juliana Menasce Horowitz, Ruth Igielnik, and Rakesh Kochhar, "Most Americans Say There is Too Much Economic Inequality, but Fewer Than Half Call It a Top Priority," Pew Research Center, January 9, 2019.

60 "Country Would Be Better If We Worried Less about Inequality," ANES.

61 Arlie Hochschild, *Strangers in Their Own Land: Anger and Mourning on the American Right* (New York: The New Press, 2016). See esp. chs. 2 and 6.

62 Katherine J. Cramer, *The Politics of Resentment* (Chicago: University of Chicago Press, 2016), back cover and p. 201.

63 Francesco Duina, *Broke and Patriotic* (Stanford, CA: Stanford University Press, 2018).

64 Ben Bradlee Jr., *The Forgotten* (Boston: Little, Brown and Company, 2018), p. 43.

65 Louis Hartz, *The Liberal Tradition in America* (New York: Harcourt Brace & Company, 1955).

66 Alexis de Tocqueville, *Democracy in America* (Chicago: University of Chicago Press, 2002 [first published 1835 and 1840]).

67 World Values Survey, items Q149 and Q150, respectively. On freedom vs. equality, the only countries in the survey whose people score freedom more highly than the United States are Serbia (82-16), Zimbabwe (80-20), and Greece (78-22). On freedom vs. security, the next-highest scores after the United States are for Serbia (55-44) and the United Kingdom (54-44).

68 GSS.

69 Richard Wike et al., "European Public Opinion Three Decades after the Fall of Communism," Pew Research Center, October 15, 2019.

70 *Wall Street Journal*/NORC Poll, March 2023.

[71] Ariel Gelrud Shiro, Christopher Pulliam, John Sabelhaus, and Ember Smith, *Stuck on the Ladder: Intragenerational Wealth Mobility in the United States*, Brookings, June 2022.

[72] "Speech of the President," Worcester, Massachusetts, October 21, 1936.

[73] See his "fireside chat" of September 6, 1936, reprinted in *The Bulwark*, September 4, 2023.

[74] Quoted in Nancy Spannaus, "The American System in Healthcare: The Path to Medicare," July 20, 2017.

[75] "Five Decades Ago, Bill Clinton Meets JFK," *NBC News*, July 24, 2013.

[76] Emily A. Shrider, Melissa Kollar, Frances Chen, and Jessica Semega, *Income and Poverty in the United States: 2020*, U.S. Census Bureau, September 4, 2021.

[77] Courtney Subramanian, "You're Not Getting Child Tax Credit Checks Anymore. Here's Why," *Los Angeles Times*, January 3, 2023.

[78] U.S. Census Bureau, "Income, Poverty, and Health Insurance Coverage in the United States: 2022," Press Release CB23-150, September 12, 2023.

[79] Bill Clinton, "Speech to the Democratic National Convention," September 5, 2012, *YouTube*.

[80] "The Conventions to the Debates: Set-Piece Moments Still Matter," Pew Research Center, November 1, 2012. See also David Maraniss, "Bill Clinton Delivers for Obama at Democratic Convention," *Washington Post*, September 6, 2012; and Greg Sargent, "More on That Obama Convention Bounce," *Washington Post*, September 10, 2012.

[81] "Approval of Presidential Handling of the Economy," ANES.

[82] Megan Brenan, "Biden's Job Rating Steady at 40%; Middle East Approval at 27%," *Gallup News*, March 22, 2024.

[83] "Bill Clinton Inaugural Address, January 20, 1993," *YouTube*; and "Final Presidential Job Approval Ratings," The American Presidency Project.

[84] Astrow and Erikson, "Overcoming the Democratic Party Brand."

[85] Jonathan M. Metzl, *Dying of Whiteness: How the Politics of Racial Resentment Is Killing America's Heartland* (New York: Basic Books, 2019); and Martin Gilens, *Why Americans Hate Welfare: Race, Media, and the Politics of Antipoverty Policy* (Chicago: University of Chicago Press, 1999).

[86] Andrew Wegley, "'I Don't Believe in Welfare'—Nebraska Gov. Pillen Maintains He Won't Seek Federal Grocery Aid," *Lincoln Journal Star,* December 22, 2023.

[87] "Iowa Won't Participate in US Food Assistance Program for Kids This Summer," *Associated Press*, December 23, 2023.

[88] "Life Expectancy by State," *Wisevoter*, 2023; Anna Fleck, "Native Americans Still Face Significant Life Expectancy Gap," *Statista*, October 9, 2023; "List of U.S. States and Territories by Race/Ethnicity," *Wikipedia*.

[89] "Life Expectancy of the World Population," *Worldometer*, 2023.

[90] "List of U.S. States and Territories by Life Expectancy," *Wikipedia*.

[91] GSS.

[92] Brandy Zadrozny, "How a Well-Timed Legal Assault Unraveled Mississippi's Stellar Record in Vaccinating Kids," *NBC News*, December 16, 2023.

[93] Christopher H. Achen and Larry M. Bartels, *Democracy for Realists: Why Elections Do Not Produce Responsive Government* (Princeton, NJ: Princeton University Press, 2017).

[94] Drew Westen, *The Political Brain: The Role of Emotion in Deciding the Fate of the Nation* (New York: PublicAffairs, 2007), p. 151.

[95] Heritage Foundation and the *Wall Street Journal, 2023 Index of Economic Freedom.*

[96] David D. Kirkpatrick and Kate Kelly, "Before Giving Billions to Jared Kushner, Saudi Investment Fund Had Big Doubts," *New York Times*, April 10, 2022; Daniel Bice, "U.S. Sen Ron Johnson Defends Pacur Sale Amid Accusations of Insider Trading by Other Senators," *Milwaukee Journal Sentinel*, March 20, 2020; and Ruth May, "How Putin's Oligarchs Funneled Millions into GOP Campaigns," *Dallas Morning News*, May 8, 2018.

[97] "Donald Trump Says He 'Gets along Great' with Tyrants," *The Independent*, December 13, 2021.

[98] Greg Miller, "Trump Has Concealed Details of His Face-to-Face Encounters with Putin from Senior Officials in Administration," *Washington Post*, January 13, 2019.

[99] Tim Weiner, "The Unanswered Question of Our Time: Is Trump an Agent of Russia?," *Washington Post*, September 21, 2020; and Natasha Bertrand, "Trump Hid His Calls with Putin. Now, Biden Has Access to Them," *Politico*, February 9, 2021.

[100] Drew Westen, "How to Win an Election," *Psychology Today*, April 29, 2020. See also Jonathan Haidt, *The Righteous Mind: Why Good People are Divided by Politics and Religion* (New York: Vintage, 2013); and "How the Democrats Can Use Moral Foundations Theory against Trump," *The Righteous Mind Blog*, July 28, 2016.

[101] Jonathan Allen and Amie Parnes, *Shattered: Inside Hillary Clinton's Doomed Campaign* (New York: Crown, 2017), p. 298.

[102] Richard Cowan and Moira Warburton, "Senate Republican Tuberville Calls White Nationalists Racist after Taking Heat," *Reuters*, July 11, 2023.

[103] See Tom Nichols, "How Are Trump Supporters Still Doing This?," *The Atlantic*, March 6, 2023; and Tom Nichols, "This is *the* Case," *The Atlantic*, August 1, 2023.

[104] Neli Esipova, Anita Pugliese, and Julie Ray, "More Than 750 Million Would Migrate if They Could," *Gallup News*, December 10, 2019.

[105] Brooks, "The Materialist Party."

[106] Muhammad Ali, "To Make America the Greatest Is My Goal," Poetry Soup.

[107] "Muhammad Ali—'I'll Show You How Great I Am' Speech," *YouTube*.

Part Four

[1] Lionel Barber, Henry Foy, and Alex Barker, "Vladimir Putin Says Liberalism Has 'Become Obsolete'," *Financial Times,* June 27, 2019.

[2] Andrew E. Kramer, "Putin Makes a Splash at the G-20 Summit," *New York Times,* June 28, 2019.

[3] "Brazil's 2022 Presidential Vote Will Be between 'Fascism and Democracy', Ex-Leader Lula Says," *Euronews,* July 10, 2021.

[4] Igor Carvalho, "In His First Speech as President, Lula Criticizes Previous Government and Declares: 'Democracy Forever'," *Peoples Dispatch,* January 1, 2023.

[5] Carlie Porterfield, "Brazilian Rioters Damaged a $1.5 Million Painting in Jan 6-Style Attack, Brazil's Government Says," *Forbes,* January 9, 2023.

[6] Tom Phillips and Andrew Downie, "Brazil Protests: Lula Vows to Punish 'Neo-Fascists' after Bolsonaro Supporters Storm Congress," *The Guardian,* January 23, 2023.

[7] "Brazil's Lula Lays Out Plan to Halt Amazon Deforestation," *Politico,* June 6, 2023.

[8] Michael Fox, "Lula Empowers Brazil's Indigenous Peoples with Their Own Ministry. But Environmental Protection Remains a Key Concern," *The World,* January 19, 2023; Marina Dias and Terrence McCoy, "Under Lula, Amazon Deforestation Is Declining. Can He Keep It Up?," *Washington Post,* July 16, 2023; and George Wright, "Lula Tightens Gun Control Amid a Surge in Ownership," *BBC News,* July 21, 2023.

[9] Tom Phillips, "Judges Ban Bolsonaro from Running for Office for Eight Years over 'Appalling Lies'," *The Guardian,* June 30, 2023.

[10] Henry Foy, "Lunch with the FT: Donald Tusk," *Financial Times,* November 28, 2014.

[11] Shaun Walker, "Opposition Leader Donald Tusk Cheered by Crowds at Warsaw Election Rally," *The Guardian,* October 1, 2023.

[12] Vanessa Gera, "Hundreds of Thousands March in Poland Anti-Government Protests to Show Support for Democracy," *Associated Press,* June 4, 2023.

[13] Walker, "Opposition Leader Donald Tusk Cheered by Crowds at Warsaw Election Rally."

[14] "Ranking of Trust in Politicians in Poland between October 2022 and October 2023," *Statista.*

[15] Charlotte Alter, "Maryland Governor Wes Moore Wants to Reframe American Patriotism," *Time,* July 6, 2023.

[16] Benjamin Wallace-Wells, "How Gretchen Whitmer Made Michigan a Democratic Stronghold," *The New Yorker,* July 17, 2023.

[17] "Planned Parenthood Thanks Gov. Beshear for Vetoing Egregious Anti-Abortion Bill," *Planned Parenthood Newsroom,* April 8, 2022.

[18] Bruce Schreiner, "Kentucky Governor Defends Photo Posing with Drag Queens," *Associated Press,* February 27, 2020.

[19] "Beshear Shares Disdain for Bill Banning Gender-Affirming Care," March 2, 2023, *YouTube.*

[20] "Gov. Andy Beshear—Briefing on COVID, 3.7.22," March 7, 2022, *YouTube.*

[21] Christian Paz, "Ruben Gallego's Ready for a Fight—Even if the Democratic Party Isn't," *Vox,* September 20, 2022.

[22] See "Rep. Eric Swalwell: Trump Went 'Lower Than I Thought' We Could Go—The Beat with Ari Melber, MSNBC," July 16, 2018, *YouTube.*

[23] Matt Fuller, "'You Are a P*ssy': McCarthy and Swalwell Get in House Floor Feud," *The Daily Beast,* June 29, 2023.

[24] Library of Congress, "Composite Nation," Speech Delivered in the Parker Fraternity Course, Boston, 1867.

[25] Kenneth T. Walsh, "The Young Presidents: John F. Kennedy Learned from Early Mistakes," *U.S. News and World Report,* December 8, 2009.

[26] Matthew Rosa, "The True Story of the U.S. President Who Kept His Disability a Secret," *Salon,* February 20, 2023.

[27] John F. Kennedy, "Remarks Intended for Delivery to the Texas State Committee in the Municipal Auditorium in Austin, November 22, 1963 [Undelivered]," John F. Kennedy Presidential Museum and Library.

[28] "Most Popular US Presidents (Q4 2023)," *YouGov.*

[29] Robert A. Caro, *The Years of Lyndon Johnson: Master of the Senate* (New York: Vintage, 2002).

[30] Lyndon B. Johnson, Remarks at the Signing of the Immigration Bill, Liberty Island, New York, October 3, 1965, The American Presidency Project, University of California, Santa Barbara.

[31] "The Last Speech of Ronald Reagan as President Was on Immigration," January 19, 1989, *YouTube.*

[32] "1986: Immigration Reform and Control Act of 1986," Library of Congress Research Guides.

[33] Perry Bacon, "The Left Needs to Win, Not Duck, the Immigration Debate," *Washington Post,* July 25, 2023.

[34] Jens Manuel Krogstad, "Americans Broadly Support Legal Status for Immigrants Brought to the U.S. Illegally as Children," Pew Research Center, June 17, 2020.

[35] "Immigration," *Gallup News,* June 30, 2023.

[36] Amina Dunn, "Republicans View Reagan, Trump as Best Presidents," Pew Research Center, December 20, 2021.

[37] "Congresswoman Annihilates Lauren Boebert during Hearing & Says She & MTG 'Lack All Substance'," *LGBTQ Nation,* June 19, 2023.

[38] "MSNBC 06 17 2023 12 36 42," *YouTube.*

[39] David Smith, "'This Is about Saving Lives': The Texas Democrat Fighting for Gun Control and Abortion Rights," *The Guardian,* May 17, 2023.

[40] "MSNBC 06 17 2023."

41 Jeremy Herb, Annie Grayer, and Marshall Cohen, "Takeaways from President Biden's First Impeachment Hearing by House Oversight Panel," *CNN.com*, September 28, 2023.

42 The Editorial Board of the *Wall Street Journal*, "'Nobody in Hollywood' Like Xi Jinping," *Wall Street Journal*, July 20, 2023.

43 Walter Einenkel, "Rep. Crockett Has 5 Minutes of Mic-Drop Moments during Impeachment Hearing," *Daily Kos*, September 28, 2023.

44 Speech at Madison Square Garden, October 31, 1936, *YouTube*.

45 Mary McLeod Bethune, "What Does American Democracy Mean to Me?," *YouTube*. The text is available at Mary McLeod Bethune, "What Does American Democracy Mean to Me?," American Town Meeting of the Air, New York City, November 23, 1939, American Radio Works, *Say It Plain, Say It Loud: A Century of Great African American Speeches*.

Index

About the Authors

M. **Steven Fish** is a comparative political scientist at the University of California, Berkeley, who specializes in democracy and authoritarianism, religion and politics, and constitutional systems and national legislatures. He writes and comments extensively on international affairs and the rising challenges to democracy in the United States and around the world. He appears on BBC, CNN, and other major networks, and has published in *The New York Times*, *The Washington Post*, *Los Angeles Times*, *The American Interest*, *The Daily Beast*, *Slate*, and *Foreign Policy*.

Laila M. Aghaie is an education consultant specializing in the development of community forums, speaker events, writing programs, and arts curricula in collaboration with school districts, government agencies, and community-based organizations.

www.ingramcontent.com/pod-product-compliance
Lightning Source LLC
Chambersburg PA
CBHW032048020426
42335CB00011B/237